BASEBALL:
IT'S MORE THAN JUST
A GAME

Personal Memories, Historical Firsts, Feats, and
Special Stories from the Great Game

by

GREG LUCAS

CHART
HOUSE PRESS, LLC.

Baseball: It's More than Just a Game
(2014)
By Greg Lucas
Houston, TX
© 2014 by Greg Lucas

This book is designed to provide information and motivation to our readers. It is sold with the understanding that the publisher is not engaged to render any type of psychological, legal, or any other kind of professional advice. The content of each topic is the sole expression and opinion of its author and not necessarily that of the publisher. No warranties or guarantees are expressed or implied by the publisher's choice to include any of the content in this volume. Neither the publisher nor the individual author(s) shall be liable for any physical, psychological, emotional, financial, or commercial damages, including, but not limited to, special, incidental, consequential, or other damages. Our views and rights are the same: You are responsible for your own choices, actions, and results.

ISBN: 978-1-63125-022-4

Chart House Press, LLC.
24044 Cinco Village Center Blvd #100
Katy, TX 77494
844-974-8348
(844-WriteIt)
www.ChartHousePress.com
www.twitter.com/GregCLucas
http://www.linkedin.com/pub/greg-lucas

DEDICATION

This book is dedicated to
my wife of more than forty-two years, Yong Ae Lucas.
I could not have a better partner in my life.

CONTENTS

Chapter III: THE BAT, THE BALL AND EVERYTHING IN BETWEEN

Foreword

Baseball, it is said, is only a game. True. And the grand canyon is only a hole in Arizona. Not all holes, or games, are created equal.

George Will

L-R: Greg Lucas, Larry Dierker, Bill Brown, 2003, Houston, Texas

I first met Greg Lucas many years ago when he was working for Fox and I was doing Astros radio and television. After doing a few Astros and college games with him, I couldn't help but notice his Cheshire cat grin. When he came up with something obscure, it tickled him and amused me as well. He wasn't really laughing, but I found it hard to take things too seriously when we worked together. Don't get me wrong—we didn't just yuk it up. I was prepared to do straight reporting, and he was too.

Fortunately for us, baseball is the type of game that gives announcers plenty of time to digress. Some of our sidebars went pretty far afield. It was a lot of fun. Within these pages, Greg does a lot of digressing. He'll tell you a fact, such as that Jeremiah Denny, whose career ended before 1900, still holds the career record for total chances by a third baseman in his career. Then he will add that Denny was ambidextrous, also holds the error record for third basemen, and played his whole career bare-handed! In fact, he was the last player to play his whole career without wearing a glove. He'll tell you of two pitchers who won more than twenty games in their single season in major league baseball, but never pitched in the major leagues again. And he will also tell you why they didn't.

This book covers a lot of little-known baseball history. It's sort of a guidebook down the sideshows of the game. It is full of obscure firsts and facts, but it also gives a stage to the great players from the Negro leagues as well as the heroes from the glory days of Minor League baseball who never made big names for themselves in the majors. As Greg points out in his introductory comments, just about every part or chapter in this book could be or has been expanded into a book of its own. His purpose was to create one place where fans of the game could find any interesting or amusing anecdotes that hopefully will create an appetite to learn more.

One thing you can do as a writer that you cannot do on the air is edit. I have been fortunate to write a couple of books myself. The first, *This Ain't Brain Surgery*, is biographical and includes stories mostly of my career. The second, *My Team*, discusses the players I have seen that are the best in my opinion. That book took hours of extra research to back up my recollections with facts.

FOREWORD

Baseball: It's More than Just a Game is a gem of diversions that has been well-researched and carefully rendered in Greg's ironic style. Talking about the great nicknames from baseball's past and the strange injuries that have sidelined players over the years will make you smile. You'll grin, too, as an improbable cast of characters parades through the pages, doing odd things or having odd things done to them. At the same time, when Greg and I worked together, there were several times when I said, "Where did you come up with that?" I think all those years of researching and writing for Astros pregame shows and finding answers to questions asked by fans through e-mail had paid off. Greg just smiled. And then a few innings later, he'd come up with something else. He is as unassuming as an accountant, just as accurate, and a whole lot more amusing.

Greg likes the spotlight, although he doesn't act that way. He would just as soon let it shine on the athletes. Some broadcasters lapse into thinking they are the show. Greg never does that. And he never forgets the game is the main course and the esoterica merely the spice. If you are new to the game or a would-be historian, this book is a great place to start. His bibliography lists some of the best sources for those who want to really go further. This book is a great introduction, but it is also fun for those who already consider themselves pretty good baseball historians. A whole lot of knowledge is available in one place.

When you plunge into the stacks of baseball history, you often find that the charm of the game is as alluring as its drama. This book does not compare players or list the best of all time. Instead, it tells a bit about the way the game has grown and the changes through which it has gone, from playing in ballparks of all sizes to the men who tried to play the game on ice. So sit back in your easy chair and kick your shoes off. You're liable to be here for a while. I was.

Larry Dierker
Author, Former Player, Broadcaster, Manager, Houston Astros

Preface

I'm going to write a book. This won't be one of those tell-all-deals like Jim Bouton's "Ball Four." It's going to be a family book. I'm just writing down a lot of things that go through my head, so there probably will be a lot of blank pages.

Doug Rader
Manager, Texas Rangers (1983–1985)

Houston Astros, First Game in Colt Stadium, 1962

PREFACE

This isn't Doug Rader's book. You won't find blank pages here. But it is for the entertainment of baseball lovers and, at times, may be as funny as Rader's quote. This book is my collection of facts and stories from the history of the longest and most colorful past of any major sport. From word of mouth to the most respected written annals in the history of the sport, this book is made up of the research that I conducted during the more than twenty-five years that I was directly connected with Major League Baseball as a features co-producer and game broadcaster and telecaster.

From Fans to Fruition: The Making of a Book

I first delved into the history of baseball professionally and in great depth in the early 1990s as the co-producer of a segment in a Fox Sports Southwest television series called "Tales of the Game." While researching, producing, and writing two-minute features for the pregame show, I stumbled upon some great and little-known stories, many of which have been expanded in this book.

Years later, I inadvertently committed myself to further research when I introduced the use of fan e-mail during the 2000 Houston Astros baseball season. I was unprepared for the explosive response to the opportunity to interact with the game—more than 4,000 questions from fans crowded my inbox on the first day alone. Some questions were very basic, while others caused me to groan at the hours or days of research that would be required before I could answer. However, I made sure to reply to each of those 4,000 e-mails. As a matter of fact, I responded to every single question either on the air or through e-mail until the day I worked my last game with the Astros. I take great pride in being the only announcer involved in games to handle that volume of mail.

To prepare for both "Tales of the Game" and e-mails from fans, I gathered information directly from written features, from word of mouth, and from carefully researched volumes, newspaper clippings, and old copies of *The Sporting News, Sport Magazine,* and *Baseball Digest*. The research led me from one fascinating story to another, revealing interesting anecdotes, small factoids, and first feats along the way.

It turns out that I learned as much from the fans as I did from the research. Not only was it fun to make a connection with fans; I also learned the sorts of things they already knew and wanted to know. They opened my mind to the concept that a lot of folks who are watching or attending a baseball game might also like to know more about the game and its origins. Ultimately, the research and the fans led me here, to the making of this book.

What This Book Is and Isn't

In a nutshell, this book is an outline of the history of baseball. It serves as a starting point for aspiring historians. Many items and stories have not been included nor greatly expanded because the history of the game is too great to include everything. Indeed, the volume of research and the millions of printed pages documenting the history of the game overwhelm all other sports. My hope is that this book instills in readers a desire to seek out the many books listed in the bibliography to allow deeper study. I point out this resource because anyone who talks or writes about baseball owes a debt to those who documented the stories before them, and I am no exception.

This book provides straight-forward truth. It is not a trivia book, although its information certainly could be used to construct some solid trivia questions. Trivia can be fun, and I frequently posed trivia questions as a longtime baseball broadcaster and telecaster. However, trivia can also leave people with a lot of misinformation if the wrong answers stick in their minds. I have always preferred to learn about history and not guess about it. In cases of historical dispute, such as the inventor of the curve ball, I have tried to tell the whole story. Yes, Candy Cummings is given credit by most, but the pitch may be a product of evolution more than of a man throwing seashells on a beach.

Most of all, this book is for your entertainment. I made sure to leave out the boring parts and didn't get bogged down in statistics and averages. I also didn't go into too much depth on any one issue—I just want to whet your appetite.

The bibliography provides a perfect opportunity to find out more. I hope you enjoy my unusual collection of quirky tales, solid facts, first feats, and irresistible stories. May this book open the door for a lifetime of fun reading about the greatest game ever invented.

Greg Lucas
Houston, Texas

Acknowledgements

The way a team plays as a whole determines its success. You may have the greatest bunch of individual stars in the world, but if they don't play together, the club won't be worth a dime.

Babe Ruth
Hall of Famer

Norm Hitzges and Greg Lucas, 1992, Arlington, Texas

ACKNOWLEDGEMENTS

I would like to acknowledge my publisher, Jeff Hastings of Chart House Press, and my editor, Ella Hearrean. Without Jeff, this book might still be in a holding pattern. Without Ella, some of my obvious composition or grammatical errors would still be in the book. I also want to thank Tom Doherty of Cardinal Publishing for his encouragement and advice as well as Dr. Bill McCurdy, an author of three baseball books who shared his advice and counsel in getting my project in print.

I certainly want to thank my wife for putting up with my holing up in my home office for hours and days working on the original manuscript.

I would like to extend a special thank you to Larry Dierker, Sumner Hunnewell, and Monte Irvin.

The countless many with whom I worked as an announcer also deserve thanks. There are far too many to name them all—I know because I tried to compile a list of former broadcast and telecast partners a few years ago and left some out. However, I will mention those with whom I worked on telecasts for the Texas Rangers and Houston Astros. The list includes announcers Norm Hitzges, Jim Kern, Dave Barnett, Jim Sundberg, Brad Sham, Bill Brown, Milo Hamilton, Alan Ashby, Larry Dierker, Jim Deshaies, Bill Worrell, Kevin Eschenfelder, Bart Enis, and Patti Smith. I also appreciate the research performed by members of the Society for American Baseball Research (SABR).

Patti Smith and Larry Dierker get double thanks. Patti was my co- producer on all the "Tales of the Game" segments, and Larry shared a booth with me on Astros and a season of college baseball. He also graciously wrote the forward. Tal Smith, Jim Deshaies, and Nolan Ryan all had nice things to say about the book before they had a chance to see the final product. I hope I have been worthy of their praise.

I also must thank television game producers and directors who made sure I got enough air time to entertain and inform the viewers with much of the material that was used in this book. That list of regulars includes David Handler, Bob Steinfeld, Jim Feldman, Dave Burchett, Mike Anastassiou, Murphy Brown, Wave Robinson, Paul Byckowski, Perry Fuhrman, Jeff Muckleroy, and Greg Maiuro.

I should also thank all the fans with whom I communicated via e-mail, Twitter, Facebook, and in person over the years. They were my inspiration to keep researching. In fact, some of their questions led directly to segments or facts in this book.

Greg Lucas and Tal Smith, 2007, Wrigley

Chapter I

WHERE IT ALL BEGAN

Baseball is the very symbol, the outward and visible expression of the drive and push and rush and struggle of the raging, tearing, booming 19th century.

Mark Twain
Author and Humorist

1903 First World Series, Game Five

BASEBALL: IT'S MORE THAN JUST A GAME

Mark Twain got it right. And what he said in the 1800s is instructive of how important the game was from its formative years. That is why the history of the development of the game is so fascinating. Anyone who is determined to trace the history of this sport back to its origins will find answers—and this chapter reveals some of those truths and legends. However, no amount of research can compare to the ultimate experience of witnessing a game of baseball. For many people, including myself, their earliest memories of baseball are still vivid today.

McLane Down Memory Lane

Former Houston Astros owner Drayton McLane remembers the first time he attended a major league baseball game. He and his father had taken a train trip from their home in Central Texas to St. Louis. When he first entered Sportsman's Park, he was in awe of the large field with the green grass. He had no idea that he would eventually own a major league team. In fact, he wasn't really even a fan until years later. When McLane wound up buying the Astros, the memories of his trip to St. Louis and his first ballgame returned. He caught the fever late, but he caught it nonetheless.

"Big Klu"

The circumstances of my first ballgame are just as indelibly etched into my memory as McLane's is in his. I was nine years old in 1955 when my maternal grandfather, Charles Small, took me to Crosley Field to see the Reds play the Braves. I had never been to a major league city like Cincinnati, though my family had roots there. My grandfather had lived in the area years earlier, and my grandmother still had a sister living in Cincinnati. In fact, my mother had been born just across the river in Covington, Kentucky. The trip had ostensibly been for my grandmother to visit her sister, but for me and Grandpa Small, it was a chance to see a real major league game.

12

I remember approaching Crosley Field and staring in awe at the light towers, which stood majestically taller and held far more lights than those in our local ballpark in Kokomo, Indiana. When we entered the grandstand from the concourse, I gaped in wonder at the perfectly manicured grass and dampened soil that defined the infield and base paths.

I recall very little of the game itself except for one player: Reds' first baseman Ted Kluszewski. My grandfather knew about Ted, or "Big Klu." Ted had been a football player at Indiana University when he was discovered by the Reds' groundskeeper, Matty Schwab. The Reds were holding spring training in Bloomington, Indiana, near the end of World War II when Schwab saw Kluszewski do some hitting.

By the time I saw Klu that first time, he had been around the majors for more than eight seasons. The year before, Ted had led the National League with forty-nine home runs and 141 RBIs. He was on his way to a forty- seven home run season in his fourth straight outstanding season. He was feared as a hitter and admired as a man. But I didn't know or care about any of that. I was transfixed by how he wore his uniform.

Ted was 235 pounds of all muscle and was impossible not to recognize. He liked to cut the sleeves off his jerseys to give his overly large shoulders, biceps, and triceps some room. I couldn't keep my eyes of this man with the bare arms who might hit a home run with any at bat.

Split Loyalties

From that first trip, I was hooked on major league baseball and became a Cincinnati Reds fan, though I learned that I was not in the majority back home. You see, the Reds, Cubs, and White Sox were all about the same 150-mile distance from Kokomo. Detroit and St. Louis were only a little bit further. There were more Cubs than Reds fans in my town.

We even had different loyalties within my family. My dad was a St. Louis Cardinal fan all his life. His first idol was Joe Medwick and, later, Stan Musial. His father had been a White Sox fan. I don't think I ever asked him why, but White Sox broadcasts with Bob Elson, Don Wells, and, later, Milo Hamilton always blared from the radio in his barber shop during day games.

Annual Pilgrimage

For years after that first trip to Cincinnati, I made it back at least once a year, usually for a Sunday afternoon doubleheader. My best friend, Richie Spay, his father, Bob, and his grandfather, Brick, were all Cubs fans who would try to make it to a series against the Reds. Because getting in and out of Crosley Field was far easier than handling the environs at Wrigley Field in Chicago, the three Spays would invite me and my dad to ride along.

The Reds' opponent wasn't always the Cubs, though. While I did see Ernie Banks, I also saw the Giants' Willie Mays and Orlando Cepeda. Mays was the greatest, but Cepeda had a special place in both Richie's and my heart. We had seen him play in our own hometown of Kokomo in 1955 when he was a seventeen-year-old, second-year pro. He had hit .393 while playing third base for the Kokomo Giants of the Class D Mississippi Ohio Valley League.

In those days, the ballparks opened much earlier before games than today. It was possible to get in even before batting practice started. We always timed our drives to Cincinnati to arrive right when the gates opened. And once I got there, I never left my seat. I wanted to see everything on the field—I watched every hitter take every swing.

Richie, on the other hand, liked to collect autographs under the stands where the players walked between the clubhouse and field. He and his dad tried to attract the attention of the players, hoping that they would sign autographs on scorecards. Many times, Richie remembered to ask a player to sign a second scorecard just

14

for me. That's how I got autographs of Ernie Banks, Willie Mays, and Orlando Cepeda.

The "Zippo" Line

Richie's dad had gotten Cepeda's autograph by calling out his little-known nickname, "Zippo." Cepeda had been known as "Zippo Cepeda" when he played in Kokomo, though the name didn't stick. When Cepeda heard the old name, he immediately knew the Spays were from Kokomo and graciously came over to sign.

Years later, I had an opportunity to surprise Cepeda with his old nickname again. I was announcing an Old-Timers' game for the Texas Rangers, which was organized by the late Bobby Bragan. Bobby did a great job of drawing really big names—I'm talking about people like Joe DiMaggio, Bob Feller, Willie Mays, Ernie Banks and Orlando Cepeda. During the telecast game and the regular game that followed, some of the stars visited us in the booth, including Cepeda. When I referred to him as "Zippo," he knew I was from Kokomo.

Cepeda opened up to me about his time in Central Indiana. He had been only seventeen, had spoken very little English, and had felt lost in a foreign land, except when he was on the baseball field. Cepeda had suffered from homesickness that could have ended his career, had it not been for the encouragement from his manager, Walt Dixon, and from the lady in whose home he lived. Not only did Orlando Cepeda stick it out, but we know now that the seventeen-year-old boy I first saw in my own hometown would ultimately become an MVP, World Champion, and a member of the Baseball Hall of Fame.

What I Know Now

I know now that my first special experience as a nine-year-old boy in Cincinnati would spark a life-long love for and ultimately a career in baseball. I made many more boyhood trips to Cincinnati and, later, to both Chicago parks and St. Louis. I remained a Reds fan until I started working for other teams as a broadcaster and telecaster, but even then, I've always kept up with how my "old" team is doing. Throughout my life, I have played and followed baseball longer than any other sport. I believe that to fully appreciate a sport and its pioneers, one must go back to the beginning—to its origins.

Humble Beginnings for Baseball

Every summer, followers of baseball turn their attention to Cooperstown, New York, for the annual Baseball Hall of Fame induction ceremony. Cooperstown has long been recognized as the supposed birthplace of baseball by Abner Doubleday in 1839. However, historical research has exposed that information as legend.

The truth is that neither Cooperstown nor Doubleday had anything to do with the birth of baseball. The sport we know today is actually a result of an evolutionary process from a number of games played in many countries of the world that employed a ball, a bat, and some form of bases. In fact, more of the game has been tied to the British game of rounders, with some elements of cricket, but still lacks enough of a connection to give full credit to any prior game.

It's All in a Name

Some of the confusion is purely based on semantics. The name "baseball," or "base-ball," exists for games that don't resemble the current sport at all. Some of those games predated even well-established games like rounders and cricket. John Thorn, a noted baseball historian, digs into the actual formation of what we now know as baseball in his book, *Baseball in the Garden of Eden*. In it, Thorn presents thorough research and superb details about real, likely origins of the sport and the early development of the game. David Block, author of *Baseball Before We Knew It,* is a bit more scholarly in his approach. He explores the game and its forebears, who may have come from places other than just the British Isles.

In my opinion, Thorn's and Block's works are the most fully developed histories of the game. Another great scholarly reference is Peter Morris' *A Game of Inches*. These books provide much greater detail, background, and thought-provoking reading about the roots of baseball than can be addressed here. Suffice it to say that they and other sources all point to one conclusion: Baseball is a product of evolution. It was not really invented by anyone; rather, the administration and method of the game were simply modified over time.

Ball-and-Bat Games Common Worldwide

Games using some form of a bat and ball can be found in the histories of many countries around the world. So, the basic concept of hitting a ball with a bat is certainly no American invention. The big question is, how did the sport become baseball as we know it now? For our purposes, we will focus on the American development of the sport.

Early Ball Games Played in America

The earliest known written reference to baseball in the United States is in a document dating to 1791. It bans baseball from being played near the town meeting hall in Pittsfield, Massachusetts, for fear of broken windows. However, several sources make significant references to a bat-and-ball game well before the first documentation of baseball in America.

For instance, some sources reference soldiers in the American Revolution playing a form of baseball. A Princeton undergraduate diary mentions a pastime called "baste ball" in 1786. A children's book published in Worcester, Massachusetts, in 1787 includes an illustration of playing ball.

The word "baseball" also appeared in Great Britain in *The Little Pretty Pocket Book* and in Jane Austen's *Northanger Abbey*. The game that is referenced in those books may have been more like a modified version of cricket or rounders, not what we associate with the word today. In a discussion about the roots of baseball, it is better to include club ball, tip cat, and stool ball as ancestors of all bat-and-ball games without giving cricket or rounders too much credit.

Two Significant Forms Preceded Baseball Today

The full team game that is played in the United States originally began in two main forms: the "Massachusetts Game" and the "New York Game." While the Massachusetts Game originated first and continued to be played for a while, it would ultimately be supplanted by the New York Game, which is closer to the form that has endured. There were significant differences between the two styles of the game.

The game in Massachusetts was often referred to as "town ball." This is the game closest to what had been played in Great Britain. Town ball consisted of a box-shaped field and wooden stakes spaced sixty feet apart that served as bases. Pitchers threw overhand with balls that weighed only about half as much as today's baseball. Outs were recorded when fielders hit runners with balls when they were off base, and only one out retired the side. The winner was the first team to score seventy-five runs.

In contrast, the New York Game consisted of four ground-level bases, not wooden stakes, which were spaced approximately ninety feet, or forty- two paces, apart in a square-diamond shape. Pitchers threw underhand, and three outs were required before a side was retired. The elimination of "plugging" or retirement of offensive players occurred by hitting them with thrown balls when they were between bases. The winner was the first team to score twenty-one runs.

The Massachusetts Game Hung On for a While

The first collegiate Massachusetts game played was reportedly between Amherst and Williams on July 1, 1859, in Pittsfield, Massachusetts. The game involved baseball's most unusual challenge as well as charges of professionalism.

After Williams lost to Amherst with a score of 73 to 32, the school challenged Amherst to a chess match. Amherst won again. Soon after, Williams accused Amherst of having used a "ringer" as its pitcher in the baseball game. Supposedly, a local, nonstudent blacksmith named Harry Hyde had been making the tosses.

There is no report of the chess match having any ringers, and nothing came of the charges of professionalism. However, a lot came of Mr. Hyde, who became a prominent lawyer in Boston and later served as a trustee of Amherst, his alma mater. There was also quite a celebration: After the two victories, Amherst backers paraded through the streets of Pittsfield.

The New York Game Won Out

Meanwhile, the New York Game developed in the New York City area. In October 1845, Alexander Cartwright published a set of rules for the new form. Although the rules were not the first nor even Cartwright's own invention, the Cartwright Rules endured as the lasting form of the sport.

The first game played under those rules has long been believed to have been on June 19, 1846. Interestingly, an unknown team from New York beat Cartwright's Knickerbockers 23 to 1. This was thirteen years before the infamous Amherst victory over Williams in Massachusetts. It was not the first organized game of baseball in that area; this form had been played in New York since at least 1830. However, the famed 1846 game on Elysian Fields in Hoboken, New Jersey, featuring the New York Knickerbockers and another New York team, gets credit because the Knickerbockers were an organized men's social club of significantly higher societal rank than many others who were playing the game at the time.

Chapter II

BASEBALL GETS ORGANIZED

Baseball is a public trust. Players turn over, owners turn over and certain commissioners turn over. But baseball goes on.

Peter Ueberroth
Commissioner of Baseball, 1984-89

Cincinnati Red Stockings, 1869

The 1869 Cincinnati Red Stockings Were First

The 1869 Cincinnati Red Stockings are often given credit as baseball's first fully professional team, but they were a long way from being the first to be paid to play. For years, many players had been paid to essentially play the game, though they were not paid openly. In 1859, for instance, the National Association of Baseball Players' rules specifically stated that "no party shall be competent to play in a match who received compensation for his services."

That rule would ultimately be hard to enforce. Some players were given rather soft, if not nonexistent, jobs in the businesses associated with club owners or members of the team's board of directors. The Washington Nationals of 1867 may have really been baseball's truly first professional team, but the truth about whether or not the team received pay was hidden. Certainly there was a large number of professional players prior to the 1869 Reds, but no team dared proclaim itself totally because amateurism was still acclaimed as the higher status.

Jim Creighton: Baseball's First Natural

Jim Creighton was a great star in both cricket and baseball. He may have been baseball's first professional. He also may have died as a result of wounds from the ball field before reaching age 22.

In baseball, Creighton exceled as a pitcher. He learned to bend the rules a bit, which made his pitches a bit harder to handle. This was in the 1850s, when the pitcher was little more than what is now considered to be a slow- pitch hurler in softball. In 1960, the Brooklyn Excelsiors reportedly paid him about $500 under the table to ply his trade.

Creighton was more than just a top pitcher. He was also the leading hitter of his time. That part of his game, however, may have led to his doom. It was reported that on October 14, 1862, while playing for the Brooklyn Atlantics, he came to the plate in the seventh inning. He took a mighty swing and drove the ball deep, then circled the bases with a home run. Creighton suffered an internal injury from the swing. Whether he tore his bladder or suffered from a ruptured inguinal hernia, there is some doubt, but the result was tragic. Four days later, he was dead.

While Creighton's story had a horrible end, his career was part of the incipient stage of what would turn into full-blown professionalism. By 1871, the National Association would be formed as a fully professional league. It was the start of what we now consider Major League Baseball. Salaries certainly were not great, but everyone received something. And it all started in Fort Wayne, Indiana.

The First Major League Game
The historic first game under the auspices of the new National Association of Professional Baseball Players was played on May 4, 1871 in Fort Wayne, Indiana. Fewer than 500 fans braved poor weather to see the home team beat the Forest City team of Cleveland, Ohio, 2 to 0. The home team "Kekiongas" were named for the Native American word for "blackberry bush," a common shrub in the area around Fort Wayne. It was also the name of the capital of the Miami tribe located in the region.

However, the Kekiongas' first win in the league was hardly a forerunner of what was to come for the franchise. In late August of that year, Fort Wayne left the league for financial reasons. It was the first franchise to fail.

The players fared better. Although James "Deacon" White played for the losing Clevelanders, he was the hitting star with three of five hits. White would go on to play for eight teams over fifteen years and finish his career with a lifetime .303 batting average.

Another notable player was the Kekiongas' pitcher, Bobby Mathews. Mathews had six strikeouts and one walk against Forest City, pitching the first shutout in organized professional baseball history. He was one of the early proponents of using the curve ball, which he used to his advantage in a successful career.

KEKIONGA B. B. C., 1871.
1. E. MINCHER, L. F.   5. B. MATHEWS, P.
2. W. M. KELLEY, C. F.   6. J. H. FORAN, 1st B.
3. P. DONELLY, R. F.   7. W. GOLDSMITH, S. S.
4. F. SELLMAN, 3d B.   8. W. H. LENNON, C.
          9. T. CAREY, 2d B.

Kekiongas Baseball Club, 1871

In 1874, Mathews had a career high of forty-two wins for the New York Mutuals of the National Association. His winning stretch continued into the early to mid-1880s, when Mathews won thirty games for three straight seasons for Philadelphia of the American Association. He would eventually win a total of 297 games over ten seasons in three leagues—the National Association, the National League, and the American Association—before ending his career in 1887 at age thirty-six.

In 1889, Mathews claimed the Philadelphia Athletics owed him $600 for his services as a "coacher" the previous year. He sued the team and won, thus being credited as the first paid coach in baseball history. Later, in 1907, Arlie Latham of the New York Giants would be credited as the first "contracted" base coach.

The "Real" First Major League Game

Actually, one game was played earlier than the game in Fort Wayne, but it was deleted from the records. On April 22, 1871, the Washington Olympics of the National Association hosted the Washington Nationals. The Olympics beat the Nationals 36 to 12.

However, the Nationals were thrown out of the National Association because they failed to pay their $10 league dues. As a result, all of the Nationals' games were removed from the records and standings.

Davy Forced Some Important Decisions

In the 1876 season, the stability of the National Association was threatened by some teams' unrest in response to new rules. Some teams had violated new bylaws in the Association regarding the signing of players from other teams, including one which stated that no player could sign a contract for the next season until the current season was over. For years, players had jumped teams after or during seasons, and the National Association hoped the new rules would keep players committed to their place.

Davy Force

The rules led to a division within the league after a violation by the Chicago White Stockings regarding their shortstop, Davy Force. Force was an interesting player. He was only 5'3, weighed 130 pounds, and was not much of a hitter. His lifetime average was only .249 over fifteen seasons. However, his fielding skills were outstanding for a shortstop at the time. His career fielding percentage of .897 in 1,046 games may not seem very good, but it was very impressive for shortstops who wore no gloves and who played on fields that were not uniformly smooth.

His fielding skills also include a worthy baseball trivia note: On September 5, 1881, Force was the first player to turn two unassisted double plays from the second base position while playing for Buffalo. The feat would be duplicated eighteen years later by Claude Richey of Louisville but not achieved in the American League until October 10, 1978, by Mike Edwards of Oakland.

The Chicago White Stockings were so nervous they might lose their shortstop to big money clubs in the East that they signed Force to a renewal contract during the 1874 season. Big clubs had stolen top players before with offers of more money, like when the Boston club took Albert Spalding from his native Midwest to Boston. However, the White Stockings' early contract with their own player was just as much against the rules as if another team had signed Force. As a result, the renewal contract was declared void, as well as another Force signed in November to stay in Chicago that had been backdated to September. In December, Force signed as a free agent with the Philadelphia Athletics.

Albert Spalding

To turn the tide back in their favor, the White Stockings offered Spalding a chance to come back to Chicago as president of the team. To get revenge for losing Force, the owner of the White Stockings at the time, Wilbert Hulbert, went a step further. He raided Boston and hauled in four or five other key players in addition to Spalding. But he wasn't out of the woods: He had signed the contracts in midseason for delivery in 1876. The National Association would surely deem them void. What was a powerful owner to do? Why, form a new league, that's what! And that new league would eventually spell doom for the National Association.

Actually, the National Association was dying a slow death anyway. As early as May 1875, teams started dropping when the Philadelphia Centennials ceased playing. In June of that year, an organized gang of toughs interrupted a game in Philadelphia. They were upset because they had all bet on the Athletics, and Boston was winning. On July 5, the Washington club had no money to return from St. Louis to Washington. Washington disbanded, but players were given travel money by the Browns so they could get home. On July 20, the *Chicago Tribune* reported that the league powerhouse in Boston would shut down after the season. Something new was needed if professional baseball was to survive.

Here Comes the National League

After the 1875 season and amid the impending death of the National Association, the western portion of the National Association decided to formally disassociate and form the National League of Professional Baseball Clubs. The new league, shortened to National League, consisted in part of teams that wanted to skirt the rules of the National Association. It would certainly not just be a western association, however. Eighteen cities or clubs were listed as original members. The list included Chicago, St. Louis, Cincinnati, Louisville, New York (two teams), Hartford, Boston, Philadelphia (3 teams), New Haven, Brooklyn, Buffalo, Cleveland, Washington, and Burlington.

Needless to say, not all of those franchises made the opening day cut. Eight teams opened in the first season of the National League. They were in Chicago, St. Louis, Louisville, Cincinnati, Boston, Hartford, New York and Philadelphia. But only six finished the season because two teams were expelled: The New York Mutuals and the Philadelphia Athletics failed to finish their schedules when they skipped season-ending road trips. For six years, the National League would not have teams in either New York or Philadelphia.

Both Louisville and St. Louis dropped out prior to 1878, which could have ended the National League. During the off season, the National League had only four teams. Then Hartford also left. But the league hung on, as Indianapolis, Milwaukee, and

Providence joined the fold to keep the loop afloat.

Challengers to the National League

Things were not easy in the early days. The National League was not stable. It suffered from many of the same problems with misbehavior by players and fans as had the National Association. Gambling continued to be a problem, and labor disputes started as players received limited salaries and experienced less freedom to decide where they would play.

New leagues formed, including the American Association, which was often called the "Beer and Whiskey League" because it allowed beer and alcohol sales that had been prohibited in the National League. The major league version of the American Association would only last from 1882 to 1890, but it accomplished two things in that short time: It put teams back into New York and Philadelphia, and it quickly gained a foothold in larger cities than the National League. By 1890, the American Association faded as a major league as teams folded or shifted to the National League.

In 1884, a third league existed, which was called the Union Association. Whether or not it was really a major league has been questioned, but it lasted only that season.

First Interleague Post-Season Series

From 1884 through 1890, teams from both the National League and American League met in a post-season series, which was the forerunner to the World Series. Clubs in the National League won five of the seven series.

In 1890, the Players' League was formed to give players an alternative to the National League and its attempts to bind players to their teams. The league lasted only one season but included many top National League stars who were not happy with the ownership of the National League.

During that one season, twenty-seven teams were classified as major league, more than any time in history until 1993, when the National League added the Miami and Denver markets for a total of twenty-eight teams in Major League Baseball. Even though the Players' League did not last, it led to the demise of the American Association. Four of the former franchises from the American Association were absorbed by the National League, making the National League a twelve-team loop until 1900, when the league dropped Louisville, Baltimore, Washington, and Cleveland.

Enter the American League

Still, the desire to compete against the National League was not dead. A new minor league—the Western League—was formed in the late 1890s. By 1900, its founder, Ban Johnson, changed the name to American League and sought designation as a major league. It achieved major league status in 1901 with Baltimore, Philadelphia, Boston, Washington, Cleveland, Detroit, Milwaukee, and Chicago as original teams.

Three cities—Philadelphia, Boston, and Chicago—had teams that competed against each other in the new American League and the National League. Before long, two more cities would have teams in both leagues. Milwaukee would move to St. Louis to become the Browns, and Baltimore would be transferred to become the Highlanders, later known as the Yankees. That lineup would remain in the American League for the next fifty years, from 1903 through 1953. There would be sixteen major league franchises in just nine cities in the East and Midwest.

After the formation of the American League and the stability of both leagues, America's national game began to mature. Some rules were improved to help the players, and the players continued to get better. Playing equipment and field conditions also got better.

The National League, which included New York, Brooklyn, Philadelphia, Boston, Pittsburgh, Cincinnati, Chicago, and St. Louis, would also be stable until the Braves moved to Milwaukee for the 1953 season. The American League's decision to move the

Browns from St. Louis to Baltimore and to move the Philadelphia A's to Kansas City the next two seasons ended the stability of the junior circuit, but the next moves would be far more wide-reaching as baseball moved West and ultimately expanded.

Rules and Other Changes for the Next Fifty Years

With the standardization and improvement of equipment over the next fifty years, baseball offered a few adjustments to rules regarding the strike zone, field, and scoring during the period.

One rule that was eliminated dealt with the "courtesy runner." The rule had allowed a substitute runner for a player with a temporary or minor injury. The courtesy runner could be used later in the game or could be a player already in the game. The last courtesy runner was Indian catcher Jim Hegan, who ran for Ray Boone in July 1949. Later that year, the use of courtesy runners was eliminated from professional baseball. Today, a courtesy runner can still be used in high school and college games to speed up the pace of a game. He normally runs in place of the catcher, enabling him to get into his catching gear quicker for the next inning.

The rules on home runs and sacrifice flies were also altered during the first fifty years of the twentieth century. For a while, balls that left the field of play by bouncing over fences were considered home runs. The exception to that rule was the scenario in which a ball drove in a winning run by a player that was already on base—that was not credited as a homer. Hitters only got credit for the number of bases needed to get the runner home with the winning run.

The rule concerning whether or not a sacrifice fly was credited as an at-bat was changed several times. In 1908, the batter who got credit for a sacrifice fly was not charged with an at-bat. In 1926, hitters got an even better break. They got credit for a sacrifice fly and were not charged with an official at-bat when any runner advanced. In 1939, the rule was amended again: Batters were only credited with a sacrifice fly for advancing a runner that scored. By

29

1940, there was no such thing as a sacrifice fly. It was wiped off the books, whether a runner scored or not. Finally, in 1954, the rules we know today concerning sacrifice flies and at-bats were reinstated. Several hitters between 1940 and 1954 would have added points to their batting averages, including Ted Williams who would have had an even higher average than his .406 in 1941 if the sacrifice fly rule had been in effect. It has been computed that Ted would have hit .411 in 1941 had the current sacrifice fly rule been in effect that year.

One other new rule of interest in 1954 stated that players could no longer leave their fielding gloves on the field when they went in to hit. While not often a problem, there had been some interesting incidents in the past. Nellie Fox was said to have once doubled into his own glove. He hit a liner that smacked into his glove, which was resting in the grass behind his usual second base position. The ball took a side hop and Nellie was able to leg out a double while defenders tracked down the ball. Other cases occurred in which players tripped over opponents' leather.

In addition, warm-up mounds for starting pitchers were removed. They had been located in front of the teams' dugouts near the on-deck circles. Starting pitchers would now have to get ready in the team bullpens. And of course, the strike zone, balk rules, and the pitcher's mound were slightly changed. More detail is provided on these changes in the pitching section.

Chapter III

THE BAT, THE BALL AND EVERYTHING IN BETWEEN

There was no paraphernalia in the old days with which one could protect themselves. No mitts, not even gloves. And masks? Why, you would have been laughed off the diamond had you worn one behind the plate. In the early days, the pitcher was only fifty feet away from the batsman, and there was no penalizing him if he hit you with the ball.
Jim O'Rourke
Hall of Famer

USS Maine Baseball Team Poster, 1898

Remember the first time you put on a baseball uniform? Maybe it was in a youth league. Maybe you got one as a gift before you even played ball. Whenever it was, you probably remember that uniform. I do.

My first was as a gift when I was ten years old. I think it was to help me feel better. I had played in the Little League farm league when I was nine, but the next winter I was diagnosed with rheumatic fever. I was put on bed rest and even had to have a tutor come to my home with my fourth grade work. I was lucky. My case was mild, and I only missed six weeks of school. But I had to take it easy when I returned to class because a heart murmur had been detected. I was not cleared by my doctor for Little League tryouts and would not be able to play that summer.

That is when I was presented with my own uniform. I wore it all the time, and when I was given the go-ahead to resume normal activities, I started playing catch and hitting in our back yard with neighborhood friends.

I got my first real team uniform the next spring in Little League and wore one each summer through Babe Ruth League, high school, American Legion, and amateur and college baseball until I was twenty-one years old. Some of them I liked better than others, but I never forgot that first one. And I can tell you that my first uniform was much further up the evolutionary chain that much of the stuff early ballplayers were wearing in the 1860s.

The Uniform

In many respects, the uniform worn for baseball has changed less than any other part of the game. A cap, shirt, pants, and socks have been part of it since the New York Knickerbockers organized. Certainly the look has gone through some adjustment, but the basic elements have not.

Knickerbockers Wore Straw Hats

The Knickerbockers' uniform included white flannel shirts, blue woolen pantaloons, and was topped with straw hats. The hats were impractical since they would fly off when players were on the run. Soon caps replaced them. They were hardly all alike, though. Some were pill box styles with bills; others were skull caps with bills.

Red Stockings First in Knickers

The first team to wear knicker-style trousers was the Cincinnati Red Stockings. That makes sense: It allowed the red stockings they wore to be prominently displayed.

Worst Uniform Experiments

Baseball teams have tried two experiments in uniform wear that were rather poor decisions. In 1882, teams tried coordinating uniforms to the positions played. Each position had a designated color, so the field was a kaleidoscope of color. Only the color of the stockings identified one team from another. Fans called them "clown costumes," and they didn't make it through the whole season. They tried something different with color-coded caps and stockings, too. All attempts at looks that were less than "uniform" eventually faded.

First Pin-Stripers Were Not the Yankees

Three teams were first to wear uniforms featuring pin stripes. Washington and Detroit of the National League and Brooklyn of the American Association wore them in 1888. The New York Yankees adopted them for the first time in 1912.

Collars or Not

Until 1906, baseball uniform shirts all had collars, and most had lace-fronts. The New York Giants introduced the collar-less jersey in 1906, and the lace-front died when the two teams in Boston became the last two teams to scrap the design in 1910.

Numbering Players

Several teams have a hand in the move to put numbers on uniforms to identify players. The first major league team to try it was the Cleveland Indians, who put small numbers on one sleeve in 1916, but the experiment did not last.

In 1929, The New York Yankees was the first major league club to number all players on the back of the shirt and keep the system in place. Originally, they numbered the players to correspond to their regular spot in the batting order. For example, Ruth was number three and Gehrig was number four. That proved to be an impractical method. By 1933, every team wore numbers except the Philadelphia Athletics, who held out until 1937.

But numbering had been considered in the minor leagues before the major leagues. The manager of the Atlantic League Reading Roses, Alfred Lawson, planned to have his team wear numbers in 1907. Number thirteen would not be issued for superstitious reasons.

In 1909, the Cuban Stars, who performed in the Negro leagues, put numbers on their uniforms. The numbers were on the left sleeve.

Names on the Back

The first team to put player's names on the back of the shirts was the 1960 Chicago White Sox. It was probably no surprise they led the way, since they were owned at the time by baseball's all-time top showman, Bill Veeck. Some teams were reluctant to follow since it was feared the names might hurt scorecard sales. A few major league clubs held out from putting names on the back, but most clubs had them by the 1990s.

Wool

The material used in baseball uniforms was mostly wool, with a few exceptions. It was not always a heavy wool but often flannel, which is a wool-cotton blend. The combination was less prone to wrinkling, was durable, and was easy to launder.

In the 1970s, wool finally gave way to man-made, double-knit materials, which met all of the requirements and were lighter and cooler to wear. They could also be fitted to streamline the look. Pictures of players from the 1960s and 1970s show many wearing uniforms that look almost painted on. They were that tight, but they stretched with movement.

Stockings

Once baseball started wearing knicker-type pants, the socks were a key component of the uniform. Not only did they show off the team's colors, or even identify the team during the "clown costume" period of 1882, but they also protected the legs of sliding players. At first, the woolen stockings were worn without stirrups, as many players do today.

Stockings Named the Teams in Boston

Due to fear of blood poisoning caused by the red dye in 1907, the National League Boston Red Stockings quit wearing the red socks, and then they dropped the longtime team name. They became the Beaneaters to start, eventually settling in as the Boston Braves in 1912. Meanwhile, with the name Red Stockings so well known in Boston, the young American League franchise in the city quickly adopted it. Up to then, the team had been known as simply the Boston Americans.

Ultimately, players in baseball started wearing long white

cotton stockings under their uniform socks. They were called "sanitary socks," or "sanitaries". Players still wear them under their baseball stockings today, even if the socks never show with the current trend to wear pants low to the shoe tops.

Once players moved to wearing sanitary socks, the colored overstocking was modified to include a stirrup. This lengthened the life of the colored stocking. During the 1960s and 1970s, a baseball fashion was wearing the stirrups very high, with little colored stocking showing.

Do They Even Wear Socks?

The advent of players wearing soccer-style stockings with no stirrups in the 1980s evolved from the no-sock-visible style. The first noted player to wear his pants so low that no stocking was visible was George Hendrick. He played for several teams from 1971 through 1988. By the 2000s, most players wore their uniforms in that style.

The Sleeveless Vest

The Chicago Cubs introduced both the zipper front jersey in 1937 and the sleeveless jersey in 1940. The idea of jersey was to give players more shoulder and arm freedom. Chicago stuck with the style for three seasons, and then it would be revived by the 1956 Cincinnati Reds. The Pittsburgh Pirates, Cleveland Indians, and Oakland A's also joined the club later. The sleeveless style used by those teams was different that the design brought back later and in use into the twenty-first century. The latter style was less of a vest look and more of a simple cut-off sleeve look.

Gray on the Road

Although all clubs had their own colors, actual baseball uniforms were toned down; for many years, gray uniforms were used on the road and white uniforms were used at home. Many clubs still follow that guideline, but with the advent of different colored jerseys, the colors of uniforms are not universal.

Charlie Finley Brought Color

Kansas City and Oakland A's owner Charlie Finley was the man who brought color back to baseball. He introduced multiple uniform styles for his team. He also introduced the solid color jersey. Baseball purists objected, saying Major League Baseball teams now looked like Friday night slow-pitch softball teams. But most teams got with the program, especially when it was shown that the more uniforms or caps a team might wear translated to more duplicate uniform and cap sales to fans.

The Ultimate Color Was in Houston

Perhaps no uniform in the history of baseball can match that of the Houston Astros between 1975 and 1986. During the first season, the orange, yellow, and red rainbow-striped jersey was worn both home and road. It was panned in most circles but made the Astros stand out for sure. The Astros toned things down in 1987 by limiting the rainbow stripes to the shoulders. Years later, however, the rainbow Astros jersey became quite a collector's item.

The Caps

From the early straw hats of the New York Knickerbockers came the baseball cap. The design was simple. The lightweight cap consisted of a bill on the front helped to shield the players' eyes from the sun and a cap firmly fitted to the head to protect against direct rays of the sun while running. The shape of caps and the size of bills changed over the years, but the basic cap was always on players' heads. Today, the baseball cap has reached universal status. Coaches of all sports wear baseball caps. Golfers wear them. People of other nations where baseball is not a primary sport wear them. If the sport of baseball has one enduring legacy, it will be the baseball cap.

The Batting Glove

At many times during the history of baseball, players had worn gloves during especially cold days. Thin leather gloves—often driving gloves— were the first choice. But other than on cold days, players on the offensive team were barehanded. That started to change by accident in the 1960s.

The story that most frequently circulates involves Ken Harrelson. An outfielder with the Kansas City Athletics in 1963, he was also a frequent golfer. One day that season, he played twenty-seven holes of golf because he did not expect to be in the lineup that night. He played too many holes for his hands and was extensively blistered. When he got to the park that night, he discovered he was in the lineup against the Yankees. He elected to wear his golf glove to protect his left hand—the one that would pull the bat through the right-handed hitting zone. Whenever anyone asked, he would say it was to give him firmer grip on the bat. It worked that day, since Ken hit two homers in the game against the Yankees.

He also heard a lot of razzing for wearing a glove. The next day, according to Harrelson in a 2007 MLB.com article, the Yankees had bought a number of red gloves like he was wearing and waved them at him. Some even tried them in batting practice. When the players realized the gloves afforded a better grip on the bat, the use of batting gloves was born.

Before long, more and more players started wearing golf gloves, and soon an industry was born to make gloves specifically for baseball hitters.

The Harrelson story has been verified, and he is thought to be the first to wear a golf glove in a game. However, some sources credit Bobby Thomson with first wearing a glove or gloves

38

during spring training of 1949. And Ted Williams was wearing golf gloves while hitting to get back in shape after his return from the Korean War in 1953. Neither wore them in a game.

To Wear or Not to Wear a Fielder's Glove

In the early days of baseball, no players wore gloves on defense, let alone at bat. In reality, they were rarely needed because the balls were soft and the pitching was slow. But as the equipment got better and the game faster, it soon became apparent some protection might be a good idea, even if some of the veteran players might have scoffed.

In 1875, Charles Waitt of Boston reportedly used the first glove on defense. Since he didn't want it to be obvious to fans or foes, he wore two flesh-colored, fingerless gloves—one on each hand. Whether Waitt was really number one or not is quite disputable.

The question of whether Waitt was number one hinges on whether catchers are considered as in the same category. Waitt, you see, was playing first base at the time. It is believed some catchers may have started wearing protective gloves prior to 1875. But even that is in dispute.

Cincinnati Red Stocking catcher Doug Allison may have had a saddle maker sew him buckskin mittens as early as 1869. But it was not until Jim White actually started catching from right behind the plate in 1875 that nearly all catchers started needing some help for their hands. It is known that when the National Association started operating in 1871, there was no rule against players wearing gloves if they liked. Those that did wore half-gloves that covered the palm and first joints of their fingers.

It is quite possible that Waitt was not the first to wear hand protection.

He just gets credit for it by many sources.

There are reports that some minor league backstops started

cutting fingers off brick layers' gloves in the early 1870s. By 1890, it is known most catchers were wearing mitts after Harry Decker invented the first padded catcher's mitt the year before.

However, that was still not the case with most fielders. In fact, it was not until 1901 that baseball's last gloveless player left the game. That man was pitcher Gus Weyhing, who won 264 games in a fourteen-year career. That total might have been higher had he tried wearing a glove since his lifetime fielding percentage was only .881 with 128 errors.

Bid McPhee: Last to Go Gloveless

Second baseman Bid McPhee was the last position player to not to wear a glove on defense in major league baseball. He was also one of the best fielding second basemen of his era. McPhee played between 1882 and 1899 for the Cincinnati Red Stockings. If Gold Gloves had been awarded in his day, he would have been a multiple winner. He would annually either lead the league or be near the top in putouts, assists, and fielding percentage. One of his secrets was that he would regularly soak his hands in salt water to toughen them.

For the final four seasons of his eighteen-year career, McPhee did wear a glove. His lifetime fielding percentage was .944. That was extremely good for his era, yet starting to wear a glove made him even better. In his last gloveless season, 1895, his percentage was .955. The next season, when he started using a glove due to an injury sustained in spring training, his fielding percentage jumped to .978, and his errors were cut from thirty-four to fifteen. That percentage would be the highest for a second baseman for the next twenty-nine seasons! McPhee could "pick it," with glove or not.

Jeremiah Denny: The Last He-Man

The last regular defensive player to play his entire career gloveless was third baseman Jeremiah Denny. He played fourteen years in the majors, finishing in 1894 with Louisville. Denny was ambidextrous and fielded and threw with whatever arm was handy. This skill was the primary reason he never wore a glove. Being able to field and throw with either hand or arm gave him great range. Of course, that brought both good and bad results.

His record of an average of 4.2 chances per game and 1.6 putouts still holds. His sixteen total chances in one game, an 18-inning contest on August 17, 1882, still stands as the record for third baseman.

He also holds the National League career record for errors at third base with 533. Denny concluded his career before Bid McPhee but never wore a glove. McPhee was the last to quit wearing one, but Denny was the last to never wear one.

Lave Cross Used What was Comfortable

While Denny was going barehanded, Lave Cross was going to the other extreme. He was playing third base with a catcher's glove until it was outlawed in 1895. Cross would use the glove to knock down grounders and hard-hit balls then pounce on them to make the throw. Cross was primarily a catcher early in his career, and he was used to wearing the mitt.

The Catcher's Mask—A Harvard Product

When Jim White started catching right behind the batter in 1875, it did not take long for catchers to realize they needed some protection other than just a padded mitt. It wasn't until 1875 that Harvard player Fred Thayer came up with a cage-like face protector. He devised it so that teammate James Tyng would agree to move to catcher.

The catcher's mask evolved from the original Thayer device. Most historians claim that Jim White was the first pro to start wearing a mask. White also is credited by some with being the first to wear a chest protector. Others say it was John Clements of the Philadelphia Keystones in 1884 who wore a sort of protector under his uniform shirt. Others say it was Charles Bennett of Detroit in 1886. The early wearers of all the protective devices—even gloves— were ridiculed as being soft. They were actually just ahead of their time.

Shin Guards Came Next

Once catchers started wearing face masks and chest protectors, their legs were next to be covered. Some catchers had been wearing pads or cushions under their socks for a few years. Some wore soccer shin guards.

It was not until 1906 that catchers had outer protection for their legs, when Roger Bresnahan of the New York Giants appeared on the field with shin guards modified from those worn by cricket players. Bresnahan did not invent anything. He was just the first to try something. His manager, John McGraw, correctly predicted that every catcher in baseball would be wearing leg guards within less than six months.

The Batting Helmet

Baseball fans who are old enough can remember when players did not wear helmets while batting. Helmets have evolved over the years and only became mandatory for all players in the major leagues in 1971. It has been obligatory in the American League since 1958. Up to then, players who had begun their careers without helmets did not have to wear one, but new players did. In 1994, a flap covering the ear on the side facing the pitcher was required. Helmets for bat boys, ball boys, and base coaches were made mandatory in the 2000s. It is not that helmets only became a good thing in the last fifty years; it just took a long time to design good ones.

Bresnahan Tried to Use a Head Protector

The first known helmet produced and used by a major league player was the Reach Pneumatic Head Protector, which was designed by Frank Pierce Mogridge of Philadelphia. It was somewhat goofy, like wearing a boxing glove on one's head, but was actually used by Roger Bresnahan around 1905, a year before he tried shin protectors. One drawback was it had to be inflated with air before each at bat. It never caught on.

In 1932, a batting helmet that fit over the cap and looked sort of like a turban was conceived by a Washington inventor. It didn't make the grade, either. Modified football helmets were tried, but it would be years before suitable helmets could be devised.

The Dodgers were the first to try using plastic inserts that fit inside their caps. They offered little protection unless the ball hit right on the insert. For years, however, players could use inserts in place of full batting helmets, if they wished, when head covers became mandatory.

In Negro National League baseball, Willie Wells used a batting helmet in 1942 after he had been beaned in a game. *The Sporting News* credited Willie with being the first to use a helmet, but that was incorrect, of course.

Remember Roger Bresnahan, who used head protection around 1905? Wells was actually wearing a construction worker's helmet anyway.

The problem was finding a way to make a usable, light, but strong batting helmet. Once moldable synthetic plastics were developed, it was only a matter of time.

43

Safety Only One of Reasons Rickey Pushed Helmets

The batting helmet became common in Major League Baseball in the early 1950s when Branch Rickey, then running the Pittsburgh Pirates, had all his players wearing plastic hats. The helmet moved to the American League when Yankee shortstop Phil Rizzuto

ordered one. By 1953, the use of fiberglass made helmets even lighter.

Rickey made a lot of money off them. He was President of American Baseball Cap, Inc., which made the helmets. Rickey showcased them by having all the Pirates wear them at all times in 1953. No one does that any longer, although former first baseman John Olerud wore a helmet at all times after he underwent brain surgery during his college years.

Phil Rizzuto and Joe DiMaggio

The Ball

Baseball cannot be played without the ball. Over the early years, the quality of the balls used varied a great deal. They were made by hand but not always by the most skilled workers.

Baseball pioneer Doc Adams admitted in 1896 that the old New York Knickerbockers and other clubs in the area back in the 1840s and 1850s had trouble getting balls made. For six or seven years, Adams had the balls made himself using three or four ounces of rubber cuttings, wound with yarn and covered with horsehide. The early balls were quite soft and light.

Ellis Drake Came up with a Better Baseball Cover

As baseball evolved, standards for the balls became more uniform. The fact is that, like the game itself, the ball likely started as a ball used in other sports. Maybe it was a cricket ball, or maybe it was a simple hand ball. No one really knows.

However, the Baseball Hall of Fame ultimately gives credit to the figure- eight style and cover of the ball used today as having being designed by a boy named Ellis Drake. Until Drake came up with the design, balls were often coming apart at the seams. Early balls used in the Massachusetts game often consisted of an ounce or so of lead with yarn wound hard around it and covered with chamois. Using chamois as a cover was a problem, as was the way the ball was held together. Drake introduced the leather cover, according to credit given by the Hall of Fame. All historians are not quite as sure.

Horsehide was used as a cover from the beginnings of professional baseball until 1974. However, in the early days prior to the 1870s, it was not exclusively so. The cover was changed to cowhide in 1974 since quality horsehide was harder to find. For trivia buffs, let it be noted that the cowhide baseball was first used in a game played by the Reds in Cincinnati on April 14, 1974.

Once baseball players decided they needed a ball of their own, they used a number of products for the inside. Anything from twine, leather, yard, and even sawdust would be compressed inside the horsehide cover. Eventually, a small rubber ball was used as the center, with yarn wound and wound around until the proper size and weight was reached. The degree of the hardness of the ball varied, and it often did not last past a few well-hit balls.

Of course, as baseball spread, the need for standardized balls was great. Many people tried to come up with the best way to make a good baseball, including a couple of men in the New York area named John Van Horn and Harvey Rose. Their ball was constructed of old rubber shoe parts melted and wrapped with sheepskin. It was a bit light, weighing about three ounces, and hard to throw for any distance. It didn't last long.

Others tried, too. An 1875 patent, the earliest found for a baseball, called for a heart of palm leaves wrapped with wool yard, cotton thread, and a rubber cover. There was no sewing involved and, thus, no seams. It did not take long to discover that baseball needed balls with seams.

Removing Stitches Didn't Work

Ben Shibe

Two men who would become baseball's primary ball-makers initially failed when they came out with a seamless baseball in 1883. Alfred Reach, a former player, and Ben Shibe, who had been making baseballs for a few years, teamed up to open a sporting goods company. Baseballs in those days had seams which tended to break, so Reach and Shibe decided to come up with a seamless ball. They hired an engineer named Sam Castle to invent it.

The balls were made internally as before but were dipped into a liquid solution of gutta-percha for the cover. The ball looked good, but without seams, curve balls could not be thrown and further experimentation showed that neither knuckleballs nor even the then legal spitball would not work. Exit the seamless ball. Rubber-covered balls were devised for youth play and batting machines, but they had simulated seams pressed on to allow the balls to act more as hide-covered balls.

Balls More Standard by the 1900s

The last decade of the 1880s found the baseball much improved. The stitching pattern was standardized, as was the use of horsehide for the cover. For the most part, the size and weight of balls were uniform. The biggest remaining problem was durability and consistency in the degree of hardness.

Inventors from near Cincinnati and Bridgeport, Connecticut, came up with methods in which balls were filled with the proper material—a bit oversized—then put into molds where they were pounded into shape. Then the contents were heated to solidify the balls. By the 1890s, the proper way to make baseballs was discovered. A small spherical object was wound tightly with yarn until the proper size was reached, and then the cover was sewn on. Since then, both machines and individual workers have made balls.

No matter how they were produced, though, the balls were quite dead. They became deader as a game progressed, since every time the ball was hit, the winding would loosen. Back then, one ball to last a whole game was norm. Teams were reluctant to change balls, for they were expensive. They could cost as much as three dollars. That would be more than ten dollars at today's prices.

Rubber-Coated Cork Center Changed the Game

In 1911, the cork center replaced the rubber ball center. Cricket had been using a cork-centered ball for fifty years. The change from rubber to cork is credited by many as the beginning of the "lively ball" era. Physicists pointed out that rubber is bouncy, of course, but it doesn't return to its original shape until after the ball hits the bat. The bounciness does not translate. It was Ben Shibe who suggested playing with the same cork center as had the cricketers. It started the change of the game.

In 1910, the New York Giants had baseball's highest team batting average at .274. The next season, with the cork centered baseball in use, the Philadelphia A's led the majors with a .296 mark. Home runs went from 214 to 316 in the N.L. and from 147 to 198 in the A.L. The game was changing because the ball had been.

Balls Now Okay, but Rarely Changed

Even with the improvement in the ball over the years, it was the custom to use as few balls in a game as possible. Sometimes the same ball went all nine innings. Fouls into the stands were returned to play. Unless a stitch in the seam broke, the chances are only one ball would be used.

This was the era in which pitchers could do almost anything to the ball to make it move: They could throw spitters; they could apply foreign substances. They could work the seams for a better feel for throwing a curve ball. And during play, the balls became softer, dirtier, and darker.

As a result, they were hard to see late in games. Unfortunately, because of this, the major surge in the long ball in the major leagues began with a tragedy. It was Carl Mays' pitch to Ray Chapman that ended Chapman's life on August 16, 1920. Most observers didn't think Chapman even saw the ball.

Spalding, Reach, and Rawlings

From 1876 through 1976, Spalding was the official supplier of major league baseballs. Until the last two years, the American League used a ball stamped with the name "Reach," and National League balls were stamped "Spalding." They were exactly the same ball. Reach was the original sporting goods company name formed by A.J. Reach and Ben Shibe, which later merged with Albert Spalding's firm.

When the Spalding name left Major League Baseball in 1977, there was no noticeable difference. The reason was simple: Spalding had purchased Rawlings of St. Louis more than twenty years before. For a while, the name Rawlings was stamped on American League baseballs, and Spalding remained on National

League balls.

Legal reasons forced Spalding to divest its interest in the Rawlings Company, but Spalding continued to contract with Rawlings to make the baseballs from 1968 through 1973. Then Rawlings took over independently. Until 2000, some balls were stamped "Official Ball American League" or "Official Ball National League." Since 2000, all balls are stamped "Official Major League Baseball."

REACH, PRESIDENT OF THE PHILADELPHIA BASE BALL CLUB.

Al Reach

Rawlings originally made the balls in Haiti, but the operations were moved to Costa Rica in 1987. About 50,000 baseballs are produced weekly.

All major league baseballs are between 9 to 9.25 inches in circumference and weigh between 5 to 5.25 ounces. The cowhide covers are held in place by exactly 108 stitches. The weight of the baseball is about twice what it was in the 1840s when the game was first being organized

Despite the standards, each baseball can be slightly different. Pitchers can tell, and that is one reason why a hurler may throw out a perfectly good-looking ball for another. If the stitches are not quite right or the weight or size feel a bit off, pitchers can tell.

The cork center coated with pink rubber and wrapped tightly with yarn has not changed for over a century. During an average major league game, seven dozen balls are prepared for each game, with each ball averaging about six pitches before being replaced.

Ball Prep—The Mud

New baseballs are bright white, shiny, and slick. But the ball doesn't enter a major league game in that condition. The balls selected to use in a game are rubbed down in the umpire's room before each game. When they are put into play, they have a slightly yellowish hue. That is because they are rubbed down with mud.

It is not just any mud. It is a special mud discovered on a tributary of the Delaware River. Although the Lena Blackburne Rubbing Mud website does not name the location as it is a very closely guarded secret, other sources say the special mud hole is off the Pennsauken Creek in New Jersey. But even those sources do not know the exact location.

The discoverer of the mud, Lena Blackburne, was a former player who was coaching third base for the Philadelphia A's in the late 1930s when umpire Harry Geisel complained that the method of rubbing down baseballs was not suitable. The day's third base ump would have the duty of rubbing down the balls with dirt from the field mixed with water and tobacco juice. Geisel didn't chew tobacco except on the day it was his duty to rub the balls.

Blackburne remembered the mud from past fishing trips as being different and experimented with it—eventually adding a secret ingredient that made it smooth and non-staining. The next spring, he gave a can to Geisel. Word spread, and before long, the mud could be found in umpire rooms all over baseball.

The mud mixture has been used in both major leagues since 1950, when the National League starting using what the American League had been using since 1938. Now the mud is shipped to leagues all over the world. It is even used in football. The San Francisco 49ers were reportedly the first to buy a bucket of the mud to take the shine and slickness off new footballs.

What About the Hitters—and Their Bats?

In the early days of baseball, almost any piece of wood could be used as a bat. Some used flat-sided cricket bats, which was not outlawed until 1893. Others used heavy, rounded hunks of lumber that could barely be swung due to their weight. Over the years, the cricket bat and any flattened piece of wood were banned. But the size and length of bats widely varied for many years.

It was not until 1852 that there were any restrictions on what a player used to swat at the ball. By 1859, however, the rule-makers for the new game decided that, while bats could be of any length, they could be no more than 2.5 inches in diameter. When the Cincinnati Red Stockings became the first all-professional team in 1869, the length was limited to forty-two inches. In 1895, the diameter was increased to 2.75 inches. To this day, those are the limits. There is no limit on anything other than maximum length and diameter. It must be noted, however, that fully round bats were not required until 1893. Before that, some hitters would plane one side of their bat—especially those that liked to use the bunt as an offensive weapon. They were legal between 1885 and 1893.

Who Could Swing a 42″ Bat?

Since it is rare for a current major league player to use a bat longer than 36 inches, and most are in the 34″ to 35″ range, what kind of a player could tote the maximum-sized, 42″ bat? For the most part, they were the big guys, since the conventional wisdom in the early days was the heavier the bat, the better. Now we know that bat speed is more important than weight. History does not record any hitter consistently using a 42″ bat, but Al Simmons regularly used one that was 38″ long.

Babe Ruth used one that weighed 42 ounces for much of his career. Ruth, as we know, hit 714 home runs. Joe Sewell swung a 40-ouncer. Edd Roush is credited with using the heaviest bat in baseball history—a whopping 48 ounces. Roush, a fellow Hall of Famer, had a lifetime batting average of .323. He hit only sixty-eight HR in an eighteen-year career.

There is a historical note from August 22, 1894, when Bill Lange of the White Stockings came to the plate with a bat nearly six feet long. And the umpire, John McQuad, let him use it! The bat, which was actually 5'10" long, had been given to New York Giants manager Jimmy Ryan by a theatre manager as a souvenir. Ryan gave it to Lange to use with the Giants leading by six runs in the eighth inning.

Lange was facing Giants pitcher Jouett Meekin and had struck out in his first two appearances. Amazingly, with the huge hunk of wood, he actually made contact this time. But his soft grounder to first base resulted in an easy out.

Clubs Are Much Lighter Now

In addition to most players today swinging bats no longer than 35 inches, most don't tote lumber to the plate that weighs more than 34 ounces, either. The most popular measurements are 31 to 32 ounces and 34 inches. This also includes tapered handles, in many cases very thin. Until Rogers Hornsby popularized thinner-handled bats in the late 1920s, most hitters used thick-handled bats. Breakage was much less frequent. In fact, Babe Ruth reportedly used the same bat for twenty-one of his sixty home runs in 1927. That, however, is not the record.

Joe Sewell Never Bought a Bat

Joe Sewell had a fourteen-year major league career using the same bat and recorded 2,226 hits with it. Sewell was a contact hitter and not a big slugger, but his bat made a lot of contact. The day of his major league debut, September 10, 1920, new teammate George Burns gavehim a 40-ounce Louisville Slugger, which Sewell never broke.

Sewell only struck out 114 times in 7,132 at-bats over his career, including an astounding three times in the whole 1932 season when he had 524 official at-bats. For five seasons in his career, he struck out no more than four times! Forget all of Nolan Ryan's or Barry Bond's or Cy Young's records. If they keep using wood bats in Major League Baseball, no one will ever play that many games again with one bat. By the way,

Joe Sewell

Sewell's "Black Betsy," as he named his bat, is on display at the Alabama Sports Hall of Fame in Birmingham.

Not All Old-timers Used Heavy Wood

While Tony Gwynn won eight National League batting titles swinging a very small bat, he was hardly the first to go small. Gwynn used a 31-inch, 30-ounce bat, but Wee Willie Keeler reportedly used a bat a half inch shorter than Gwynn's. That makes sense, considering that Wee Willie really was wee. He was listed at 5'4½" and 140 pounds in the Baseball Encyclopedia. There is no record of the weight of his bat, but since he played his career in the thick-handled era, it is unlikely it weighed less than the 29 ounces used by Solly Hemus in the 1950s.

CHAPTER 3: THE BAT, THE BALL, AND EVERYTHING IN BETWEEN

The Bat Evolved Like the Sport

As mentioned earlier, there were few restrictions on bats in the first decade or so when baseball was played, other than they had to be made of wood, so there were there many sources for those bats. Most players made their own bats or supervised the manufacture by others. There was no one type of wood that was most popular, although many players thought oak could be made into a good bat because it was a very strong wood.

However, through trial and error, it was discovered that white ash actually made a better bat. Ash had more "give" on contact and was actually less prone to break. It was also not as expensive, since ash trees are quick to reproduce. However, before that discovery was made, bats were made of willow, old wagon tongues of undetermined origin, and other recycled lumber.

Enter Pete Browning and Bud Hillerich

Pete Browning was a star hitter for the Louisville Eclipses of the American Association in 1884 when he broke his bat during a game. As the story goes, among the spectators for that game was a teenager named John Hillerich. Hillerich's father was a woodworker and, since Hillerich knew how to use the lathe, he offered to make Browning a new bat. With Browning looking on, Hillerich took a piece of white ash and started shaping the bat on the lathe. Once it started looking like a bat, Hillerich took it off the lathe and gave it to Browning for a feel. Browning then asked Hillerich to take a little off here and there.

The next day, Browning had three hits in the game. Word spread to his teammates, and soon John "Bud" Hillerich was getting orders. His father didn't see much future in the side business; his main business was in bedposts and porch railings. It was not long, however, that players from most of the teams in the league were stopping by to have some bats made when they made the Louisville trip.

But Was That the Real Story?

There have been differing stories published regarding the origins of the company as a bat manufacturer. One claims Bud Hillerich only modified an existing bat to bring good luck to Pete Browning. Another says that his father, John Frederick Hillerich, actually turned the first bat and that it was Bud who showed it to some other professional players who wanted John Hillerich to make them some. At first, the elder Hillerich agreed, but then he told the players he wanted no more requests. He was in the business of bedposts, butter churns, and balusters.

In some accounts, the name Arlie Latham comes up. Latham, who was a seventeen-year major leaguer as a player starting in 1880 and, after that, the first salaried third base coach, claimed that the first bat turned by the Hillerich duo was for him. He was a third baseman for St. Louis in 1883 or 1884, and he recalled that he broke his bat while in Louisville. So, unable to find another, he stopped into the nearby Hillerich shop and asked that a bat be turned for him. Latham claims that pre-dated Pete Browning.

Good Business Decision

While all the facts may be in some dispute about the origins of the birth of mass production for baseball bats, one thing is certain. John and Bud Hillerich made a solid decision when they took the company in that direction. We still have baseball bats, but butter churns are rarely in demand.

The company saw the light by 1894 when the brand "Louisville Slugger" was born. By then, bat manufacturing had become a major part of the woodworking shop. In 1905, Honus Wagner became the first player to have his autographed name affixed to a bat after he signed a contract with the company.

The J.F. Hillerich and Son operation eventually added an astute businessman to the ownership, Frank Bradsby, to help market and promote the brand. Soon, the Louisville Slugger was dominating the baseball bat market. The company even expanded into golf equipment and, during later years, manufactured rifle stocks, hockey sticks, and more, including aluminum bats!

Others have Jumped In

However, it would not be too long before others would get involved in the baseball bat business. Companies like Adirondack, Hanna Batrite, and more came on the scene in the late 1940s and early 1950s. Sporting goods companies like Spaulding, Wilson, Cooper, and from other parts of the world starting making bats.

By the early 2000s, more than thirty-five wood-making baseball bat companies were listed in business for U.S. consumers. Nearly thirty of them had bats approved for use in professional baseball. When Barry Bonds started assaulting home run records, the bat he was using drew attention far before any possibility of the use of performance-enhancing drugs. Barry was using a bat made of maple that was turned in Canada. Barry said it was harder wood and less prone to breakage. Soon, the Sam Bat Company was receiving orders all over baseball.

The maple bat, still used by many players, turned out to be hardly perfect. It would break, and when it did, it often did more than just crack as ash. The bat would slice in two, with the end flying toward the field or stands. Major League Baseball collected broken bats for a few years to study the problem, but no changes were forthcoming.

As with ash before, a problem cropped up with wood quality. In the 1940s and 50s, there had been stories of Ted Williams inspecting his bat shipments so closely that he might reject twenty or twenty-two out of a shipment of twenty-four. Finding top-grade, quality aged and dried wood was a problem. It still is. Bat breakage is rampant. Long gone are the days when a player could play his whole career with one bat like Joe Sewell.

Nowadays, it is not uncommon for a player to run short of bats on a single road trip. They just don't hold up for whatever reason—thinner handles, lighter weight, harder swings, or just lack of good wood.

In addition to the measurements for maximum bat size as stated in the rule book, there is also the phrase "solid piece of wood." And that is important. That is why bats with holes drilled in them with cork or rubber balls inserted are illegal. It is why bats that have had small nails driven into the barrel are illegal. It is also why laminated wood bats are illegal. They may be made of wood, but the glue used in laminating is not. The "single piece of wood" part of the rule wasn't always there. Laminated bats have been used in the past.

A story in Leigh Montville's *The Big Bam* tells of a run by one of baseball's greatest while using a questionable hitting tool. The great Babe Ruth used a laminated bat in 1923 until American League president Ban Johnson ruled it illegal. Ruth had used it from July 2 until it was banned on August 11.

During that time, Ruth had come out of a slump—which prompted him to use the bat being marketed and sold by former player Sam Crawford in the first place—and was hitting near .400 with twenty-eight home runs. Johnson ruled that, while the bat was essentially wood and within the rules since the phrase "single piece of wood" was not in the rule yet, it was harder and not suitable for use due to the glue, which kept the four pieces of wood stuck together. The rule was eventually amended. A new laminated bat was given a trial again in 1954, but did not pass muster and was banned once again.

Ruth was not affected by the loss of his favorite "Betsy Bingle"—the name used for the bat in advertising. The day after the ban, he used a normal bat and went three for four with his twenty-ninth home run.

Hitters are always looking for new ways to hit the ball harder.

Legally they can "bone" their bats. That involves using a real bone or, nowadays, usually a soft drink bottle or other hard, round implement to try to tighten the grain. They can alter the gripping area with pine tar, rosin, or any other material, as long as it does not go too far up the handle. They can shave the handle or put on gripping pads. They can also tape the handle.

What they cannot do is cut holes in the barrel. They cannot apply anything to the barrel. They cannot alter the barrel from its round shape. And they must use a bat that has been approved by Major League Baseball.

There can be no "Wonderboys" carved at home off a lathe or machine shop as featured in the movie, *The Natural,* unless that bat goes through testing and is stamped as approved by MLB. Hitting a moving baseball hard enough to reach base safely nearly forty percent of the time may be the single hardest thing to accomplish in sports. No one is going to get any artificial aides anytime soon to help.

Chapter IV

BRINGING A NATION AND ITS PEOPLE TOGETHER

There is no room in baseball for discrimination. It is our national pastime and a game for all.

Lou Gehrig
Hall of Famer

Jackie Robinson sliding into base, 1947 World Series

Lou Gehrig was right, but he was also ahead of his time. He never played in a major league game with a black player. The modern color line wasn't broken until eight years after his final game and six years after his death.

Black Baseball

While Major League Baseball was finally settling down into two leagues, players of color would continue to struggle to find a place to play for more than another 100 years. The first player of color that would open up the modern major leagues to all races would not debut until 1947. Until then, their only options were to play in countries south of the border or in leagues or traveling teams built just for them.

The National Association had actually banned black players "on political grounds" on December 9, 1868, while the NA was being formed. When the National Association died and the National League and, later, the American League were formed, there were no written bans by either league. However, the ban was still implied.

Despite official or implied bans, black players and teams had been part of baseball since its earliest days. As far back as the 1870s, Bud Fowler was well-known in nonleague circles as being a strong player, but he never played with one of the organized white teams in the National Association. He did, however, play for a number of minor league clubs. From 1878 through 1895, his name can be found on teams' rosters across the country, as far west as Pueblo, Colorado, and Sante Fe, New Mexico. Fowler hit .308 with 190 stolen bases in 465 documented minor league games, including forty-five steals to lead the Nebraska State League in 1892. He was forty- five years old at the time.

There had been some black players in major league baseball and a few in the minors before Jackie Robinson played in the minor leagues in 1946 and cracked the majors with the Dodgers the next year.

Fleetwood Walker Was Really the First

The first black player on the major league level was actually Fleetwood Walker. There is a catch, however. He debuted in 1884 in the American Association, then a major league. Walker was actually of mixed race. His father was the first African American physician in Mount Pleasant, Ohio, and his mother was Caucasian. He had played baseball at both Oberlin College and the University of Michigan. His major league experience consisted of one season with the Toledo Blue Stockings of the American Association in 1884. However, some teams and players refused to take the field if he played. Because of their response, the black race was doomed to second-class status on the field of play as in daily life at the time. Although Walker hit .264 and was acknowledged as one of the best defensive catchers of the day, he and his younger brother, Weldy, who played in six games that season, were banned from both the American Association and the National League. Walker was relegated to play in the minors until 1889.

Bans Against Nonwhite Players

The conflict over Walker led to actual bans against nonwhite players that were written into the minor league bylaws by owners and players of the time. One of the instigators of these written rules was also one of the greatest players of his day, Cap Anson of the White Stockings. In 1887, Anson flatly refused to play against black pitcher George Stovey in an exhibition game.

Stovey, like Fowler, played minor league baseball. Stovey was in six different leagues, a different league in each of his six seasons between 1886 and 1891. Stovey won sixty and lost forty of 102 games and had an earned run average of just 2.17. Stovey's greatest season was with Newark of the International League in 1887. He won thirty-four games and lost only fourteen with a 2.46 earned run average.

Despite his success, Stovey's career was doomed. On July 20 of his best year, the International League passed a ban on black players. After the season, no black players would be allowed to play in the league. In the meantime, black players who loved the game were limited to playing weekend pick-up games among themselves. Those who wanted to play the game in an organized way formed their own teams.

Major league baseball teams in both the National and American Leagues never put anything down in writing, but an unwritten agreement of total exclusion of black players from baseball was in effect until 1946.

Charlie Grant Came Close to MLB

In 1901, Baltimore Orioles manager John McGraw watched a pick-up game near his team's hotel during spring training in Hot Spring, Arkansas. One player named Charlie Grant caught McGraw's eye. Grant was a light-skinned, mixed race African American. McGraw knew Negro players were not accepted in the major leagues, so he attempted to pass Grant as an American Indian. He even gave Grant a different name—Charlie Tokohama of the Cherokee nation.

Charlie Grant

However, the plan failed when the team traveled to Chicago and word got out that Grant was coming in with the team. He had played with two black teams prior to being "discovered" by McGraw. Many of his fans turned out for the game with the White Sox and even presented him with gifts before the scheduled game.

White Sox owner Charles Comiskey charged that Tokohama was actually Charlie Grant. McGraw backed off, and shortly afterwards, Grant was released from the team. Grant played with black teams through 1916, but never in the major leagues.

Black Baseball Organizes

The first black professional team was the Cuban Giants. They weren't really Cuban or giants, for that matter. They were a group of black players from the New York City area, with a few native Cubans mixed in. They played in a local white league, which was a big reason why they chose the name Cuban Giants. They were billed as being foreigners and not African Americans.

Shortly after 1890, more clubs were formed. The two strongholds were in the Chicago and New York-Philadelphia areas. Some made early attempts to form Negro leagues but never succeeded for long. However, an effort toward full organization was made in 1920.

Rube Foster: Father of Organized Black Baseball

Rube Foster, a native Texan living in Chicago, founded the Negro National League in 1920. Foster was a very talented pitcher who had reportedly spent some time working with the great white star Christy Mathewson. Foster's Negro National League was joined by the Eastern Colored League in 1923. Together, they hosted an annual Negro World Series between 1924 and 1927. But when Foster died and the Great Depression hit, black baseball joined the list of businesses that were severely threatened.

A league called the East-West League rose from the ashes in 1932 and eventually became a second Negro National League. Its annual All Star Game—mostly played at Chicago's Comiskey Park—was a highlight of black society. The Negro American League came along in 1937, and the champions of those two leagues competed in a new Negro World Series between 1942 and 1948. While the Negro leagues existed, they would produce many great baseball players.

Josh Gibson: Man of Many Legends

No player boasts a greater legend and less statistical records than Josh Gibson. The burly, power-hitting catcher played between 1929 and 1946 for the Homestead Grays and Pittsburgh Crawfords in the Negro leagues, as well as in Santo Domingo and in the Mexican League.

Josh Gibson

His supposed credits are many. For example, Gibson is credited with 962 home runs by one historian and 832 by another. He is also credited with eighty-four home runs in 170 games in 1936, seventy-five home runs in 1931, and sixty-nine home runs in 1934. However, none of those numbers are accurate. They are merely estimates. Published records for league games only show Gibson's career high as seventeen home runs during the 1939 season. The fact that he led the league in home runs eight times over a seventeen-year period verifies his power—just not some of the numbers attributed to it.

The confusion over Gibson's achievements is due to the fact that statistics from regular season games were mixed with other statistics. The regular season numbers included barnstorming games against local teams of dubious ability, as well as league games. Teams in the Negro leagues did not play 154 game league schedules as in the white major leagues. They may have played more than 200 total games per year, but that included barnstorming games. An actual league schedule of between fifty and eighty games was most common.

We know two things for certain about Gibson. We know he hit .483 in nine Negro All Star games because the box scores for those games are available. This statistic may prove he was a very good hitter—even as good as advertised.

We also know from those who played with and against him that Gibson had tremendous power. He reportedly hit the longest balls ever at both Yankee Stadium and old Griffith Stadium in Washington. Could he have been the best catcher and power hitter in baseball history? We will never know. But he was very good. He just came along too soon. Unfortunately, by the time the color line was broken, he had died at age thirty-six of a brain tumor.

DiHugo Was a Multiple Hall of Famer

Martin DiHugo was not African American; he was black player born in Cuba. In the United States, he played for the Cuban Stars, Homestead Grays, and the Baltimore Black Sox. He also played in the Mexican League and in Puerto Rico. As a 6'3 and 190-pound athlete, he played virtually any position. He was possibly the most versatile player in all of baseball history.

In 1938, for example, he led the Mexican League in both batting and pitching. He hit .398 while going 18 and 2 with a 0.90 earned run average. He also pitched no hitters in Venezuela, Puerto Rico, and Mexico. He was such a feared hitter that major league star Johnny Mize said that when they were teammates in the Dominican Republic, opponents would walk DiHugo to pitch to Mize. In Negro league ball, DuHugo led leagues in hitting and home runs. His average was reportedly .386 in 1929, but he had bested that two years before at .421. He also pitched on occasion, but not as much as he did when he left the country.

Alas, as with Josh Gibson, some of DiHugo's statistics may be irregular, but the comments from those that saw or played with him leave the impression that he may have been the best overall baseball player that ever lived. He just never got to prove it on the biggest stage—a fate of many during that period of history. DiHugo was inducted into the Hall of Fame in Cuba, Mexico, Puerto Rico, and, ultimately, by Cooperstown. He is the only player so highly honored.

Stars in Multiple Countries

During the winters, the top players in Negro league baseball played in Cuba, Mexico, and other southern points. They became widely recognized as stars. Many of the greats from the Negro leagues were also recognized as great by other players—and not only on their own level. Many major league players like Dizzy Dean, Bob Feller, and Ted Williams played on post-season barnstorming tours with or against black stars and expressed their support.

Ted Williams, for example, always had great respect for the top black pitchers. Bob Feller was outspoken and said what he felt. He thought Satchel Paige was wonderful but did not think Jackie Robinson would make it. He turned out to be half right.

Jackie Robinson was the first in modern MLB

Jackie Robinson was the first African American to play professional baseball in the modern era when he debuted with Montreal of the Triple A International League in 1946. He was promoted to the Brooklyn Dodgers in 1947 and the color line was broken once and for all. When Branch Rickey signed Robinson and later brought him to the major leagues he was not violating any rules but was breaking the unwritten and unspoken ban that had been in effect for sixty years. This was after Bill Veeck had "scared MLB" a few years earlier with his plan to buy the Phillies and fill the roster with the best black talent he could find.

66

His purchase was never approved.

Before signing Robinson, Rickey had also strongly considered making Monte Irvin the first black player. And he had his scouts looking at other players of color as well. Both Irvin and Robinson had nearly the same qualifications and were the same age. At the time, many felt Irvin was the superior player. Rickey actually signed both to minor league contracts, but Irvin was let go after a dispute between his Negro National League team owner and Rickey. The timing was simply off for Irvin. Irvin would eventually become the New York Giants' first black player in 1949. He would not be forgotten. The combination of his performances in the major league and the Negro National League would eventually lead him to be inducted into the Baseball Hall of Fame.

The signing of Jackie Robinson was the beginning of the end for Negro leagues. Larry Doby followed in Robinson's footsteps to be the first black player in the American League, also debuting in 1947 during the season. Satchel Paige was past age forty when he finally got his shot at the major leagues a year later, and he still performed well. Now that the best black players had an opportunity to move to organized ball, businesses run by people like Cum Posey and Gus Greenlee in Pittsburgh or Effa Manley in Newark no longer had as much value.

Many black players with Negro league experience like Robinson, Doby, Ernie Banks, Hank Aaron, and Irvin would become stars in MLB. Other than the barnstorming Indianapolis Clowns, which was a baseball version of basketball's Harlem Globetrotters, Negro baseball was gone by 1960.

Greats Who Never Got an MLB Chance

The Baseball Hall of Fame in Cooperstown has attempted to recognize many of the great stars from the Negro Leagues. Plaques acknowledge their accomplishments as best as they can because records were incomplete. Unfortunately, many greats never had the chance to become well-known due to the timing of the opportunity for black players to join the major leagues. Most of the great stars were more legends who barnstormed across the country in nonleague games than written fact.

Great players from the Negro leagues who did not have an opportunity in MLB include Bullet Joe Rogan, Cool Papa Bell, Oscar Charleston, John Henry Lloyd, Buck Leonard, Smokey Joe Williams, Willie Wells, Rube Foster, Biz Mackey, Willie Foster, Double Duty Radcliffe, Leon Day, and Martin DiHugo. The names of great players who could have starred in major league baseball are too many to list.

Chapter V

FIELDS TO BALLPARKS TO STADIUMS

You know those parks in those days—St. Louis was a rock pile. Ebbets Field in Brooklyn was built on a city dump. In Baker Bowl in Philadelphia, the owner apparently couldn't afford water, and Cincinnati was always flooded.

Babe Herman
Former Dodger outfielder

Shibe Park

In its infancy, baseball was played on just about any open space. There were none of the amenities fans have almost taken for granted today. But as the game developed and, most importantly, as tickets were sold, enclosed facilities were needed. The evolution of the game from fields to ballparks to stadiums includes quirky obstacles and little-known challenges.

William Cammeyer Was a Pay-for-Play Pioneer

While the American Civil War was raging, William Cammeyer came up with the idea of making money from the infant game of baseball. In 1862, he converted the Union Skating Pond grounds in Brooklyn into a totally enclosed, summertime baseball and cricket facility so he could charge admission for fans who wanted to watch the two sports.

Even though admission had first been charged in a game played between teams from New York and Brooklyn on the infield of the Flushing Race Course on July 20, 1858, the introduction of ticket sales did not catch on right away. Part of the reason may have been the initial cost of fifty cents. In 1862, one dollar was worth about twenty-two dollars by today's standards. That would have been the equivalent of about $11 today.

Cammeyer had a better idea. First of all, his ballpark would be built for the game. Seats would be constructed to make it easier to follow the play. The first games he staged at Cammeyer's Ice Rink was on May 15, 1862, and featured clubs representing Eckford, Putnam, and Constellation. Those games were free of charge to motivate fans to come to the park. Starting the next day, fans would pay only ten cents to get in and watch the action, which is equal to about $2.20 in today's money. True professional baseball—as far as the fans were concerned—had begun.

Cammeyer was not just an entrepreneur. He owned the New York Mutuals and even served as manager in 1876 during the first season of the National League.

The Evolution to the Modern Ballpark

From Cammeyer's first enclosed field, improvements for fans came next. They ranged from simple benches and chairs along the sidelines to grandstands modified from those already seen at race tracks. Benches were created for the players and then enclosed benches were added to protect players from overly exuberant fans. The playing field itself changed little after the 1893, when the current pitching distance was established, except for more modern grounds-keeping techniques that maintained its smooth texture and improved the condition of the grass.

Outfields were huge in the early days. At William Cammeyer's Union Grounds, the distance to the outfield walls measured 500 feet, although a strange pagoda-type building existed in deep center field. That was no problem since any ball headed that way would certainly already be rolling.

Only Lipman Pike was said to have ever hit the building on a fly, and his drive reportedly left a dent. The home run was not a significant or common occurrence except for the inside-the-park variety. The game was meant to be played inside the field. While those parks that had room often had very large outfields, those built in large cities had to conform to the availability of the land. Thus, while the baselines were a standard, defined length, there was no such conformity for distances to outfield walls. The baseball itself was dead and couldn't be hit very far, so conformity wasn't necessary.

Ballparks were anything but uniform. Some parks had hills or terraces in the outfield. Some even had trees that over hung the walls. Flag poles were inside the fence. Grounds-keeping equipment might be kept in the outer reaches as well. Ballparks were built of wood, which made them vulnerable to fire, and many succumbed.

Some of the Ballparks of History

While the Union Grounds has the distinction of being the first enclosed facility constructed with baseball in mind, by the 1880s the construction of ballparks was a booming industry. Somewhat ironically, their construction coincided with the closure of the Union Grounds in 1883 to make room for a new city street. New parks were springing up because baseball executives had discovered there was money to be made from the sport. During that decade, new ballparks were built in Buffalo, Cincinnati, New York, and Cleveland, including a prominent enlargement in St. Louis.

The St. Louis enlargement deserves a footnote since the grounds used for baseball were used longer and had more major league games played than any other location in history. The grounds were located on Grand Avenue, a major street which was the location of what was later called Sportsman's Park or Busch Stadium. The site had been used for games of town ball as early as the 1860s. By the 1870s, the site called Grand Avenue Grounds was home to the St. Louis Brown Stockings of the National Association. Ultimately, a new stadium was built on the site when the National League returned to St. Louis. The first game in the new stadium was played in 1881, and the park was used through 1965. It was at this park in 1884 when a tarpaulin was first used to cover the field in inclement weather. There were some gaps in the usage of the area, but for many years in the twentieth century, both the Browns of the A.L. and the Cardinals of the N.L. shared Sportsman's Park. The park was used a total of seventy-eight years for major league play when it closed after the 1965 season.

The Original Polo Grounds Was Used for Polo

The original Polo Grounds was not the facility built on 155th street, which was the last home of the New York Giants and first home of the New York Mets. The first Polo grounds was actually located just north of Central Park on Fifth Avenue between 110th and 112th streets. In 1880, the owners of the semipro New York Metropolitans leased part of the grounds for a ballpark. The area was still used for polo until two years later, when the polo folks moved to a new location. John Day, the owner of the New York Mets of the new American Association, grabbed the chance to make it their home.

Union Prisoners

John Day: One City, Two Teams, Different Leagues

When John Day moved his team to the Polo Grounds, the National League was not in New York. However, to compete with the American Association, leaders of the league needed a team in the big city.

To cover his interests, Day bought the Troy franchise of the N.L. and transferred it to New York. He now owned both the American Association Mets and the N.L. Gothams. Both of his teams played at the Polo Grounds—just not at the same location exactly.

You see, the Grounds were divided into two parts by a canvas curtain which separated their fields. Apparently, the N.L. Gothams got the better end of the deal. The Mets side may have been the worst ballpark in the history of the game. According to Mets pitcher Jack Lynch, quoted in the book *Diamonds* by Michael Gershman, "a player may go down for a grounder and come up with six months of malaria." The Mets moved out the next season.

The original Polo Grounds disappeared after the 1888 season for the same reason the Union Grounds in Brooklyn was shut down: The city wanted to put a street through the middle. It would become what is now 111th street. The Giants, as the Gothams were now known, moved further away to Coogan's Bluff. Two stadiums would be built there, which would be used by both the N.L. Giants and the Giants of the Players' League. Both teams used the same nickname, and for one year they played in adjoining parks at Coogan's Bluff.

Lakefront Park in Chicago Was Unique

Other cities had memorable homes in the early days. In Chicago, a park named Lakefront Park seated as many as 10,000 and was marketed for its grandeur. It included the first luxury boxes well before the Houston Astrodome introduced them to modern baseball in 1965. The park was located just off Lake Michigan in downtown Chicago. Michigan Avenue was just over the left field fence. The park was cozy, too. The left field line was just 180 feet from home plate. Right field was only 196 feet.

It was here that Ned Williamson set a major league record for home runs when he slugged twenty-seven in 1884. He never had another season with double figures in home runs during his thirteen-season career. He did have another footnote, though. During an 1889 game in Paris as part of a world tour by baseball, he suffered a knee injury while sliding that helped end his career in 1890 after a .190 season with the Chicago team of the Player's League.

As for Lakefront Park, its unusually short dimensions led to baseball instituting a rule. Starting in 1885, fences were required to be no closer than 210 feet. Any ball hit over a barrier closer than that was counted as a ground rule double. As a result of the rule, Chicago was forced to move to the new West Side Park.

Pittsburgh and Boston Had Historic Locations

Pittsburgh has a storied history regarding its ballparks. The site of present- day PNC Park, along the Allegheny River across the bridge from downtown, is very close to the site of Exposition Park. Exposition Park was home to baseball from 1882 until the Pirates moved to Forbes Field in 1909 and stayed through 1970. When the Bucs got their next ballpark, which was called Three Rivers Stadium, they were almost exactly on the same spot as Exposition Park. Now the original site is the parking lot for Heinz Field and PNC Park.

In Boston, only one double-decked ballpark has ever existed. It was not Braves Field nor Fenway Park. It was Boston's South End Grounds. It only seated about 5,000, but the seats were split between two decks. South End Grounds was the home field for the Boston National Association and National League franchises from 1872 until it burned down in 1894. Like Lakefront in Chicago and the all the variations of the Polo Grounds, the ballpark had an outfield that was deeply centered. The park was cavernous; its center field was as far as 500 feet deep with foul lines in the 250-foot range. The park was destroyed by a fire that started in the bottom of the third inning during a game between Boston and Baltimore on May 16, 1894. The fire, which originated with some boys setting fire to trash under the stands, consumed not only the ballpark but 177 homes.

Wooden Ballparks and Fire Did Not Get Along

Actually, fire was a big problem for baseball in the 1890s. The parks in St. Louis had six documented fires, and up to two dozen others around the country burned. The worst year was 1894. In addition to Boston, ballparks in Baltimore, Chicago, and Philadelphia were all damaged in fires.

People wondered how many of those fires were set deliberately by drunks, losing bettors, pranksters, or those opposed to Sunday baseball. That's right—there were some accusations that people who were violently opposed to the 1892 National League voting to allow baseball in their ballparks on Sundays might be behind the fires. Nothing was ever proven.

Sunday Was Not Common

Baseball games had been scheduled on Sundays since the National Association in the 1870s, but some of the teams escaped the laws of the time which forbade Sunday baseball by playing their Sunday games in different—and often rather shoddy—facilities outside the city, county, or even neighborhood limits.

Some teams didn't escape the law even when they went out of town. Both teams in Ohio tried and failed. The Reds moved games to Hamilton, Ohio, in 1889 after authorities in Ludlow, Kentucky, had reneged on an agreement to host them. Originally, Hamilton had said everything was in order, but protests from a civic group changed that. On one Sunday, when the visiting Brooklyn team was hitting in the top of the fourth, the local police chief arrived to arrest the players. Many escaped, but a half dozen were sent to jail, and the Reds were fined just under $150. Likewise, the Indians moved a Sunday game to Collingwood, Ohio, in 1898, but in the bottom of the eighth inning, police raided the park and arrested the players. The Washington teams played Sundays in Virginia. The New York clubs played Sundays in New Jersey. Others played in their home city, but in different jurisdictions where baseball on Sundays was not banned. Cincinnati, St. Louis, and Chicago teams were legally playing on Sundays before the turn of the nineteenth century. In fact, the National League's first Sunday game was played on April 17, 1892, when the Reds beat the Cardinals 5 to 1. It wasn't until 1919 that Sunday baseball in New York City was considered admissable. In Philadelphia, Sunday baseball took even longer to become acceptable. The first legal Sunday match was played on April 8, 1934, between the A's and Phillies in an exhibition game.

Before long, Sunday became baseball's busiest day as doubleheaders were routinely scheduled to take advantage of the one day in the week when more fans could make it to the park.

The first "two games for the price of one" doubleheader was played in Worchester, Massachusetts, on September 25, 1882, between the National League Worchester Brown Stockings and the Providence Grays. It was not on a Sunday, but a Monday. The purpose of the doubleheader was to help increase attendance and interest, but it didn't help any. In a game earlier in the season, only twenty-four people paid at the gate to watch the Brown Stockings. After the doubleheader, they held a game three days later, on September 28, which drew only twenty-five people. The next day, on September 29, they pulled in only eighteen spectators. That would be the final major league game to be played by the Worchester Brown Stockings.

Despite the ineffective doubleheader in 1882, doubleheaders would ultimately become regular Sunday features in many major league parks on Sundays until the 1970s. Around that time, they were no longer cost- effective as clubs were regularly drawing greater crowds and playing double headers actually cost teams money. Now a scheduled doubleheader is very rare. Two games in one day on the same ticket is limited to rained-out makeup games late in the season.

The Mound and Baselines: A Ballpark's Only Standards

One of the beauties of baseball is that no ballpark ever has or will be exactly the same. The most important distances—the measurements between the bases and from the mound to home plate—have been the same for more than 120 years. A lot of other things have been changed, though. Ballparks kept getting enlarged and improved—and finally replaced.

Because the average age of major league parks in 1952 was thirty-nine years, it would not be long before replacements to original ballparks were needed. But most of the next round of ballparks would not be like the old timers.

After the Dodgers and Giants moved west, both needed new homes. The Dodgers opened Dodger Stadium in 1962. It was state of the art and kept that status for many years. The stadium featured more amenities than fans had ever seen, just as the Astrodome in Houston revolutionized the possibilities for locations of games when it provided the comforts of indoor games for the first time.

The round Astrodome also revolutionized the style of ballparks as multipurpose facilities. During the 1960s and 1970s, a number of new ballparks were built in that mold. RFK Stadium in Washington was first, then the Astrodome, although the Astrodome was unique in many more ways.

Soon, multipurpose ballparks were built in St. Louis, Atlanta, Cincinnati, Philadelphia and Pittsburgh. The outdoor oval or circular ballparks were almost exactly alike and all but Washington were located in National League cities. Except for the air conditioning and unique roof of the Astrodome, they were all essentially the same. Foul lines were the same in left and in right. Most had artificial turf. They were boring, but necessarily so to accommodate the National Football League, which had grown and no longer comfortably fit within existing baseball parks. Cities were not ready to build separate facilities, certainly not football stadiums, which were used only eight to ten times per year for that sport.

Soon came a procession of "cookie cutter" stadiums. All of the round or nearly-round stadiums had large sections of movable seating to configure for baseball or football games. All of the new stadiums provided clear views for fans, but the seats were further away from the actual field than the old ballparks. Most also had artificial turf instead of grass to handle the extra use. Turf had been invented primarily for use in the Astrodome after it was discovered that grass could not grow under the roof, even with its skylights. The fake grass was soon used in all of the new parks, even in the park in Kansas City built solely for baseball.

The park in Kansas City, originally named Royals Stadium and, later, Kaufman Stadium, should be listed with the first of the stadiums of the 1990s even though it was built in 1973. It was built only for baseball, with a football stadium built separately on the same grounds. Like Dodger Stadium, the park essentially had standardized outfield distances and did not feature any real idiosyncrasies on the field. However, it was identified as unique because of a large water display over the outfield and the fact that it was built solely for baseball. It would be more than twenty years after its construction that other cities would opt for separate stadiums for the NFL and MLB if they could afford it.

In the 1960s, the game changed in the National League because standardized outfield dimensions and artificial turf mandated a faster game. Speed replaced power. The Cardinals won championships thanks to that speed. The Reds won titles when they learned how to combine speed with power. The N.L. owned most of the new parks and played the "new" game of speed.

Round, dual-purpose stadiums did exist in the A.L. In Oakland, the A's were moved into the existing home of the NFL Raiders. In Anaheim, the park was retrofitted to also host the NFL Rams. Cleveland was still playing in Municipal Stadium, considered for years as too large to host baseball, but eventually it became the full-time home of the Indians.

Here Comes the DH for Real

By the late 1960s, as the boom of the construction of stadiums was beginning in the National League, the American League was not doing well. The Yankees were not winning. The stadiums were old. Attendance was not growing. Pitching was dominating the hitting.

What was the American League to do? To regain attention, they considered a rule that had first been voted upon by the N.L. in 1891 and then considered again by that league in 1930 but rejected both times. The American League voted for the designated hitter.

First introduced as a temporary test rule in the minor league International League in 1969, the rule was voted by the A.L. to be added to the major leagues. In 1973, the American League would remove the pitcher from the batting order and replace him with a player who did nothing else but hit.

Rule was Tested in the Minors

The modern fathers of the designated hitter were Tidewater Tides president George Sisler, Jr., and team general manager Dave Rosenfeld. According to Sisler, it took a lot of thought before the rules for using the DH were ready to be proposed to baseball's rules committee. The new DH rule was approved, but only for a one-season experiment in the International League. After that, the rule would be evaluated and possibly put to a vote for all of professional baseball.

In later years, Rosenfeld admitted that, as a baseball purist, he really preferred the game without the DH. However, as a general manager, he realized the potential of the rule to improve offense and, thus, attendance.

That argument about offense still holds more than forty years since its introduction in the American League. Annually, the American League has higher annual team averages and more runs scored than in the National League. The offensive rule has not

80

held as an attendance boost between the two leagues in recent years, however. The average attendance of National League games in recent years, even without the DH, has been as many as 3,000 fans per game higher than in the American League.

The DH has been a permanent rule in the American League since 1975, although the National League continued to oppose adding it. Compromises were worked out between the leagues for interleague, spring training, and postseason play.

More than the DH Rule Was Needed to Revive Baseball
In spite of the new round, artificial, turf-carpeted parks of the National League and the DH rule of the A.L., the game was not progressing well in comparison with the professional football boom in the early 1970s. It took the 1975 World Series between the Reds and Red Sox to bring the game back.

Once the Reds-Red Sox seven-game series awakened the sleeping giant, which occurred at the same time the Yankees were about to return to prominence, the financial aspects of the game became front and center.

Free Agency Changed the Game
Baseball was forced into a new way of thinking in the 1970s when the long held reserve clause was broken and players could become free agents after their contracts expired. Teams also had to deal with the very strong Major League Baseball Players Association, which had led the fight for free agency behind the leadership of Marvin Miller. Now the union was seeking a greater and greater share of the revenue brought in by owners. All baseball teams had to find new revenue sources with ways to put some limits on team spending; otherwise, the stronger clubs could just sign as many of the top players as their rosters would hold.

Owners found new revenue sources. One source was better local television packages, which included more games on television than ever, from paid television through cable systems at first and, later, through satellite and other methods. Another source of revenue came from more inventive marketing and advertising plans. Money also came from yet another round of new stadiums, this time led by the American League.

Thirty Years Later—New Parks with a New Concept

The stadium developments were truly innovative with a look to baseball's early 1900s. There would be no more shared, cookie-cutter designs. It would be a time to recognize the unique status of baseball and its fans and to build ballparks more fitting for the sport.

White Sox Led the Way

The Chicago White Sox was one of those American League teams that had struggling for years. For years, the second team in Chicago to the Cubs, there were moves to transfer the club to St. Petersburg if a new stadium could not be built to replace White Sox Park, which had originally been built as Comiskey Park in 1910. It was the oldest park in baseball, and it showed.

A last-ditch vote by the Illinois legislature allocated funds and allowed for the construction of a new park on the south side, adjacent to White Sox Park. It opened in 1991. Now known as U.S. Cellular Field, the home of the Sox had seating arranged just for baseball. It featured private suites, clubs, restaurants, and all the amenities that would soon be expected in future stadiums. Originally, the grade of the upper deck caused fear with some fans, but the tradeoff was that the Sox had a new home in their old hometown and would not be shipped off to Tampa Bay. They were grateful for the new park, even though fans who had sat in the last rows of the upper deck at old Comiskey Park had been closer to the field than they would be at the new park.

Over the years, the home of the Sox was modified and

improved to the point that it became one of the best venues in baseball. But it was the first of the new parks built in the 1990s and didn't have one feature that would become very popular: It did not bring back memories of the past. It was a very good new ballpark, but it lacked character.

Here Comes Oriole Park at Camden Yards

Lack of character was not a problem when the folks in Baltimore left old Memorial Stadium on 33rd Street for a new facility closer to the heart of the city. Orioles Park at Camden Yards amazed fans when it opened in 1992.

It was asymmetrical in the outfield. In addition to all of the modern amenities for fans as introduced in Chicago, the park was built in area that was rich with baseball history. A tavern once run by Babe Ruth's father was located in the vicinity of center field, and Ruth's birthplace was only a short walk away. Beyond right field loomed the old B&O Railroad warehouse. The city skyline is visible over the left field stands.

Camden Yards was baseball's real jewel. It stood out alone until the construction of competing parks that followed the same concept.

The Ballpark Boom Continued

In 1994, two more new ballparks were added to Major League Baseball. They were called originally The Ballpark in Arlington, home of the Texas Rangers, and Jacobs Field in Cleveland, home of the Indians.

Both had all of the amenities that were expected of new ballparks of the era. Both also had characteristics that differentiated them. The park in Arlington was built on a rise next to a man-made lake, which made the outer shell seem massive. Inside the park, a right field grandstand reminded many of Detroit's Tiger Stadium. Its right field foul pole was closer than that in left field. In Cleveland, Jacobs Field featured a distinctive left field area where fans could stand near the top of the elevated wall. They could view downtown Cleveland behind that left field.

In 1995, a new park opened in Denver. Another new one, first used in Atlanta as the Olympic Stadium, was retrofitted to become the new home of the Braves. And the building never stopped.

From 1991, beginning with the opening of what is now called U.S. Cellular Field in Chicago, to 2013, twenty-two new ballparks were opened. Dodger Stadium, which was constructed in 1962, was the third oldest ballpark, behind Fenway Park and Wrigley Field. Only the Oakland Coliseum, which was originally constructed for football, still shares its grounds with an NFL team.

Ballpark Stories

From William Cammeyer's first enclosed ballpark in Brooklyn to the most modern of the current facilities, there have been many interesting differences between the locations of games.

Differences in outfield distances are most noticeable, but so have been distances from home plate to the back stops, and from the foul lines to the seating area. There have been obstacles such as flag poles, inclines in the outfield, and the use of equipment related to batting practice and grounds keeping. There have been significant errors in design. It is not just the major leagues that have offered unusual facilities either.

Outfield Size Certainly Never Standard

From the incredibly short 186' left-field lines and 197' right-field lines at Chicago's Lake Front Park to the outfield dimensions of several parks that reached 500 or more feet in centerfield, there has been no "standard" over time. The rules state that no foul line should be less than 325' now. But those rules were in place when new parks in Houston and San Francisco were built. Each has one foul line that is shorter than 325'.

The biggest ballpark in terms of field acreage in use over the last sixty years was Braves Field in Boston. While its distances were changed, it contained more acreage than any park in major league history. At its largest, it measured 402' to the left field line and 375' to the right field line. The distances in the middle of the field started from 402' in left center, 461' in center, and 542' in right center. When Braves Field was opened in 1915—three years after Fenway Park—it was the largest ballpark ever with 40,000 seats.

Because of its size, the Red Sox played their home World Series games there in both 1915 and 1916. They also played their Sunday games at Braves Field from 1929 to midway in the 1932 season because Fenway Park was less than 1,000 feet from a church. One infamous incident occurred on Opening Day in 1946, when about 5,000 fans left the park with green paint on their clothing since new paint applied to the park had not yet dried. The club reimbursed those fans.

Before the Red Sox moved to Fenway Park, they also had huge playing grounds in Huntington Grounds from 1901 to 1911. Measurements of left center to right center were 433', 530', and 412'. That park was on part of the current grounds of Northeastern University and is commemorated by a statue of Cy Young, who had played on that field in baseball's first AL- NL World Series.

Locations Were Rarely Prime

Most ballparks were not built in the best part of town. Land was cheaper if you put a park on an old garbage dump, and many did. The original Polo Grounds in New York, just north of Central Park, was located on an old garbage dump. So were Lakeside Park and Comiskey Park in Chicago, Ebbets Field in Brooklyn, as well as a couple of notable minor league parks. Sulphur Dell in Nashville was build next door to a dump. So was Ruppert Stadium in Newark, where the Yankees played their great minor league teams of the 1930s. Maybe that was why Babe Ruth declined an offer to manage in Newark!

In Chicago's Comiskey Park, White Sox shortstop Luke Appling reportedly found an old copper tea pot buried in the ground near his position.

Hills, Lumps, Bumps, and Worse

Some aspects of the old parks—exclusive of their fence distances—are hard for modern fans to believe. When Houston's then-named Enron Park was opened in 2000, there was much commentary about the hill in deep center field. Tal Smith, the club president at the time, recognized it as an homage to ballparks of the past.

The most famous hill in play was at Cincinnati's Crosley Field. The outfield there had a terrace that originally covered all three outfields, but was later only evident in left field and center. The slope was always in play at Crosley. It started only about 300 feet from home plate.

When Fenway Park in Boston was new, it had a very steep slope in left field. It was used almost as an early warning signal that the wall was near. However, it was in play, and any ball caught was counted as an out. Duffy Lewis became expert at handling the incline, which was soon dubbed "Duffy's Cliff."

Smead Jolley Was No Climber

Smead Jolley was not as fortunate as Duffy. Jolley was an outstanding minor league hitter. He had a .367 average for sixteen seasons. In all or parts of four years in the majors, he hit .305. But Jolley was a DH thirty years before the position existed.

Once, before a game at Fenway Park, much time was spent teaching Jolley how to climb the embankment to catch fly balls. In the game, however, Jolley went back for a long fly, climbed the hill, and suddenly realized the ball was going to be short. He reached back for the ball, fell down the hill, and was sprawled flat.

When he was asked about his adventure after the game, he blamed his coaching. "They taught me how to climb the hill but forgot to teach me how to come down," he said. His outfield misadventures did not need uneven playing fields. During a game in Cleveland, he made three errors on the same play when a ball got through his legs, hit the wall, and bounded back between his legs again. Then when he finally got to the ball, he threw it wildly.

Some Ballparks Were Just Not Right

Other parks just had uneven playing surfaces, like Philadelphia's Baker Bowl, nicknamed "The Hump." Its nickname was derived from a hump in centerfield. The park had been built on top of a train tunnel. At Detroit's Bennett Field, which pre-dated Tiger Stadium, cobblestones were under the field and often worked their way to the surface.

In Orioles Park in Baltimore, which was used by the original Orioles in both the American Association and National League, right field was not level. It sloped down toward the fence. The field was also often very mushy since water seeped in from a nearby stream.

Well before the Braves were in Atlanta, the minor league park there was Ponce De Leon Park. It had a Magnolia tree in play in right center field in front of an embankment that served as the fence. The tree still lives behind a shopping center built on the site. Ponce De Leon Park is also known as the site of the most traveled home run of all time. When Bob Montag homered to right field in 1954, the ball landed in a train coal car. It went all the way to Nashville, which was about 518 miles!

Brooklyn Had Multiple Sites

The borough of Brooklyn included more than just Ebbets Field as historic baseball locations. Union Grounds, of course, was the first. Built in 1871 over an ice skating rink, it featured a pagoda building in the deep outfield. That was no problem since all outfield distances were over 500 feet from home plate.

The second baseball home for Brooklyn, Washington Park, featured a clubhouse that had formerly been used by George Washington as his headquarters at the Battle of Long Island during the Revolutionary War. It was at Washington Park that Archibald "Moonlight" Graham made his only major league appearance. Moonlight Graham became famous as played by Burt Lancaster in the movie, *Field of Dreams.*

Ebbets Field was Originally Another Dump

Many stories surround Ebbets Field, which was built on a former dump site. When it was opened in 1913, builders realized they had forgotten to construct a press box, and team management had forgotten to get an American flag. The outfield walls angled at the base for about ten feet then went straight up. This resulted in a ground ball home run once. In 1916, George Cutshaw of the Dodgers hit a sizzling ground to right that rolled up the incline and jumped over the wall for a homer.

The ballpark also featured a sign by tailor Abe Stark that read, "Hit it Here and Win a Free Suit." The sign was about three feet high, thirty feet long, and was located at the bottom of the right center field wall. The only winner of a suit was Woody English of the Dodgers.

Another time, the scoreboard clock was smashed by a drive off the bat of Bama Rowland of the Braves. The incident was the inspiration for the climactic moment in the motion picture *The Natural* when Roy Hobbs hits the clock. Glass shattered and fell at Ebbets Field just as in the movie.

Clark Field Had a Limestone Cliff

Two ballparks receive special mention for quirky features. The first, Clark Field at the University of Texas in Austin, was only used for major league baseball exhibitions. The outfield included an incline in left field toward center which was made up of limestone and only accessible by traversing a goat path. Outfielders had to decide whether to play on the cliff or in front of it. It was quite often in play. One memorable moment involved Yankee great Lou Gehrig in an exhibition in 1929. He reportedly hit a home run that cleared the cliff and the fence well behind it. No one before or since accomplished that feat.

The Play is the Thing on Staten Island

But the most unusual ball park of all was in the major leagues. Officially known at the St. George's Cricket Grounds, but unofficially as "Mutrie's Dump," the Staten Island location was another dump site that had been turned into a ballpark! The American Association Mets and National League New York Giants used the park during 1887 through 1889. This was after the original Polo Grounds north of Central Park had been taken over by the city for construction of 111th Street.

The field on Staten Island had been used for ball playing since 1853 but was useful in other ways as well. A stage play, called "Fall of Babylon," was held there in 1887, which forced the field to be moved a bit west. The move made the field slope a bit from third base to left field. The real problem was in right field: A huge stage structure sat there, so all balls hit to right field were deemed singles. In addition to the complications from the play, the field was unusually uneven after some camels and elephants cut through the outfield during batting practice on their way to a nearby zoo.

In 1889, the last season either team dared try to play on the field, a stage production called "Nero, The Fall of the Roman Empire" had just concluded. The field was left in a bare and stony condition, so some scaffolding boards were used to cover the swampy, muddy outfield. While the St. George's Cricket Grounds may have had the most cluttered outfield, there have been many unusual incidents of more than just outfielders in the outfield.

Flag Poles, Batting Cages, and Monuments

The original Yankee Stadium had the centerfield flag pole plus monuments and plaques in deep center field and in play. Center field was as far as 467 feet from home plate, so they were rarely a problem.

The same was the case at Forbes Field in Pittsburgh, where the Pirates parked batting practice in deep center field during games. The cage may not have usually been a problem, but there was one problematic incident in right field. History records a home run once granted to Ed Abbaticchio when he hit a ball in the "tank where horses dive."

Flag poles in play used to be common. Houston's Minute Maid Park has the American Flag pole inside the wall, which has factored only once in a game since the park opened in 2000 through 2013. On July 1, 2003, Milwaukee's Richie Sexson hit a long drive to deep center field that nicked the pole and fell in play inside the field. He had to hustle to leg out a triple.

Years before, in 1915, Bill Hinchman of the Pirates hit a ball off the flag pole at Forbes Field. He was faster than Sexson and sprinted for an inside- the-park home run. Flag poles were also in play at Detroit's Tiger Stadium and originally at Detroit's Comerica Park. At Comerica, the flag was moved to outside the park when the walls were moved after the first three seasons.

The bullpen at the last Polo Grounds was actually in the outfield. Since the fences were already so short down the lines, the bullpen could not be enclosed, otherwise the distances would be far too short. So, bullpen personnel had to keep aware of what was happening and get out of the way if the ball or an outfielder was headed toward them.

For many years, ballparks had pitching mounds in foul territory in front of the dugouts where starting pitchers would warm up in front of the fans. That mound could sometimes be treacherous for catchers chasing foul balls. While the mounds are no longer there, some bullpens down the left and right field lines can still offer problems for outfielders chasing fouls. The days of storing stage show props in the outfield may be gone, but playing the outfield can still over more challenges than just the wind or sun.

Shibe Park In Philadelphia Was Fireproof

It wasn't until April 12, 1909, when baseball built its first park solely of steel, concrete, and brick. (Forbes Field in Pittsburgh was also built with those materials, but did not open until June 30, 1909.) Shibe Park was built for the Philadelphia A's and would be their home until they moved to Kansas City in 1955. Starting in 1938, the park would host the Phillies as well. Its name was changed to Connie Mack Stadium in 1953 in honor of the longtime owner and manager of the A's.

Chapter VI

WINNERS AND LOSERS
NOT ALWAYS THE STORY

There are three types of baseball players: Those who make it happen, those who watch it happen, and those who wonder what happens.

Tommy Lasorda
Former Manager, Los Angeles Dodgers

Crowds watching the 1914 World Series, Philadelphia

Now time for a little fun. The next few pages include some of the fun notes that I found during my years of looking specifically for answers to rather off-beat historical notes. We aren't going to talk about wins and losses but, rather, show why baseball is far more than that.

From Long to Short Games

Modern baseball is rarely played in less than three hours. That was hardly the case throughout history. For a long time, a game lasting more than even two hours was considered a bit long. But with the advent of radio and television and enforced time breaks between half innings, things started to lengthen. Before that, a few notable games were played at almost break- neck speed.

The quickest game in modern major league history was played on September 28, 1919, between the Philadelphia Phillies and New York Giants at the Polo Grounds. New York won the game in just fifty-one minutes.

Before the National Association started major league ball in 1871, one game had been recorded as having been played in fifty minutes. On August 4, 1868, at Brooklyn's Union Grounds, the Eckfords beat the Uniques 37 to 1 behind the pitching of Al Martin. First pitch hitting had to be the rule that day!

The quickest game ever played in professional baseball was between Salem and Asheville in the Carolina League in 1916. The two teams played in just thirty-one minutes because they needed to catch a train.

Both of those "quickies" were played with standard rules. But a college experiment in Texas resulted in a doubleheader that needed twenty-one innings to complete, yet it was played in a total of two hours and twenty-six minutes. The teams did it by playing with rules that used only three balls for a walk and two strikes for a strikeout with only two outs per half inning.

It was in 1958, and the University of Houston beat Sam

Houston State in both games. The first game went twelve innings and still only lasted one hour and thirty-eight minutes with a final score of 2 to 0. The second game was also won by Houston 3 to 1 in just one hour and eighteen minutes. Afterwards, the fans were asked to vote on what they had seen. They did not care for it. They preferred baseball as it was supposed to be.

An MLB Doubleheader was Faster

Even playing with the modified rules, the Sam Houston State-Houston doubleheader played in two hours and twenty-six minutes is not the fastest doubleheader ever. In the major leagues, a twin bill between the New York Yankees and St. Louis Browns on September 26, 1926, only took two hours and seven minutes! One of the games was the second shortest in major league history, only fifty-five minutes.

Lots of Long Games

The longest major league game ever in terms of innings played was twenty- six in a 1 to 1 tie between the Reds and Cubs in 1920. Both starting pitchers, Leon Cadore and Joe Oeschger, pitched all the way.

The longest major league game in terms of time was eight hours and six minutes in the twenty-five inning game between the White Sox and Brewers on May 8 and 9 in 1984. Harold Baines homered on the 753rd pitch of the game for a 7 to 6 win by the White Sox. The game was not played from start to finish without a break. The first seventeen innings were played, and then the game was suspended and resumed the next day. White Sox catcher Carlton Fisk caught all twenty-five innings, but at least he had some rest after those first seventeen.

The longest nine-inning game by time was between the Red

Sox and Yankees on August 18, 2006. The Yankees won the 14 to 11 game in four hours and forty-five minutes.

Tigers and Rangers Needed Over an Hour for One Frame

The longest single inning by time was on May 8, 2004. The Detroit Tigers scored eight runs in the top of the fifth inning against the hometown Rangers at Arlington, Texas. The Rangers followed with ten in the bottom. The inning included 110 pitches, and eighteen runs and took one hour and eight minutes to be played. Texas won the game in ten innings with a score of 16 to 15.

Extra Innings Common for Red Sox in 1943

In the 1943 season, the Boston Red Sox set the major league record for the most extra-inning games in one season when they played thirty-one extra innings. That was just more than five percent of the total schedule. The Red Sox finished seventh with a 68 to 84 record that year.

Bill Dineen Pitched and Umped No-Hitters

Only one man has ever pitched a no-hitterin the major leagues and, later, umpired while one was thrown. The man is Bill Dineen, who pitched his no-hitter for the Boston Red Sox in 1905. Then, after he retired, he was behind the plate umpiring five more.

Dineen was a very good pitcher whose footnote should also mention that he won three games for Boston in the first World Series in 1903. His no-hitter was against the Chicago White Sox on September 27, 1905.

He became an umpire full time less than three weeks after he pitched his final game in 1909. He would hold down the job in the American League through 1937. During that period, he worked eight World Series and was the home plate umpire to open the first All-Star Game in 1933. The five no-hitters Dineen called were by Chief Bender in 1910, George Mullin in 1912, Dutch Leonard in 1918, Sad Sam Jones in 1923, and three days later in 1923, Howard Emke.

Umpires Formerly Major League Players

The list of former major league players who later became umpires includes forty names through the 2013 season. That number is not expected to increase for some time since the last former MLB player to finish his umpiring career did so in 1984.

Bill Kunkel was the last major league player to turn to umpiring. Bob Emslie was the first. Kunkel umpired in the American League from 1968 through 1984. Emslie began in 1891 and continued through 1924.

Kunkel was a pitcher who appeared in eighty-nine games for the Kansas City Athletics and New York Yankees between 1961 and 1963. Emslie played his entire career in the major league American Association between 1883 and 1885. In 1884, his best season, he was 32 to 17 with a 2.75 earned run average. He started fifty games and finished them all. That season resulted in a sore arm that never really went away, and his career was finished after the next season.

Bob "Wig" Emslie—named for the hair piece he wore—turned to umpiring as a way to stay in the game, yet it happened as an accident. The native Canadian was about to watch an International League game between Toronto and Hamilton and was asked to ump when the assigned arbiter became ill. He found he liked the job and spent three seasons in the minors before joining the National League in 1891.

During Kunkel's career, the only major change in the game was the addition of the designated hitter. However, during Emslie's career, there were many changes. In 1893 the pitcher's distance was moved to its current 60' 6". The mound was added, and full overhand pitching was allowed. When Emslie started,

96

one umpire was used. At times, the ump would position himself behind the pitcher and not behind the catcher.

In 1911, a second full-time ump was added. Emslie stopped working balls and strikes and became exclusively a base umpire. He stayed in that role until his appearance behind the plate to open the first All-Star Game. Bill Klem took over behind the plate after a few innings. Ironically, Klem always umpired the plate, and Emslie always handled the bases with a few exceptions for most of his career.

Trades of Note

Let's talk about note-worthy trades. We're not talking big, multiplayer deals or even deals involving big names. No, we are talking about strange trades for sure.

Harry Chiti Knew Who He was Dealt For

In 1962, The Cleveland Indians traded veteran catcher Harry Chiti to the New York Mets for a player to be named later. Teams will often do that when one team needs a particular player—perhaps prompted by an injury emergency— that may be expendable on his current team but there has not been enough time to arrange compensation. As it turned out, neither the Indians nor Mets could agree on the proper compensation.

Chiti had been acquired by the Mets on April 25. And on June 15, after playing fifteen games and hitting only .195, he was sent back to Cleveland as the player to be named later. He had been traded for himself. It must be noted that Harry is not the only player so dealt—he was just the first.

Youngblood Faced Two Future Hall of Famers

Several players have faced two future Hall of Famer pitchers in the same game. Any team that had a future Hall of Fame starter and closer would have offered that chance. But only Joel

Youngblood ever faced two of them playing for two different teams in two different cities in the same day.

On August 4, 1982, he started in center field for the Mets against the Cubs in a day game at Wrigley Field. In the third inning, he singled off Ferguson Jenkins. Shortly after, he was pulled from the lineup and told he had been traded to Montreal. Since the Expos had a game in Philadelphia that night and getting a flight from Chicago to Philly was no problem, he hopped a jet. By the sixth inning of the game that evening, Youngblood was in the game, and he singled off Steve Carlton. Two hits, two cities, two teams, and two Hall of Fame pitchers equaled a day to remember for Joel Youngblood and a note in baseball history.

Youngblood Not First Two Team Same Day Player

While Youngblood was the first player to hit a Hall of Fame pitcher parlay, he was not the first to play for two teams in the same day. Max Flack of the Cubs and Cliff Heathcoate of St. Louis were swapped for each other in the middle of a doubleheader. Both played for their new teams in the second game. Neither, however, had hits in both games nor faced anything but Hall of Fame pitchers.

Chapter VII

TRENDSETTERS AND PIONEERS

Do what you love to do and give it your very best. Whether it's business or baseball, or the theater, or any field. If you don't love what you're doing and you can't give it your best, get out of it. Life is too short. You'll be an old man before you know it.

Al Lopez
Hall of Famer

Craig Biggio and Greg Lucas, pregame interview, 2005

The Nine-Man Game Creates the Shortstop

Until the mid-1840's, baseball—New-York style or whatever name was used locally—was usually played with eight to eleven men on a side. In some circumstances, it might have included more men. Eight players were quite common, though variants of the game could be played with fewer than the prescribed number.

Those games used modified rules as well. For a fully manned game, the positions were pitcher, catcher, first base, second base, third base, and outfielders. There were three to five outfield positions depending on how many players were being used. There was no shortstop as we now know it. The extra outfielders were often used as relay men since the soft and light homemade ball used during the period was hard to throw for distance.

When the rules were published in 1845 by Cartwright, Daniel Lucius "Doc" Adams of the Knickerbocker Club in New York strongly pushed for a ninth regular player. That player would be positioned where players were most likely to hit the ball and be used as a relay man for throws from the outfield. Thus, the short fielder was born. Adams himself was the first. The short fielder was used mostly as a rover and relay man, sometimes filling a gap on the infield. It wasn't until Dickie Pearce came along that one player placed himself on the infield full time and the shortstop position came into its own.

Interestingly, the position of tenth player was considered for a time as a right shortstop, but the idea never got anywhere after it was used in an 1873 exhibition game.

Dickie Pearce and the Tricky Hit

As for Pearce, he is also credited with popularizing the bunt—then known as the "tricky hit" or "baby hit." One tricky thing about it in the early days was that balls bunted into foul territory could still be in play if they started fairly. Whether he was the person who

RICHARD J. PEARCE,
The Veteran Base Ball Player, and Short Stop of the Mutual Nine.

Dickie Pierce

invented it or not, Dickie certainly used it more than anyone before him. (Some sources credit Tom Barlow of the Brooklyn Atlantics with inventing the bunt, but others who cite Pearce's earlier career start are skeptical.) Barlow bunted a great deal. He even had a special small bat, perhaps only two feet long, that he would often use.

Barlow may have simply been an even more notable practitioner who played in the professional era. To defend the "vote" for Barlow was a game report from June 15, 1872, which said, "After the first two strikers had been retired, Barlow, amid much laughter and applause, 'blocked' a ball in front of the home plate and reached first base before the ball did." It is curious that New York Clipper description made it sound new or different as late as 1872. The very next season, Barlow had six bunt hits in one game. Tom Barlow's career was short: He only played between 1872 and 1875. He was a victim of drug abuse, but not originally by his own hand.

In 1874, after sustaining an injury in a game, a doctor injected him with the pain-killer morphine. It led to an addiction and an end to his career midway through the next season. He was only twenty-three years old when he played his last game.

In contrast, Pearce's career was a long one. It started before the National Association was formed in 1871, possibly as far back as 1855, and lasted through the 1877 season. He retired at age forty-one.

By the way, the term "bunt," which replaced the term "tricky hit," is thought to have originated from the same word in railroading, in which bunt means to shove a railroad car onto a side track with a soft nudge from another car or engine.

Pearce may or may not have invented the bunt but is often given credit, and Barlow may have popularized it the most. There are some other "firsts" in baseball that are also quite debatable.

Candy Cummings and the Curve

For instance, did Candy Cummings invent the curve ball or not? The legend says that the 5'9, 120-pound Cummings discovered the pitch while throwing clam shells on the beach when he was fourteen years old. His Cooperstown plaque credits him for both the invention and first use of the pitch in professional baseball.

In spite of the plaque, others have received credit for the pitch. Joe Sprague, a pitcher dating back to the underhand days in 1862, has been cited by others as having a curve well before Cummings. Yet another pitcher, Fred Goldsmith, went to his grave in 1939 claiming it was he who actually first used the pitch in 1870 and that Cummings was a self-promoter who gained credit unfairly.

Cummings' pro career did not begin until 1872, but he reportedly first used the curve in a college game against Harvard in 1867. He lost 18 to 6 that day. He was the first pitcher to have trouble controlling his breaking ball! So, Cummings is given the credit, but no one really knows if it is deserved.

Cummings may have invented the overhand curve before it was legal in the "New York Game." Using the curve against Harvard in 1867 would have been plausible since the game was of "Massachusetts Game" rules, which allowed overhand pitching. Sidearm pitching was not allowed until 1884 in the games played originally under the so-called "Knickerbocker New York rules." Early curves used prior to then in the National Association or

National League and American Association were closer to what fast-pitch softball or submarine pitchers might use now.

Regardless, Goldsmith was right about one thing: Cummings did a lot of self-promotion. He wrote a book in 1886, *The Art of Curve Pitching*, and later a sequel. Cummings' 1886 book was written just at the point when pitchers were starting to be allowed to throw from above shoulder level. He also invented a "baseball curver" device that, when attached to the palm and finger, would reportedly teach anyone how to throw a curve. Never mind that it could not be used in a game. Everyone wanted to throw curves.

The First Pinch hitter

Other firsts are a bit easier to credit. The first credited pinch hitter in professional baseball history was Mickey Welch of the New York Giants. He was sent to bat for Hank O'Day in the bottom of the fifth inning on August 10, 1889. The National League had been around since 1876, and its predecessor, the National Association, had been around since 1871, but Welch became the first pinch hitter in 1889. It took until 1889 because that was the year substitution for any reason other than injury or illness was allowed, and only one substitution per game was legal. Welch struck out. "Smiling Mickey" Welch was primarily a pitcher who played from 1880 through 1892. He had a career 307 to 210 record but never pitched from 60' 6" or from a mound. His career ended the season prior to the establishment of the current standard. He threw 525 complete games out of 549 starts and won forty-four games in the 1885 season. As a hitter, baseball's first pinch hitter was not much. He had a career .224 mark.

Welch holds the record for most consecutive strikeouts to open a game with nine, but since it was achieved prior to the 60' 6" distance, the modern record of eight straight strikeouts in 1986 by Houston Astros pitcher Jim Deshaies is considered a greater feat.

Jack Doyle: First Pinch Hitter to Succeed

It wasn't until June 7, 1892, that a pinch hitter actually got a hit. Jack Doyle of the Cleveland Spiders singled. Called upon to bat by manager Patsy Tebeau, he made his skipper proud with the hit that drove in a run and won the game. It took so long for a pinch hitter to succeed because from Mickey Welch's debut in 1889 until 1891, unlimited substitutions had not been allowed. Pinch hitting was still rare.

Marty Kavanaugh Was First PH Specialist

Marty Kavanaugh, who played in Detroit, Cleveland, and St. Louis during a five-year career, may be worthy of being credited for being the first notable pinch hitting specialist. He had ten pinch hits in 1915 and had forty-six pinch hits at bat in 1916. So, let's give Kavanaugh credit for being the first pinch hitting specialist. He once reportedly hit a home run that rolled through a hole in the fence and could not be retrieved. If true, that would have likely been his career highlight. He hit just .249 with ten home runs in a 370 game major league career.

First Pinch Hitter to Homer

On May 14, 1892, Tom Daly of the Brooklyn Bridegrooms was the first pinch hitter to hit a home run. He was used for an ill teammate, Hub Collins, and was not in the game for a strategic reason. His homer tied the game in the ninth, but his team lost to Boston in ten innings. Daly played for seventeen seasons between 1884 and 1903, mostly with Brooklyn, and was a lifetime .278 hitter. He hit forty-nine home runs.

First Pinch Hitter to Homer in First MLB At Bat

Bill Duggleby homered in his first trip to the plate as a pinch hitter on April 21, 1898. It would be thirty-eight years before another player accomplished the feat. It was on April 14, 1936, when Eddie Morgan of the St. Louis Cardinals became the second player to join the club for hitting a pinch hit home run in his first MLB at bat. The next season, Ace Parker of the Philadelphia A's became the third.

Interestingly, Bill Duggleby was a pitcher. He played for the Phillies from 1898 through 1907. He had a wonderful 3.18 earned run average but had a sub .500 record at 93 and 102. As a hitter, he hit just .165 with only six career home runs.

First Time to "Put him on"

The first intentional walk has been hard to document. The reason is in part because what is intentional must be assumed from the early game. There was no stat nor did catchers routinely step away to receive purposely errant pitches. However, history does record some cases that certainly seemed to be intentional.

Many suspect that George Wright of the Cincinnati Reds received the first walk on June 27, 1870. According to an account of that day in *The Washington Olympics*, "the Washington pitcher tried to let Wright take first every time on called balls as he preferred that to George's style of hitting." Even if that was the first intentional walk, it pre-dated the start of major league baseball, which began the next season with the National Association. The fact is, it is impossible to know who drew the first major league intentional walk. It was uncommon in the early days of baseball to use the strategy and difficult when, for a time, it took nine balls to walk!

Another problem is that the intentional walk was only officially recorded starting in 1955. Any that took place earlier were often only notations and may have been unintentional wildness. The purpose to calling for an intentional walk is strategic. It allows the defensive team to avoid pitching to a good hitter and also sets up force-out options on the bases. It is rarely used if it will force a base runner to advance into scoring position. Normally, at least one runner is already there. What is most rare is for an intentional walk to be ordered that will force in a run. It is on the record that only a precious few hitters were ever so dangerous as to be walked intentionally with the bases loaded.

Being Walked with the Based Loaded

Of only six players to be walked with the bases loaded through the 2013 season, Abner Dalrymple was the recorded first player to be so feared. He played for the Chicago White Stockings and on August 2, 1881, they led Buffalo 5 to 0 in the eighth. The rules of 1881 required seven balls for a walk. It is likely that Dalrymple may have had the first intentional walk with the bases loaded since there is no earlier reference that anyone has been able to find. Based on Dalrymple's career, the intentional walk with bases loaded would have been unexpected at the time it happened. In 1884, when playing for the White Stockings at Lakeside Park with its infamous 186-foot left field line, he hit twenty-two homers, although in 1881 when the first intentional walk may have occurred, he had hit only one home run.

Some sources have reported Jimmy Ryan as having been walked intentionally with the bases loaded in 1896, but the reports lack confirmation. It is therefore reasonably certain that the second intentional walk with full bases was achieved by future Hall of Famer Nap Lajoie of the Athletics on May 23, 1901. He was walked with the bases full and the A's trailing the White Sox 11 to 7 in the ninth.

The third recorded intentional walk was on May 2, 1928, to Del Bissonette of the Dodgers with the Giants leading 2 to 0 in the top of the ninth. The Giants were also involved in the fourth intentional walk with the bases loaded. They led the Cubs 10 to

7 in the top of the eighth in the second game of a doubleheader on July 23, 1944. Bill Nicholson was passed on purpose.

On May 28, 1998, Barry Bonds of the Giants was walked by Arizona with two outs and three on base with the D-Backs leading 8 to 6. Bonds holds both the single season and career records for being walked intentionally: 120 walks and 645 walks, respectively.

The sixth and most recent case of intentionally walking a hitter with the bases loaded happened on August 17, 2008. Josh Hamilton of the Rangers was up in the bottom of the third with his team down by five. Tampa Bay manager Joe Maddon walked Hamilton to first base.

It must be noted that in all six instances in which a hitter was walked with the bases loaded, the team that made the decision to walk a hitter went on to win the game. The strategy did not fail.

Switch-hitting debut

One of the great nicknames in baseball history belonged to the first switch- hitter. Bob "Death to all Flying Things" Ferguson—so named because he rarely muffed a line drive or fly ball—switch hit for the first time in 1870 while playing for the Brooklyn Atlantics. His introduction of switch-hitting came in the game that ended the Cincinnati Red Stockings' long winning streak. (They were said to be 65 and 0 in 1869 and may have won twenty-four games to start 1870 before losing in extra innings to the Atlantics on June

14. Most records list the Red Stockings' record before their first loss as 81 and 0.) Ferguson hit from the left side for the first time in the bottom of the eleventh inning and the Reds leading by a run. He said later that he wanted to keep the ball away from Red Stockings star shortstop George Wright and "shake things up." And shake things up he did. His roller toward first baseman Charlie Gould went through his legs, allowing the tying run

to score. But when the Reds' Gould made another misplay on a bad throw to third base to get Ferguson, Bob kept running and scored the winning run to end the Reds' unbeaten streak.

During his career on July 24, 1873, Ferguson filled in as an umpire, and he proved that he took the job seriously by breaking a complaining player's arm with a bat. He would ultimately be the only person ever to be a player, manager, umpire and league president—he guided the National Association for three years. Yet, he is not in the baseball Hall of Fame.

Switch-hitting was not important in baseball's early years. The pitchers did not throw as hard, and hitters could request location of pitches as well. Things changed when the pitchers started to throw harder and the curve ball became a factor in the 1870s.

John Montgomery Ward, a natural right-handed hitter, often batted lefty to give him a head start in running to first base. He wasn't a very good hitter lefty, but he had a good on-base percentage thanks to his speed in beating out slowly hit or fumbled balls.

First Switch-Hitter to Win a MLB Batting Title

The honor of being the first switch-hitter to win a batting title goes to Tommy Tucker of the 1889 Baltimore Orioles, who hit .372 for the American Association team. Tucker was the only switch hitter to win a batting title until Mickey Mantle of the New York Yankees hit .353 to win the 1956 American League crown. Pete Rose won three batting titles during his career—the most for a switch-hitter.

Tommy Tucker had a thirteen-year playing career, from 1887 through 1899. His career batting average was .290, and he never had another season approaching the marks he achieved in 1889. That season, he had 196 hits, including twenty-two doubles, eleven triples, and five home runs. His on- base percentage was .450, and his slugging percentage was .484. He also stole sixty-three bases. Everyone knew when Tucker was around as his two nicknames would attest: He was alternately known as "Foghorn" or "Noisy Tom."

Player Born Furthest Back in History in MLB

The player born furthest back in MLB history was Nate Berkenstock. He was forty years old when he started a game as a result of an injury to teammate Count Sensenfurder. Berkenstock struck out in three of four plate appearances but made the final put out in the 4 to 1 win by the Philadelphia Athletics over the Chicago White Stockings in the National Association championship playoffs of 1871. Nate was born in 1831 and was celebrating his fortieth birthday on October 30, 1871, the day he played.

First NL Stolen Base

The first man to steal a base in the National League was Tim Murnane in 1876. But Murnane did more than that. He later became a sportswriter and proposed a rule-change calling for a designated hitter in the early 1890s. Several others took the proposition seriously and the NL actually put it to a vote. His idea was defeated, but it came up for discussion by the National League again in 1930. It did not come to existence, however, until it was tested in the minor league International League in 1969 and finally enacted in the American League in 1973. Writing about the DH in his second career may have been a more important footnote to Murnane's career than being a trivia note for stealing the first National League base.

However, no one should give Murnane credit for first suggesting the designated hitter. It was first suggested seriously in 1891 by club owner William C. Temple. In 1891, the twelve-team National League actually voted on the change but defeated it

7 to 5. Another option suggested by James Spalding was to remove the pitcher from the batting order altogether and use an eight-man hitting lineup.

Ned Cuthbert Was Really the First

Murnane stole the first base in the National League, but it was way back in 1863 that Ned Cuthbert of the Philadelphia Keystones stole the first base ever. Everyone was surprised when he did. After he pointed out that no rule in existence prevented such a move, the steal was allowed. Cuthbert was also credited with introducing to baseball the head-first slide, although it didn't become popular until the 1930s by Pepper Martin of the St. Louis Cardinals "Gas House Gang" teams. Cuthbert, who hung around long enough to play four seasons in the National League, American Association, and the Union Association through 1876, never had a steal in those leagues. Of course, by 1876, he was nearly forty years old.

Addy First to Slide

While Ned Cuthbert stole the first base and made the first head-first slide, it was Bob "The Magnet" Addy who is credited for first sliding into a base feet-first in a major league game. He played in the National Association for the Rockford Forest Citys when the league was formed in 1871 and wound up playing with Philadelphia, Boston, Hartford, Chicago, and Cincinnati— the latter two clubs in the National League. There is no date associated with Addy's first slide, but if he had his way, there would have been even more sliding in baseball than there is now.

He tried to develop a form of baseball that would be played on ice. That experiment was actually tried for a time in both New York and Chicago, but the idea melted away.

First Man of Bruises

Being hit by a pitch in a baseball game is not a pleasant experience. If it occurs with the bases loaded and the winning run on third, the pain can be alleviated. Most of the time, however, that is not the case. The all-time record for being hit by a pitch is held by Hughie Jennings. (Houston Astro Craig Biggio holds the "modern" record with 285.) "Hustling Hughie," who played from 1891 to 1918, was hit 288 times. He led the National League from 1894 thru 1898 with twenty-seven trips, then thirty-two, fifty- one, forty-six, and forty-eight trips to first base after being hit. Jennings, almost had his career ended in 1897, however, when hit by an Amos Rusie pitch that left him unconscious for three days. It was one of a reported three times that his skull was fractured by pitches! His last major head injury occurred in 1904, when he dove into an empty swimming pool. He returned to play after the Rusie beaning, but some said he was never the same. Still, he later managed in Detroit and was named to the Hall of Fame.

First Player to Record 3,000 Hits

Baseball historians all know the two sides of Cap Anson. He was a great player before the turn of the nineteenth century, but he was also a racist who was vocal in keeping nonwhites out of professional baseball. As a player, he was the first to record 3,000 hits during his career: Anson is credited with 3,055 hits. But he had help from the rules of the time; sixty of them were acquired during the 1887 season when walks were credited as hits by the rules. For a period, record books published between the late 1970s and 2001 removed his name from the 3,000 hit list. In 2001, it was decided that records must be compiled based on the rules of the time, so his sixty questionable hits were returned to his statistics, and Anson was restored as the first man to record 3,000 hits. For the record, the man who led the list during Anson's absence was Honus Wagner, who was the second 3,000 hit man. He got number 3,000 on June 9, 1914. Napoleon Lajoie joined the club three months later. Pete Rose and Ty Cobb are the only players to record more than 4,000 hits.

First Man to Hit Twenty Home Runs

The baseball was not always uniform. They often became soft or out of shape during games. Plus, the pitchers didn't throw as hard. All of this led baseball to be a game of relatively little power-hitting for the first fifty years that it was played.

By the 1880s, the balls were better, but the home run—especially the home run that actually went over a fence—was rare. The first player to hit twenty or more homers in a season was Ned Williamson of the White Stockings in 1884 when he clubbed twenty-seven. Ned had a home field that was the site for twenty-five of his dubious long balls since the left field line was a common, current Little League distance of 186' and right field was only eleven feet farther. Between 1871 and 1919, when Babe Ruth burst upon the scene as a hitter, the mark of twenty home runs was only reached six times. Given Williamson's misshapen ball park, the first legitimate twenty-homer hitter was probably future Hall of Famer Sam Thompson of the 1889 Philadelphia Quakers. He hit exactly twenty that year in 128 games for a team that hit only forty-four home runs in total. And Sam had a long target in home games because in 1889, the Quakers played at Huntingdon Grounds. It was 500' to left field, 410' to center, and 310' to right. Fortunately, Thompson was a left-handed hitter, but the wall was 25' high all around. Three hundred and ten feet to the right field foul pole was inviting enough, but still considerably tougher to reach compared to Williamson's target in Chicago.

First Home Run In Major League History

The National Association, which began play in 1871, is recognized as the first professional major league. And the player who hit the first ever home run was Ezra Sutton of the Cleveland Forest Citys on May 8, 1871, against the Chicago White Stockings. As a footnote, Sutton also hit the second major league home run. Sutton had played in the first major league game with the Cleveland Forest Citys in Fort Wayne on May 4, 1871. He had one hit in three at bats while playing third base. Five years later, he also played in the first National League game on April 22, 1876, with the Philadelphia Athletics.

The first home run after the National League was established on May 2, 1876, and was hit by Ross Barnes of the White Stockings. Barnes' first home run was an inside-the-park homer off Cherokee Fisher of the Red Stockings in Cincinnati. It was part of a huge day by Barnes who also hit a triple and single, stole two bases, and scored four runs. Later in the game, Charlie Jones of the Red Stockings hit the NL's second home run.

Barnes was a very good player during a nine-year career. He had a lifetime batting average of .360 which would be second best of all time if not that numbers for players in the pre-1900s are not given full credit. His career ran from 1871 through 1881 and included three seasons with averages of .430, .431 and .429 respectively. He also stole forty-three bases in sixty games in 1873. The season Barnes hit the first National League home run, he did not hit another, and it would be his final +.400 season. For his career, he hit just six home runs, only two of them in the National League.

First Career Home Run in First At-Bat

The category for most home runs in the first at-bat grows almost every year. But the first player in professional major league baseball to hit a home run in his first at bat was Joe Harrington with Boston of the National League on September 10, 1895. Harrington was not around long. His major league career lasted only seventy-two games over two seasons with Boston. He hit a total of three home runs and hit just .220.

Since then, several others players who have faded into obscurity also achieved the feat. But only one player homered in his first at bat and never hit another, despite playing twenty-one years: pitcher Hoyt Wilhelm. He would make nearly 500 plate appearances and never hit another home run. He didn't have many other hits of any kind, as his .088 lifetime batting average would attest. Wilhelm's hitting highlight occurred while he was with the New York Giants on April 23, 1952.

First Player to Homer in Last MLB At-Bat

A few players have departed the major leagues by leaving the game on a home run as their final hit. Buck West of Cleveland was the first. His three-run home run off Bill Phillips of Pittsburgh on September 18, 1890, wrapped up his career. West hit only three home runs in his major league career, which was a strange one. He debuted in 1884 at twenty-three years old, then played in the minor leagues until the 1890 season.

Two Hall of Famers hit home runs in their final major league at bat. The most famous was Ted Williams of the Boston Red Sox who connected off Jack Fisher of the Baltimore Orioles at Fenway Park on September 28, 1960. Earlier, Mickey Cochrane of Detroit ended his career with a homer off New York Yankee hurler Bump Hadley on May 25, 1937.

First Player with Sixty Doubles in a Season

The all-time career leader in hitting doubles and the man who will hold the record for many more years is Tris Speaker. During a twenty-one-season career, he hit 792 doubles, which is forty-six more than runner-up Pete Rose. But neither Speaker nor Rose ever hit as many as sixty in a single season. Only six players have accomplished that feat.

The first to hit sixty doubles in a season was George Burns of the Cleveland Indians in 1926. He hit sixty-four. While his name is largely forgotten, he was a very good first baseman for more than fifteen seasons with a career .307 batting average. But he also deserves note for giving rookie Joe Sewell one of his bats. The bat, later named "Black Betsy," was used by Sewell for his entire career of fourteen years and now is on display in the Alabama Sports Hall of Fame. Sewell only struck out 114 times in his long Hall of Fame Career.

Burns has the honor of getting the first hit at the original Yankee Stadium when it opened in 1923. Near the end of his career in 1929 with the Philadelphia Athletics, he became the first pinch hitter in World Series history to bat twice in the same inning. When he hit the first time, the A's trailed the Cubs 8 to 3. He batted again in the same frame as the team scored ten in the inning.

George Burns never made the Hall of Fame but he did win the Chalmers Award, which was the early equivalent of the Most Valuable Player for the 1926 season when he collected his sixty-four doubles.

Earl Webb Set the Doubles Record in 1931

Earl Webb, who holds the single-season doubles record with sixty-seven, has held the mark since 1931.

Webb was with the Red Sox when he eclipsed the mark held by George Burns in 1926. Although Earl's career was relatively short, he was a good hitter. In all or parts of eight seasons, he compiled a .306 career average. His best season by far was 1931, when he hit his sixty-seven doubles. His batting average was also .333 and he drove in 100 runs—103 to be exact— for the only time in his career.

First to Hit Thirty Triples

Other than the rare inside-the-park home run, the most exciting play in baseball is often watching a player run out a triple. With many current ballparks, a triple is rare because the outfield distances are just not as far from home plate. Yet in the history of major league baseball, four players have been able to leg out thirty or more triples in a season. Three of those four did it before the turn into the twentieth century.

The first to reach thirty triples—thirty-one to be exact—was Dave Orr, first baseman of the American Association New York Metropolitans of 1886. His career lasted from 1883 through 1890, cut short by a stroke just after his thirty-first birthday. Orr was good while he played, compiling a

.342 career batting average. Many record books will not recognize Orr due to his mark coming in the American Association; however, most historians now do credit the American Association as being a major league. Heinie Reitz of the National League Baltimore Orioles in 1894 is given credit by others for being the first to thirty triples. He, too, recorded thirty-one triples in his big season. Like Orr, Reitz did not have a long career: He played from 1893 midway through 1899. His batting average was .292 while playing for Baltimore, Washington, and Pittsburgh. He is also known for a tragic trivia note: Reitz is the first former major league baseball player killed in an auto accident. He died in Sacramento, California in 1914 at age forty- seven.

Chief Wilson Set Triples Mark in 1912

The triples record has existed since 1912, which makes it the second- longest lived hitting record on the books. In that season, Chief Wilson of the Pittsburgh Pirates collected thirty-six.

For Wilson, setting such a record was incongruous with his

overall career, which lasted only from 1908 through 1916 and in which the Austin, Texas, native hit only .269. In 1911, he led the National League in runs batted in when he also set a Pirate home run record of twelve while hitting an even .300. The next year, he hit .300 again and added the thirty-six triples. At the time, he got little notice, since an important record book in print at the time featured a misprint. The book said Nap Lajoie had hit forty-four triples in 1903, but he really hit only eleven. Only the mark for highest batting average in a season, which is .426 by Lajoie in 1901, is a longer lasting hitting record.

As for his name? Chief Wilson was really John Wilson. He had no Native American connection but was given the nickname by Pittsburgh Pirate teammates who thought it fitting because of his visage, size and Texas roots.

First Best Player of an Era

When baseball was new, the first big-name star was Jim Creighton. He was the first pitcher to figure out how to throw the ball hard while sticking with the underhand restrictions of the period. He also was an outstanding fielder and hitter. Jim, you see, played between about 1857 and 1862, in the last and greatest amateur era.

But Creighton's baseball career ended prematurely. He died as a result of a ruptured bladder attributed to a hard swing of the bat. Because his career was so short and not during the professional era, he is only a footnote when recapping the great players in the pre-1900s.

The "Man" during the nineteenth century was Buck Ewing. In fact, during the fiftieth anniversary of the Baseball Hall of Fame in 1989, Ewing was officially given the title as the best overall player of the pre-1900s. How good was he? His batting average was good but not great at .303. But he also stole a minimum 354 bases. We have to say "minimum" because numbers only exist for the last eleven years of his eighteen-year career. Defensively, he played catcher, first base, and right field the most, but it was hard to find a spot he did not play. He also was considered to be one of the smartest players of his day.

He was inducted into the Hall of Fame by the veterans committee in 1939 but was not part of an induction ceremony at Cooperstown until 2003. That is one record that may last forever: the longest time between election and induction.

First Female Major League Scout

In 1946, Philadelphia Phillie owner Robert Carpenter hired a new scout. Baseball had been around for more than a century, but it was still making history. The new scout was Edith Houghton, the first female scout in baseball history.

It was not a joke or a case of tokenism: Edith knew baseball. She had played the game as a shortstop on an organized level with a women's team called the Philadelphia Bobbies beginning in 1923. Her team was so good, it was invited to play a series of games against men's teams in Japan in 1925. She came along too early to be a player for the All American Girl's League during World War II, but she was busy in uniform anyway by serving as part of Women Accepted for Volunteer Emergency Service.

In early 2013, Edith Houghton died at 100 years of age after a lifelong love with baseball and a footnote as the first female scout.

First Team with Head Coaches

Head coaches have always been part of teams in high schools and colleges. Managers have always led teams in professional baseball—that is, except for the Chicago Cubs between 1961 and 1965.

During that period, the Cubs had no manager. They had what they called a college of coaches. The original group contained eight baseball men. The plan was for each of them to hold the head coach job for various lengths of time. Elvin Tappe, who reportedly sold owner Phil Wrigley on the idea, was one of them. Others included Charlie Grimm, Harry Craft, Rip Collins, Bobby Adams, Vedie Himsl, Verlon Walker, and Goldie Holt. Later Lou Klein, Freddie Martin, Bob Kennedy and Charlie Metro were added.

Of that group of twelve, only six actually ever held the slot of head coach. Grimm was not one of them, but he had managed the club on two earlier occasions. For the record, Himsl, Craft, Klein, Tappe, Metro, and Kennedy ran the whole show. Kennedy spent the most time in the top job.

The Cubs had little success. Their best season was in 1963, when they finished seventh in a ten-team league. They never finished higher than that but never finished last. The idea was scrapped in 1966 when Leo Durocher was named manager. He led the team to tenth in the National League, a last place finish.

Wrigley Was Only One of Strange-Thinking Owners

Phil Wrigley's decision to forego a manager for a "college of coaches" may have been a bit different, but he was hardly the first owner to try something a bit strange. In 1925, the New York Yankees awarded one of their scouts with a raise because he did not sign anyone. Former outfielder Joe Kelley was looking for prospects all season, but did not find any. After the season, instead of being give a pink slip, he was given a raise. The club owner, Jacob Ruppert, said that Kelley had saved the club at least $150,000 by not signing anyone.

Fuchs and Turner Thought they Could Manage

Two owners with no background in playing baseball thought they could be managers. After the 1928 season and with the Boston Braves in dire financial straits, team owner Emil Fuchs sold his manager, Rogers Hornsby, to the Chicago Cubs and took over the job. The German-born Fuchs, who got into baseball as the attorney for the New York Giants, had no experience to qualify him for the job. He was the titular manager of the team for the entire 1929 season as the Braves finished 56 and 98. Johnny Evers was actually handling most of the managerial chores. The Braves hired Bill McKechnie to manager for 1930.

Years later, another owner stepped into the role of manager, but for only one game. In 1977, Ted Turner, owner of the Atlanta Braves, decided to send his regular manager Dave Bristol on a scouting trip and take over in his absence to see if he could get the slumping Braves to start winning. They had been in the midst of a sixteen-game losing streak. However, he was not able to end the slump and never got another chance. Both National League President Chub Feeney and Baseball Commissioner Bowie Kuhn cited a major league rule that barred managers, coaches, and players from owning stock in their teams.

Connie Mack Didn't Have That Rule

It was good for baseball history that the ownership rule did not exist when Connie Mack was around. It would have drastically changed his life. Mack both owned and managed the Philadelphia Athletics for more than fifty years. He took over as manager of the team in 1901 and was also treasurer and twenty-five percent owner. By 1937, his ownership share became one hundred percent while he continued to manage.

His last season as skipper was in 1950. By then, he had won nine American League pennants and five World Series titles. His teams won 3,731 games, but he lost more, a total of 3948 losses.

Mack was not the only manager in baseball's early years to have a share of the club. He was just the longest lasting and most successful to be running the management of both players and business at the same time.

The Man who Invented the Hit and Run

In modern baseball, the "hit and run" play is almost a dinosaur. They play, in which a hitter has to swing at the next pitch regardless of where it is while the base-runner heads to second, scares many managers. Instead, they are more likely to use what is called the "run and hit," where the base- runner takes off to attempt to steal second, but the hitter has the option whether to swing or not. In past eras, hitters almost always did not swing when a base-runner was trying to steal, unless it was a hit and run. Now, both the runners and hitters are given more room to decide for themselves.

Tommy McCarthy was the first to make sure everyone was on the same page while playing for Boston in the 1890s. He reportedly developed batter- to-runner signals. That opened the door for the new play that he devised: the hit and run. McCarthy and his teams were the first to use the hit and run at times when sacrifice bunts had been the only strategy in the past. McCarthy was also credited—or blamed—with perfecting the "trapped" ball to catch base runners on pop flies to the infield. That ultimately led to the infield fly rule, which made the move illegal.

Hitting for the Cycle Family Style

Hitting for the cycle means getting a single, double, triple, and home run in the same game. The first player to accomplish the feat was Curry Foley for the Buffalo Bisons on May 25, 1882. It is not overly rare; there are about the same number of cycle-hitters as no-hit pitchers. Both are in the 300 range. In both 1933 and 2009, eight players hit for the cycle during the season.

But only twice have two players from the same family accomplished the feat. When Daryle Ward hit for the cycle while playing for the Pirates on May 26, 2004, he duplicated a feat his father, Gary Ward, had accomplished for the Minnesota Twins on September 18, 1980.

There is also a grandfather-grandson cycle. Gus Bell hit for the cycle as a Pittsburgh Pirate in 1951. His grandson, David Bell, did the same for the Phillies on June 28, 2004.

From POW to Umpire

Augie Donatelli was a National League umpire for twenty-four years between 1958 and 1973. During that period, his work was rewarded with assignments in five World Series. But how he started umpiring was a unique story. He first umpired at a prisoner of war camp in Germany during World War II.

Donatelli had been a tail gunner on eighteen air corps missions during the war. In his last mission, the plane was shot down, and he was captured. He was sent to a German stalag as a POW.

The prisoners were allowed to organize and play in softball games by their captors. It was in these games that Donatelli tried umpiring for the first time. After the war, Augie decided to make umpiring his life's work. Following an apprenticeship in the minor leagues, he had one of the most distinguished careers in major league history. And it all started in a POW camp during World War II.

Steve Palermo: Good Ump, Great Hero

For fifteen years, Steve Palermo had become regarded as one of the best umpires in the American League, but it all ended suddenly one night outside of a restaurant in Dallas. His attempt to aid a woman in distress resulted in a devastating and career-ending injury.

On July 7, 1991, he and several friends, including fellow umpire Rich Garcia, were eating a late dinner at Campisi's Restaurant in Dallas. He and his crew had officiated a Texas Rangers game in Arlington about twenty miles away. An altercation started outside the restaurant as two waitresses who had just gotten off work were struggling with some muggers. Palermo and his group rushed outside. Whey they chased the would-be assailants, Palermo took a bullet into his spinal cord.

The early prognosis was that Palermo would live, but he would never umpire and possibly never walk again. He never did umpire, but through hard work and determination, he did learn to walk using a leg brace and cane. Since then, he has served as an inspiration to many others. He also has worked with Major League Baseball as an umpiring supervisor.

Chapter VIII

HITTING FEATS OF NOTE

Pitchers did me a favor when they knocked me down. It made me more determined. I wouldn't let that pitcher get me out. They say you can't hit if you're on your back. But I didn't hit on my back. I got up.
Frank Robinson
Hall of Famer

Frank Robinson

Most baseball fans know that Pete Rose had the most hits, Ty Cobb had the highest career average, and Barry Bonds had the most home runs. But how many know the names of those players who weren't so outstanding but who still stand in a class of their own?

Best Hitting Bad Team

The 1930 Philadelphia Phillies proved you just cannot win without pitching and defense. They tried to do without and finished 51 and 102. Now, that is not the worst record of all time, but it certainly is the worst record for a team that batted .315!

As amazing as it sounds, the 1930 Phillies not only hit .315 as a team but had one future Hall of Famer, Chuck Klein, who had a .386 average as well as forty home runs and a whopping 170 runs batted in. Third baseman Pinky Whitney hit .342, and two more regulars were well over .300. The team averaged six runs per game.

Oh, but the pitching and the defense was horrible! Not only did the pitchers rack up an earned run average of 7.71, but the defense made an average of an error and a half per game.

Say all you want about Johnny Vander Meer's two straight no-hitters being a record that will never be broken. You might also consider never ever again seeing a team with a .315 batting average lose over 100 games.

Best to Worst Hitting Teams

As good as the .315 was for the 1930 Phillies, it is not the record for team batting average in the National League. That record was established by the Phillies of 1894. They hit an astounding .350. The American League record was set by the 1921 Tigers at .316.

Like the 1930 team, all that hitting was not enough to win. The 1894 Phillies finished 71 and 57 in fourth place and eighteen games behind the pennant-winning Baltimore Orioles. All three starting outfielders hit over .400. Only first baseman Jack Doyle hit less than .300 at .298. Billy Hamilton stole 100 bases and the team pilfered 285 while scoring 1179 runs—an average of 9.2 runs per game! Unfortunately, the pitching surrendered an average of 7.8 runs per game, with an earned run average of 5.63.

Washington Baseball Club, 1887

The worst hitting team of all time was the 1888 Washington Nationals. They hit just .207. Their pitching was much better than the 1894 Phillies, with an earned run average of only 3.54. But the Nationals' top average was the .274 of Dummy Hoy, and no other regular batted higher than .225. The team averaged only 3.6 runs per game.

Best to Worst Hitting Players

In modern baseball, Napoleon Lajoie's .426 batting average for the A.L.'s Philadelphia Athletics in 1901 is the best ever. Of all time, however, it is only the eighth best. Tip O'Neill hit .485 for the 1887 St. Louis Browns of the American Association. Tops in the National League was Hugh Duffy at

.440 of the 1894 Boston Beaneaters. Best ever in the modern National League is Rogers Hornby of the 1924 St. Louis Cardinals at .424.

Fifteen players carried a career average of .340 or more. Of career leaders, the top players are led by Ty Cobb at .366.

So who was the worst hitter of all time? Certainly for players who were around long enough to qualify for this dubious distinction, it would be hard to beat Bill Bergan.

In eleven major league seasons between 1901 and 1911, the right- handed hitting catcher for Cincinnati and Brooklyn hit just .170. He hit just two career home runs—both inside-the-park homers—in 3,028 official at bats. Bergan had just sixty-eight extra base hits out of 516 career hits. His career on-base percentage was just .194 and his career slugging percentage only .201. He hit over .200—.227 to be exact—only once in his eleven seasons. He established a record for non-pitchers with forty-five consecutive hitless at-bats in 1909. It was later tied by Dave Campbell and Craig Counsell and broken by Eugenio Velez of the Los Angeles Dodgers in 2009 with forty-six consecutive hitless at-bats.

As one might imagine, Bergan hung around as long as he did because he was a whale of a defensive catcher. He once threw out six players attempting to steal bases in one game.

His caught-stealing percentage for his career was forty-seven percent. By the new "win shares" statistic, he was the number two catcher of all time, and he has been ranked as high as the number two best defensive catcher of all time by statistical researchers. He just couldn't hit a lick.

Longest Home Runs

There is no way to ever know who hit the longest home run in baseball history. But there are several instances in which balls traveled in the air—or accumulated an after-landing distance—that are quite memorable.

Physicists have studied the trajectory of baseballs and have concluded that any baseball that has hit its highest point will start to descend and add far fewer feet to its distance than many have estimated. Hitting a baseball on the fly much more than 500 feet under normal conditions is highly unlikely. The higher the ball is hit into the air, the closer it will descend from its most elevated point. The speed has been spent.

That is not to say some balls have not been hit prodigious distances, only that those distances may have been overestimated. Babe Ruth was superb, but could he really have hit a spring training home run that

Babe Ruth

went 612 feet? Supposedly, he did just that while still a pitcher with the Red Sox against the New York Giants during a 1919 spring exhibition game in Florida. The ball reportedly hit the far edge of a race track, well over the center field fence. Actually, the field in Plant City was built inside a race track, with home plate located at the midway point of the grandstand and the field in the infield. Historians have repeated the 612-foot distance for years, but there is great skepticism of its accuracy.

Bob Montage likely hit the ball that covered the most distance, but a train helped. He is the player who homered at Atlanta's minor league Ponce DeLeon Park in 1954 and whose ball landed in the coal car of a passing train. The train was headed to Nashville, which was 518 miles away. As interesting an anecdote as that may be, Bob does not qualify in the true longest home run category. Neither does Ernie Lombardi of the Reds, but he has the major league unofficial longest "vehicle aided" homer. He hit one into a truck outside Crosley Field. The truck went another thirty miles before it stopped.

But it could be a minor leaguer named Gil Carter who really hit the longest home run ever. He was a twenty-year-old outfielder playing for Carlsbad in the Sophomore League when he unloaded on a home run that may have traveled up to 650 feet on the fly and was found in the yard of a house 730 feet from home plate!

Carter hit the ball off Wayne Shaper of Odessa on August 11, 1959. Eyewitnesses said the ball was on the rise when it sailed over the light towers in left field at the 360-foot mark. To reach the yard where in was found, it had to cross one street, two alleys, and two lots. The owner of the Carlsbad team was the developer of the subdivision. He calculated that the ball couldn't have bounced or rolled more than eighty feet. Whether the ball was in the air 650 feet or not is an educated guess, but where it was found after its travel was not. That was 730 feet from home plate.

By the way, don't bother trying to find Carter's name in a major league record book. He never appeared in a major league game even though he hit a total of twenty-eight home runs that memorable season.

Mantle Has MLB's Recognized "Unofficial" Longest

It is not in any official record book, but the longest home run in major league history is still believed in many circles to be Mickey Mantle's 565-foot blast at Washington's old Griffith Stadium on April 17, 1953. That distance includes the ball's roll into the yard of a home at 434 Oakdale after it landed.

While the home is still there—fellow Astro broadcaster Bill Brown and I found it—the ballpark is not. The Howard University Hospital is on the grounds where Griffith Stadium once stood. Over the years, a few other balls have been "guesstimated" as either longer or with the right trajectory to go further had they not been stopped. Since Mantle's blast was actually measured, it remains major league baseball's "unofficial" longest.

On June 8, 1926, Babe Ruth may have hit one longer. He sent one all the way out of Detroit's Navin Field, which was later known as Tiger Stadium, that landed an estimated 602 feet from home plate then came to a stop 800 feet away. That's the legend, at least, and a legend it will remain. Pitcher U.S. Grant

Stoner surrendered the monster blow.

The perfect scenario to challenge the Mantle or Ruth distance would involve a ballpark with a wind blowing out at a good clip with a very hard- throwing pitcher on the mound. Wrigley Field would be a good location candidate if the hitter could put the ball over the bleachers and land it right in the middle of Kenmore, which intersects with Waveland Avenue in left field. Hitting on the concrete would give the ball a lot more chances to keep rolling, especially if there were no traffic on the street for the ball to hit.

Actually, Dave Kingman could have claimed the longest home run ever, had a ball he did hit at Wrigley been just to the left and landed in the street. As it was, he is credited with a ball that wound up 530 to 550 feet from home plate on a porch roof on the east side of the street, three houses down on Kenmore past Waveland. The ball was hit while Kingman was with the Mets on April 14, 1976. In the street, with extra roll—who knows how far it could have gone?

Bobby Lowe: First to Hit Four HRs

Four home runs in one game by a single player is the major league record. It has been achieved by more than fifteen players. No player has ever done it more than once. The first time the feat was accomplished was on May 30, 1894, by Bobby Lowe of the Boston Beaneaters off Elton "Icebox" Chamberlain of Cincinnati. Primarily a second baseman, Lowe hit .346 with seventeen home runs and 117 runs batted in that season. He had an on-base percentage of .401 and a slugging percentage of .520, which made his season one of the very best by a second baseman of all time. Only Rogers Hornsby, who came around almost thirty years later, would put up those sort of offensive numbers while playing second base. Lowe's career, however, did not sustain that level of offense. In eighteen seasons, he carried a lifetime .273 average and hit a total of only seventy-one home runs.

Nig Clarke Hit More

On June 15, 1902, Canadian-born Jay "Nig" Clarke may have hit eight home runs in a minor league game. His team, the Corsicana Oil Citys, beat the Texarkana Casketmakers 51 to 3. The game was played on a short field in Ennis, Texas, since Sunday blue laws did not allow baseball in Corsicana. The right-field fence was only about 210 feet away from home plate.

When reports of the game started to circulate, newspaper editors were sure there must have been a mistake and someone had made a "3" look like an "8." No one could hit that many home runs in one game, could they?

Later, however, the full box score indicated that the eight was likely correct. Clarke himself never denied hitting eight home runs in one game even if some were not much to boast about with the short fence. And his whole team hit twenty home runs in the rout.

It was Nig Clarke's most famous note in history. He only hit a total of eleven home runs in 109 games that season. In a fifteen-year major league career, he hit a total of nine homers. But he did have one other highlight: He was the catcher for Addie Joss' perfect game on October 2, 1908.

Lipman Pike Hit Six in a Game

The record shows that Lip Pike hit six home run in a July 16, 1866, game, though when he did it there was no professional baseball and the competition for his Philadelphia Athletics, the Alert Club of Philadelphia, might have been suspect. He hit five of them in succession. Offense dominated the game which was won by the A's 67 to 25.

Lipman Pike has been declared "America's First Home Run King" in a short book of the same title by Richard Michelson, and the facts back up that assertion. In addition to the six-home-run game in 1866, Pike deserves recognition for being one of baseball's first paid players. He, along two other teammates, was reportedly paid twenty dollars per game, which caused animosity among his nonpaid teammates. He was voted off the team for that and for his Brooklyn Jewish background. The excuse given was their fear of his disloyalty when the A's might play a New York or Brooklyn team.

Pike continued to play through the mid 1887 season once the game became totally professional. As a professional, he played with Troy, Baltimore, Hartford, St. Louis, Cincinnati, Providence, Worcester, and New York. He won home run championships the first three years of the National Association, from 1871 to 1873. In 1877 in the National League, he was known as the "Iron Batter" with a career .322 batting average over ten seasons. His season home run leading totals never exceeded seven, which he hit in 1872. His other league leading home run seasons included just four home runs each year. In Pike's day, no season included more than seventy games, and it was a far different game then. Yet, relatively speaking, Lipman Pike could take credit for being "America's First Home Run King."

Chapter IX

PITCHING ACHIEVEMENTS TO REMEMBER

I became a good pitcher when I stopped trying to make them miss the ball and started trying to make them hit it.

Sandy Koufax
Hall of Famer

Roger Clemens and Greg Lucas, pregame interview, 2005

CHAPTER 9: PITCHING FEATS TO REMEMBER

Baseball's history includes many playing legends, from Cy Young, Ty Cobb, and Babe Ruth to Willie Mays, Pete Rose, and Barry Bonds. But a great many baseball legends don't involve just the great hitters. Many of them were pitchers. Fans know that Cy Young won the most games, Nolan Ryan had the most no-hitters and struck out the most batters, and that Bob Gibson and Roger Clemens may have been the most intimidating pitching stars in the game's history. Since most fans already know most of that, what about some of the others who also toed the rubber?

Who Threw Hardest?

For instance, who threw the ball harder than anyone who ever lived? This is impossible to factually present since radar guns never timed Walter Johnson, Smokey Joe Wood, Bob Feller, Jim Maloney or Sandy Koufax. Furthermore, what counts? And are all radar readings equal? We know that Mark Wohlers of the Braves was first to be clocked at 103 miles per hour in an exhibition game in 1995. Since then, a few others have reached that number, including Joel Zumaya of Detroit, who reached that number more than once in 2006 and has been reported as reaching 104 in a stadium radar gun display. Red's Cuban-born lefty, Aroldis Chapman, was clocked at 105 in 2010.

The unofficial record for most pitches at 100 mph or more in a season is held by Joel Zumaya of the Detroit Tigers in 2006. He was clocked at that speed or greater 233 times. Kyle Farnsworth of the New York Yankees was second with twenty-six. Billy Wagner of the New York Mets led the National League with only five. Until 2006, Wagner had held the single season record when he was measured at over 100 mph 159 times in 2003 while with the Houston Astros.

Measurement Systems are the Problem

We may never know who actually has thrown the fastest pitch since there is no consistently calibrated system in play at the ballparks.

Even the scout's radar gun readings are predicated on which point in the balls flight is caught.

Bob Feller once raced a motorcycle with a pitch. He was clocked at 98.6 mph. Walter Johnson had done the same years before and was timed at 99.7 mph. Feller also threw into an electronic measuring device that clocked him at what has become a legendary 107.9 miles an hour. Unfortunately, other than from Feller's memory, there was no known record of the test. More contemporary reports of a photo cell test showed the speed to be 96.8 miles per hour.

In 1917, Johnson threw into a speed meter at an arms laboratory in Bridgeport, Connecticut, at 134 feet per second. That calculated to just 91.3 miles an hour, but it still was the quickest of any recorded that day. The list of those tested included Christy Mathewson at 127 fps, or 86.59 mph, and Smokey Joe Wood at 124 fps, or 84.5 mph. It is easy to see with the conflicting reports and measurements that pinning a "fastest ever" on a single pitcher is impossible.

They Threw Very Hard

The two hardest throwers in baseball history may have been minor leaguers who never made it to stick in the majors. Longtime baseball scouts say Steve Dalkowski had to throw the fastest of all time. Except Steve never was quite sure where his heater was headed. A Baltimore farm hand, he once threw 283 pitches in a complete game, which featured 120 pitches in just two innings. He once walked twenty-one in a minor league game. In another game, he struck out twenty-one.

Respected baseball men like Paul Richards, Harry Brecheen and Earl Weaver contended that Dalkowski could fire it up at least 105 miles an hour. Weaver said he was the fastest he ever saw. Ted Williams concurred after seeing just one pitch in a spring training game.

In 1962, while pitching for Stockton, he struck out 262 in just

170 innings. Unfortunately, he walked exactly the same number. Dalkowski was only measured for speed once, and he only reached 93.5 miles an hour.

There were some reasons for his low speed. He had pitched the day before, and he was not throwing from a mound. In addition, he had to pitch forty minutes before the machine could measure his speed. He had to throw the ball through a tube-like target and it took him a long time to actually hit it!

Umpire Doug Harvey was working in the California League while Dalkowski was there. The Hall of Fame major league umpire said, "I've umpired for Koufax, Gibson, Drysdale, Maloney, Ryan, Seaver, Marichal, and Gooden, and they could all bring it, but nobody could bring it like he could. In one season in the minors, he broke my bar mask, split my shinguards, split the plastic trim on my chest protector, and knocked me back eighteen feet. He was the fastest I had ever seen."

Cal Ripken, Sr., who caught Dalkowski in the minors, said hitters didn't need to be afraid. Dalkowski was wild, but only high or low. He just was wild in those areas a lot. In one game, he was relieved after 120 pitches. He was only in the second inning. He got as high at AAA twice, but not for long either time. He could throw it hard—maybe harder than anyone who ever lived. He just never quite knew where it would go.

Dalkowski never played in a single major league game. Ron Necciai did, but not many. Necciai once fanned twenty-seven hitters in a minor league game and in his next start struck out twenty-four more. That was in 1952 for a Pittsburgh Pirate low minor league affiliate. When he cracked the majors with the Bucs later the same season—jumping five levels as a twenty-year-old—he was hardly as impressive. He was 1 and 6 with a 7.08 earned run average. In fifty-four and a third innings, he fanned thirty-one and walked thirty-two. He never appeared in a major league game again.

The First No-hitter

When talking of no-hitters pitched in baseball, the name of Joe Borden should be remembered. He not only won the first game in National League history but also pitched the first no-hitter in the National League on May 23, 1876, for the Boston Red Stockings under current rules, thus making major league baseball history.

He had also pitched the first recorded no-hitter in any professional league the previous season, while still in the National Association. He twirled that one for the Athletics against the Chicago White Stockings on July 28, 1875. Borden's no-hitter in the N.L. is not recognized officially because he walked two batters. In 1876, walks were counted as hits. But he actually gave up no hits as we now know them. Borden's career lasted only those two seasons; he never played again after 1876. He was only twenty-two years old. Pitching two no-hitters in his only two seasons is a record, even if one of them is questioned. He was also the winning pitcher in the first N.L. game ever played. He threw a complete game for Boston and beat Philadelphia 6 to 5 on April 22, 1876.

The first recognized no-hitter in the NL was tossed the same season by George Bradley of St. Louis versus Hartford on July 15.

The first known no-hitter of all time anywhere was pitched on May 29, 1875, by Princeton's Joseph L. McElroy Mann. He beat Yale 2 to 0.

Then There Was Bumpus

Bumpus Jones made his first major league start on October 15, 1892. He pitched a no-hitter. It was his only appearance that season with Cincinnati; the next year he started the season with the Reds but finished with the New York Giants. He was 1 and 4 and never appeared in the major leagues again.

Bumpus had an excuse. You see, his no-hitter occurred in the last regular season game ever played with a flat pitcher's box that allowed the hurler to release the ball as close as 50' from the plate.

The season after he pitched his no-hitter, the pitcher's mound was established, and the distance was moved back to 60' 6".

Don't Forget Bobo

Bobo Holloman's name is found on the major league baseball no-hitter list, but not much of anywhere else. That is because his career lasted only one season and totaled only three wins. His no-hitter came in his first major league start. He won 6 to 0 for the St. Louis Browns over the Philadelphia.

Athletics and had two hits and three runs batted in as well. When he opened his career with a no-hitter, he was the third player to do so. Fewer than 3,000 fans saw the game played on the drizzly night of May 6, 1953. And Holloman was not seen in the major leagues ever again after that season.

The Tough Luck King

You won't find Tommy Bridges on the list of pitchers with no-hitters. But no one was ever closer or had more chances. On September 24, 1933, he lost a no-hit bid in the ninth inning while pitching for Detroit against Cleveland. That has happened to any number of pitchers. But it was the third time in the same season he had lost a shot at a no-hitter in the ninth. It was also the fourth time in his career. He never threw a no-hitter.

Ryan is the King

Most baseball fans are aware than no one has pitched more no-hitters than Nolan Ryan. He threw seven of them spread out over his long career with the Mets, Angels, Astros, and Rangers. Sandy Koufax had four in his career. Ryan bested Sandy with number five for Houston, and then padded his lead with two more for the Texas Rangers. The interesting note of Ryan's no- hitters is that no catcher caught more than one of them. Seven different backstops had the honor.

Ryan the Oldest, Rusie the Youngest

When Nolan Ryan threw his seventh no-hitter at age forty-four for the Texas Rangers against the Toronto Blue Jays on May 1, 1991, he set yet another record. He became the oldest hurler to author a no-no. The youngest was Amos Rusie at twenty years and two months old. His no- hitter came in 1891 for the Giants against the Dodgers. That was during the pitcher's box era with the front line fifty feet from the plate and the back line at fifty-five and a half feet.

Vander Meer Still in Class of His Own

One of baseball's achievements that has yet to be tied and has the longest odds of ever being broken is Johnny Vander Meer's back-to-back no-hitters in 1938 for the Cincinnati Reds. To break it, one would have to throw three in a row. Vander Meer achieved his feat in Cincinnati against the Braves on June 11, winning 3 to 0, and against the Dodgers in Brooklyn's first home night game on June 15, winning 6 to 0. Ironically, Vander Meer, who threw hard but often was wild, had begun his pro career in the Dodgers' organization then the Braves' organization. His next start saw him throw three more hitless innings; finally Debs Garms of the Braves singled, ending Vander Meer's hitless streak at twenty-one and two-third innings. That record also still stands. He won the game allowing only three hits.

Vander Meer Could Have Been Number Two

Beating the Vander Meer record may be nearly impossible, but tying the mark is not. In fact, had Howard Ehmke had any luck in 1923, it would have been Vander Meer tying his record.

Ehmke, then with the Red Sox, pitched a no-hitter against the Philadelphia A's on September 7. It deserved an asterisk because he did surrender what would normally be a hit when Slim Harris lined a ball over shortstop that rolled all the way to the wall. But Harris had missed first base. When the Red Sox called for the ball and touched the bag, he was out and not credited with so much as a single.

Four days later, Ehmke was on the mound again. His third baseman, Howard Shanks, failed to make a play on a ball that was ruled a hit rather than an error. That would turn out to be the only hit of the game.

Blackwell the Closest Since Vandy

The closest to duplicating Vander Meer's feat was turned in by the Reds' Ewell Blackwell in 1947. He threw a no-hitter against the Braves then followed with eight and a third no-hit innings against the Dodgers.

No-Hitters in Two Major Leagues

Into the 2014 season, only six pitchers have thrown no-hitters in two different major leagues. Ted Breitenstein did it first. Ted also did it in his first major league start for the St. Louis Browns against Louisville, after being only used in relief up to that point in his rookie season. The date was October 4, 1891, on the last day of the season. It was the last no-hitter thrown in the American Association, which dissolved before the next year.

His second no-hitter was pitched in the National League for the Cincinnati Reds on April 22, 1898. He beat the Pirates. Breitenstein had to share the headlines, though. For the first time in baseball history, two no- hitters were thrown on the same day. Jay Hughes of Baltimore no-hit the Boston Beaneaters. In spite of the feat, Breitenstein's career was mediocre and over early in 1901. He finished with a 160 and 170 record along with a 4.04 earned run average.

Cy Young, Tom Hughes, Jim Bunning, Nolan Ryan, and Hideo Nomo make up the rest of the exclusive list. All threw one in each league except for Ryan, who had six in the American League and one in the National. (Kevin Millwood pitched a no-hitter for the Phillies in 2003 and was part of baseball's second six-man effort for the Mariners in 2012.)

Most Pitchers Teamed in Major League No-Hitter: Six

Twice have teams of six major league pitchers pitched a no-hitter. The first was pitched by the Houston Astros at New York in an interleague game with the Yankees on June 11, 2003. Roy Oswalt started but had to leave with a groin injury after the first inning. He was followed by Pete Munro, Kirk Saarloos, Brad Lidge, Octavio Dotel, and Billy Wagner. Lidge was given credit for the win and Wagner the save. Munro went the longest, two and two-third innings, but walked three. Lidge went two full innings with two strikeouts and no walks.

Octavio Dotel pitched the eighth and struck out four. A wild pitch on strike three to Alphonso Soriano allowed him to reach base, but Dotel struck out both Derek Jeter and Jason Giambi to end the inning. Houston won 8 to 0.

Mariners Match it in 2012

The second pitching staff to team up for a six-pitcher no-hitter was in another interleague matchup featuring the Seattle Mariners against the Los Angeles Dodgers on June 8, 2012. Mariner starter Kevin Millwood went the first six innings before had to leave with a groin injury, like Roy Oswalt nine years earlier. Charlie Furbush, Steve Prior, Lucas Luetge, Brandon League, and Tom Wilhelmsen made up the rest of the six-pack. When Millwood, left the game it was still scoreless. The only run was scored in the bottom of the seventh by Seattle, giving Prior the 1 to 0 win. Wilhelmsen got the save.

Seven No-Hitters to Seven Different Catchers

Ryan pitched seven no-hitters for three different teams: the Angels, Astros, and Rangers. The first four were pitched for the Angels. Seven different catchers were behind the plate for Ryan's no-hitters.

Jeff Torborg, Art Kusnyer, Tom Egan, and Ellie Rodriguez caught him for the Angels. Alan Ashby had the honor in Houston, and John Russell and Mike Stanley were behind the plate in Texas.

Using a Bat Won't Help

Ryan's second no-hitter for the Angels on July 15, 1973, is worth noting. Not only may it have been his most dominant, since he struck out seventeen hitters, but the game ended unusually. After totally handling the Detroit Tigers, he had two out in the ninth, and the hitter was to be slugging Norm Cash. Cash had fanned his three previous at-bats. So, he came to the plate carrying a table leg instead of a bat.

When home plate umpire Ron Luciano saw the weapon, he asked Cash about it. His reply was that the table leg would work as well as anything else that day. Luciano made him come back to the plate with a bat. Ryan got his no-hitter when Cash hit a soft pop fly for the final out.

Strange as it may seem, though, history records one other player trying to use something other than a bat. In 1929, Rabbit Maranville took a tennis racquet to home plate to see what he could do against Dazzy Vance. The umpire would not give him a chance to use it, either.

Varitek Most Experienced

Jason Varitek has the record for catching the most no-hitters. He had four starting with Hideo Nomo in 2001. Then he caught no-hitters by Derek Lowe in 2002, Clay Buckholtz in 2007, and Jon Lester in 2008. All were with the Red Sox.

For a while, Ray Schalk was credited with four as well, but in 1991, Major League Baseball changed the definition of a no-hitter, stating that games must be at least nine innings long, and even pitchers who allow no hits for nine innings but surrender hits after that will not be credited with no-hitters. That cost Schalk credit for a game pitched by Jim Scott in 1914. He had given up two hits in the tenth.

Thirteen catchers have caught two no-hitters into the 2014 season, but only one catcher has caught two perfect games: Ron Hassey, for Len Barker in 1981 and for Dennis Martinez in 1991.

Zip Zabel Super Reliever

On June 17, 1915, George "Zip" Zabel was probably not expecting to see any action. Bert Humphries was starting the game for his Chicago Cubs and had spun a complete game shutout in whipping the Phillies 2 to 0 in his last outing six days before. Zip was wrong. Before the day was over, he would pitch 18.1 innings in relief to set a record that stands to this day. He also won the game over the Dodgers 4 to 3 in nineteen innings.

No one knows if the strain of that day had anything to do with it, but Zabel, who was only twenty-five years old, never appeared in another major league game after the 1915 season.

Record for Most Innings Pitched in a Game

Zabel holds the record for relief innings pitched, but two starters share the mark for most innings pitched in a single start. And Leon Cadore of Brooklyn and Joe Oescher of Boston did it in the same game. Both threw twenty-six innings in a game that ended in a 1 to 1 tie on May 1, 1920.

Phil Paine: First American In Japan

Japanese baseball has long been a spot for major league players past their prime or not able to get a break to continue their careers. But it was pitcher Phil Paine that was the first. In 1953, the Braves hurler, on leave from an Air Force assignment, appeared in nine games for the Nishitetsu Lions. He was 4 and 3 with a 1.77 ERA. In 1954 he went back to the Braves and finished his career with the Cardinals.

Only Woman to Pitch to Major Leaguers in a Game

Jackie Mitchell was the first female to pitch in a major league game. It was only an exhibition game, and no one knows for sure if Babe Ruth and Lou Gehrig took her presence seriously. Mitchel was a seventeen-year-old, left- handed high school student who was signed to a contract by the minor league Chattanooga Lookouts in 1931.

That spring, the New York Yankees played the Lookouts in an exhibition on their way north. In the first inning, with two on and two out, manager Bert Niehoff made the call to bring in Jackie. When the count on Babe Ruth reached 2 and 2, she let go a big, slow curve that caught the plate while Babe was frozen. He was called out. The Bambino slammed his bat on the ground in what most thought was mock anger.

Jackie still had to deal with Gehrig. She struck him out swinging. Were they both taking it easy on her? Or did Jackie really have their number? We would never know for sure since, following the game, Baseball Commissioner Kenesaw Landis voided her contract.

One other female tried to play professional baseball with the men. Eleanor Engle was signed by the Harrisburg Senators as a shortstop in 1952. However, she never appeared in a game before her contract was voided by Ford Frick, the baseball commissioner at the time.

Best Pitcher's Season Since 1940

It would be hard to top what Bob Gibson did for the St. Louis Cardinals in 1968. Other pitchers have had better records, even though 22 and 9 is quite good. But Gibson allowed only 1.12 earned runs per game. He started thirty-five times and completed twenty-eight of them. Thirteen of those games were shutouts. He struck out 268 and walked only sixty-two in 304.2 innings pitched. Gibson was so dominant that his season had a lot to do with baseball deciding to lower the height of the pitcher's mound from

15" to 10" for 1969. Over the years, it has been returned to 15" , but due in large part to what Gibson did in 1968, it was lowered, and Gibson can be credited with requiring the adjustment. He was just too good.

Best Single Game Ever Pitched

For a number of reasons, many think former Chicago Cub right-handed pitcher Kerry Wood pitched the greatest game ever. It happened on May 6, 1998, at Wrigley Field against the Houston Astros. In that game, Wood struck out twenty hitters and allowed only one hit—a ground single by Houston shortstop Ricky Gutierrez in the third inning.

Wood's game is somewhat lost in history because it was not a no-hitter nor a perfect game, but it certainly was the most dominating outing ever. It was thrown against an Astros team that would finish the season with 102 victories and that had all the regulars in the lineup that day, including players like Craig Biggio, Jeff Bagwell, Moises Alou, and Derek Bell. Wood never pitched another game in his career that even approached what he did that afternoon. But then, neither has anyone else.

Strikeout Records

Nolan Ryan holds the career record with 5,714 strikeouts, followed by Roger Clemens and Randy Johnson. Ryan also holds the single season record of 383, set with the Angels in 1973—that is, if you discount Matt Kilroy and Hoss Radbourne. Since both played before the turn of the twentieth century, neither Kilroy nor Radbourne are normally remembered. But they should be, if for nothing more than as interesting footnotes.

Matt Kilroy Fanned 513 in Sixty-Eight Games

Matt Kilroy played for Baltimore in the American Association in 1886, a major league at the time, when he struck out an average of

145

7.5 batters per game. That does not compare with Ryan's average of 9.3 per game. But Kilroy was pitching in an era when throwing overhand had only been legal for two years and batters could still request high or low pitches.

Kilroy had a couple of major advantages, though. The pitching distance was only fifty feet, and it took seven balls to walk a hitter. He also could take a running start as long as his delivery released the ball while he was still inside the pitcher's box. Even so, in his sixty-eight games, he walked 182 batters in 583 innings. His record was 29 and 34, as the twenty-year-old pitched every other game. The next season, when the rules were changed to require four strikes for an out and only five balls for a walk, Kilroy only struck out 217 in 589 innings. But he won forty-six games and lost only nineteen. Although he hung around for parts of ten major league seasons, he was only a part-timer after his first four seasons.

Radbourne: A Legitimate Star

Hoss Radbourne also had a season with more strikeouts than Ryan's record of 383. He fanned 441 in 678 innings in seventy-five games in 1884 in what may have been the greatest single season for any era. He won sixty and lost twelve. The year 1884 was the first in which overhand pitching was legal, but Radbourne never varied from the submarine style he had already developed. When Radbourne's career ended after 1891, he had 311 wins in just eleven seasons. He was inducted into the Baseball Hall of Fame in 1939.

Who Fanned the Most in a Nine-Inning Game?

There is no question of who fanned the most in a single nine-inning game between the early ages of baseball and recent times. Roger Clemens holds the record with twenty in a nine-inning game with Boston in 1986. Clemens tied his record in 1996, as well as Kerry Wood of the Chicago Cubs in 1998 and Randy Johnson of Arizona in 2001. Johnson got his in the first nine innings of an eleven-inning game.

But What about Tom Cheney?

While pitching for the Washington Senators on September 12, 1962, Tom Cheney actually struck out twenty-one in a game. But he had to pitch sixteen innings to do it. While Clemens and Johnson are bound for the Hall of Fame and Wood might have been, had not injuries cut his career down, Cheney is a great unknown. He played for the Cardinals, Pirates, and Senators in an eight-year career. His best two seasons were with Washington in 1962 and 1963 when he went 7 and 9 and 8 and 9, respectively. The latter season included a fine 2.71 earned run average. He was out of the major leagues after 1966 when he was only thirty-two years old.

Running up the String

Houston Astro lefty Jim Deshaies was not known as a strikeout pitcher. But in 1986 he started against the Los Angeles Dodgers and struck out the first eight players in the lineup, setting a modern major league mark for strikeouts to open a game. Jacob deGrom of the Mets tied Deshaies' feat on September 15, 2014 against the Marlins. Deshaies' chance to fan the whole lineup was destroyed when Dodger manager Tom Lasorda sent Jim Lett to pinch hit for his pitcher in the third. Lett flied out, which was quite ironic. In three career appearances by Lett against Deshaies, Lett struck out in two of them...not just this time. DeGrom gave up a hit to pitcher Jarred Cosart to end his string. Those ninth place hitters prevented Deshaies and deGrom a shot at tying the pre1900 record of nine strikeouts to start a game by Mickey Welch in 1884. Mickey was a strikeout pitcher, with 345 of them in 1884, when he won thirty-nine games in the first season when pitchers did not have to throw underhand and from only fifty feet.

Eight strikeouts in a row is also the American League record for a whole game. Nolan Ryan did it for the Angels twice. Ron Davis, Roger Clemens, and Blake Stein also fanned eight in a row. The major league record for consecutive strikeouts in a game is ten by National Leaguer Tom Seaver with the Mets. More on this later.

147

Four Ks in One inning

Something wrong has to happen for a pitcher to strike out four in one inning. But it has happened over sixty-five times in major league history. The first pitcher to have to fan four in one frame was Ed "Cannonball" Crane of the New York Gothams on October 4, 1888. In the minor leagues, Kelly Wunch fanned five in one inning.

Only two pitchers have struck out four in a frame more than once. A.J. Burnett did it twice and Chuck Finley three times.

Fanning the Side on Nine Pitches

If striking out four in one half inning is quite a feat, so is striking out the side on nine pitches. It has been done fewer times that having to fan four, but it became far more common when the game started changing in the early 1920s. That was when the big swing started to replace "small ball" as the primary offense. Fewer than fifty pitchers have struck out the side on nine pitches in baseball history. Only three of them occurred before 1921. It should be no surprise that the three pitchers who were the first to perform the feat twice were Lefty Grove, Nolan Ryan, and Sandy Koufax. Ryan was the first to do it in both leagues.

Pete Richert Deserves Some Love

When lefty Pete Richert broke in with the Los Angeles Dodgers in 1962, he set a rookie record by striking out the first six hitters he faced, including four in one inning. Four years later, he struck out seven straight in a game with the Washington Senators to tie the then AL record.

Tom Seaver is the King

It is Tom Seaver with the New York Mets who holds the major league record for consecutive strikeouts. He fanned ten straight San Diego Padres over the sixth, seventh, eighth, and ninth innings on

April 22, 1970. Eric Gagne also fanned ten in a row, but as a relief pitcher, it took him four games over five days in 2003.

But There is a Higher Number

There is a higher number, but the catch is that it happened in the minor leagues. Baltimore farmhand Luis Ramirez playing for the Aberdeen Firebirds struck out twelve straight on June 23, 2004. He pitched five innings and struck out twelve of the fifteen hitters he faced, including the last twelve. Then he was removed from the game. Why? He was on a pitch count.

Speaking of Pitch Counts

It is not known who threw the most pitches in a single game. Records were just not kept until the last forty years or so. Since 1990, however, the most pitches thrown in a game by a single pitcher is 172 by knuckleballer Tim Wakefield of Pittsburgh versus Atlanta in 1993. Fernando Valenzuela was also credited with 172 pitches for the Dodgers in 1987.

Many historians are fairly certain that either Nolan Ryan or Cy Young threw the most pitches in their careers. Ryan is thought to have the edge as a result of his high strikeout and walk totals and the changes in how the game was played. However, there is no conclusive proof. Ryan has said that he believes he once threw 241 pitches in a single game while with the Angels.

Even That Total May Be Short

There have been published reports of a sixteen-inning duel between pitchers Juan Marichal and Warren Spahn on July 2, 1963, that featured 462 pitches between the two men, with Marichal throwing the ball toward the plate 261 times and Spahn 201 times. In his next start, Marichal went seven innings and allowed only five hits and two earned runs. Spahn, who was forty-two years old in 1963, finished that season with twenty-one wins and a 2.60 earned run average, but he never had another good season. However, in his next start after going sixteen innings versus Marichal, he tossed a nine-inning complete game shutout of the Houston Colt 45s. In the 4 to 0 win, he scattered five hits in going 12 and 4 for the season.

Red Barrett Was the Most Efficient
The recognized record for fewest pitches thrown in a complete game is held by Red Barrett of the Boston Braves on August 10, 1944. He beat the Cincinnati Reds 2 to 0 in a game that took only one hour and fifteen minutes to play. He threw only fifty-eight pitches.

Cy Young is Worthy of an Award
Cy Young was not a strikeout pitcher. He averaged just over three strikeouts per game in a 906-game career. But he knew how to pitch, as demonstrated by his 511 wins, including fifteen seasons with twenty or more victories. Looking behind the numbers and at when Cy played shows his greatness even more. His career began in 1890 when the pitching distance was just fifty feet. After the 1892 season, the distance was moved to its present 60' 6" , and the pitching rubber was established. Did it hurt Cy? Not much. In 1892, he was 36 and 12 with a 1.93 earned run average and nine shutouts. Having to work further back the next season, he was 34 and 16 with a higher 3.36 earned run average and only one shutout. By 1901, he was 33 and 10 and a 1.62 earned run average. Cy knew how to adjust.

We Must Remember Jack Taylor
Records that never will be broken in baseball are many, but Jack Taylor had another one. When he started between June 20, 1901, and August 6, 1906, he finished what he started. Taylor threw an incredible 188 consecutive complete games. His career included

278 complete games in 286 starts. Taylor's record is officially listed at thirty-nine in a row because he appeared in relief on a few occasions. But when he started, you couldn't get him out of there.

The Many Changes in Pitching

In addition to coming up with all sorts of ways to keep hitters from making solid contact with the ball, the pitchers in the history of major league baseball have had to make the most adjustments. The ball has gone from soft and dirty to very hard and easy to see.

The style has gone from almost slow-pitch, underhand softball to fastballs thrown over 100 miles an hour. The bases have been ninety feet apart since the 1840s, but the pitching distance was quite different during baseball's infant years.

Pitchers Have Had to Adjust

When the pitching distance was established in 1893 at 60' 6" with a pitching rubber, the pitchers discovered it was easier to throw the ball hard if they could do it downhill. Mounds of dirt were constructed to help give them an edge. In the beginning, there was no rule allowing or disallowing the practice, and many teams had changeable mounds when different pitchers started. In 1903, the rules were solidified, calling for a standard 15" rise from field level. That remained the case, although often abused by teams who wanted it a bit higher, until 1969 when the rise was limited to 10" to help hitting. Currently, the rise is a maximum of 18" for all professional baseball.

The fastball has always been baseball's primary pitch. Thrown with four seams biting the air on release, it typically will have what appears to be a rise. Actually, it just loses height less, and compared to a ball gripped with two seams cutting the air, which actually does sink and move a bit. The four-seamer was often called a "riser."

Who Invented the Other Pitches?

If Candy Cummings, Joe Sprague, or possibly Fred Goldsmith invented the curve ball, who came up with the slider, knuckleball, split finger, or screwball?

The Nickel Curve

The nickel curve was the original name for all the pitches now in the slider family. That includes the cut fastball, the cutter, slurve, and slider. The term was derived from the fact that early sliders had a break on them, but not nearly as great as the best curve balls of the day. The slider and its variants did not appear until the 1930s. George Uhle of the Tigers and George Blaeholder of the Browns were early proponents. The Uhle slider was more often called a sailor due to the way it acted.

The Fadeaway

The fadeaway was the famous name given to Christy Mathewson's reverse curve, or screwball as it was later named. It may be the most difficult pitch to master. Carl Hubbell became most noted for his screwball; Warren Spahn and Fernando Valenzuela also threw excellent ones. Nolan Ryan threw a changeup that, due to the way it was gripped and its speed, had a lot of screwball tendencies.

The Knuckleball

Only a few pitchers actually grip the ball with the knuckles. Most use the finger tips with the knuckles bent. Famed Chicago White Sox pitcher Eddie Cicotte, who was banned from baseball after the Black Sox scandal, was the first pitcher of note to use the pitch extensively. In the 1950s, Hoyt Wilhem made the pitch popular again and was the first knuckleball Hall of Famer. Later, Wilbur Wood, Phil, and Joe Niekro all had great success with the pitch. Tim Wakefield was one of the few to keep the pitch alive into the twenty-first century. Knuckleballer R.A. Dickey won the 2012 N.L. Cy Young award.

Forkball Evolved to Split Finger Fastball

The forkball may have been devised by Joe Bush after an arm injury had made it impossible to throw a good curve. He needed an off-speed pitch and discovered that, by spreading the grip on his pitches, the ball would have a significant drop in velocity and actually have some sink when it neared the plate. He started throwing the pitch in 1921. Reliever Elroy Face of the Pirates in the late 50s and early 60s was known for his forkball.

Bruce Sutter Threw it Harder: a New Pitch was Born

Roger Craig is given credit for being the father of the split finger fastball, but it was a pupil, Chicago Cub reliever Bruce Sutter, that became famous—and ultimately a Hall of Famer—for throwing it. The split finger fastball was gripped even wider than the forkball and thrown with more velocity. That made it drop quicker and later.

Houston Astro starting pitcher Mike Scott had great success with the pitch in the mid and late 80s. Roger Clemens learned the pitch to help extend his career several seasons. Some pitchers who threw it were often accused of doing other illegal things to the ball to make it move more.

Other Pitches Evolved

There is no single way to throw a change of pace pitch—or changeup. Thus, there is no single pitcher credited with inventing it. In fact, the change up, along with the fast ball, was one of the two original pitches dating back to the underhand, straight-elbow days. A.G. Spalding was an early practitioner, but some have credited Amos Rusie as being the inventor of the modern change of pace.

Today, a change can be thrown with a tighter grip or a split finger fastball type or forkball grip. It can be thrown with only the palm or with the thumb and forefinger forming a circle and the third, fourth, and fifth fingers doing the actual gripping. A "slip" pitch is a changeup. Paul Richards often tried to teach the pitchers in his Baltimore Orioles and Chicago White Sox clubs a pitch he called that. It just means that the ball "slips" out of the hand on release and has less velocity coming to the plate.

Now Illegal Pitches

Everyone has heard of the spitball. History gives pitcher Elmer Stricklett credit for inventing it but Jack Chesbro for making it famous. Chesbro learned the pitch from Stricklett and used it for the first time in 1904. He won forty-one games that season! Chesbro earned Hall of Fame induction in 1946. Elmer was a good teacher—he also taught Ed Walsh—but not a great pitcher. His career record was just 35 and 51 in just four seasons.

The spitter was generally thrown by wetting the fingers or a side of the ball and then thrown with the grip over the wet spot. The ball would slip off the fingers giving it a different aerodynamic. It would often sink but sometimes, depending on the delivery, was hard to control. While quite effective, it was obviously not very sanitary and, as shown in the fatal beaning of Ray Chapman, could be dangerous.

Most Unsanitary for Sure

Was their ever a more disgusting advocate of the spitball than Pittsburgh Pirate pitcher Marty O'Toole? For a while, Marty actually licked the ball. Well, he did until a member of the opposing team, Phillie first baseman Fred Luderus, decided to rub liniment on the ball every time it came to him. As early as the third inning, O'Toole's tongue was inflamed and he had to leave the game. Today, the average life of a baseball is only about six pitches. In 1912, the same ball could last the whole game. That was plenty of time to get revenge on a pitcher like O'Toole.

Eventually the Legal End to It

The spitter and pitches that were delivered after applying any foreign substance, including liniment to the ball, were banned by baseball under a grandfather clause in 1920. Pitchers who had used it successfully in the major leagues were allowed to continue doing so the rest of their career. The last legal spit baller was Burleigh Grimes, whose career ended in 1934.

When the spitter was outlawed, so were a number of other pitches that involved doing something to the ball other than just grip it. No pitcher could apply any foreign substance to the baseball. That eliminated slippery elm, sweat, dirt, pine tar. The rules also stipulated the ball could not be intentionally marred with cuts or scratches or by altering the seams by packing them with mud. The rules did not eliminate the spitter and its ilk after Grimes, but it reduced the pitch to an oddity that some pitchers might throw on occasion but certainly not blatantly.

Any number of hurlers in the post-Grimes era, from Preacher Roe to Lew Burdette, Don Drysdale, Whitey Ford, Mike Scott, Don Sutton, and Gaylord Perry, have been accused of throwing spitters or defaced baseballs during their careers. It took ten years from the last legal spitball from Grimes to the first ejection for a pitcher accused of throwing a spitter in a major league game. On July 20, 1944, pitcher Nels Potter of the St. Louis Browns was ejected by home plate umpire Cal Hubbard for violating the rule. Potter contended he was not spitting on the ball but only blowing on it.

But that is only the tip of the iceberg. As pitching has evolved, the men in the middle of the diamonds have always looked for an edge. At one point, as many as one third of the pitchers on major league teams in the 1960s were suspected of at least occasionally "doctoring" the ball. Nothing has changed in ensuing seasons, but the preferred method shifted from grease to making small cuts or scuffs on the ball to help it move.

Adjustments Have Always Been For the Pitchers

From the day baseball was born with underhand pitches intended primarily to allow the hitters to put the ball in play, to the 100-mile-an-hour, overhand blazers intended to embarrass the men with the bats in their hands, pitchers have had to make adjustments.

As the skill of players improved, so did the men who served up the pitches. In 1871, when major league baseball was born with the National Association, the pitchers' job was to put the ball in play. Hitters could take a running start toward the pitch until 1874.

From then on, they had to stand in a box. Meanwhile, pitchers were throwing from only forty-five feet but had to throw underhand or sidearm. They also had to ask hitters where they preferred the ball. High? Low? Or at the belt?

It took as many as nine balls for a hitter to walk. Those numbers, thankfully, were reduced within twenty years to the current four. Foul balls were eventually counted as strikes for the pitcher's benefit. While the job of the pitcher was still to put the ball in play, many started experimenting with putting a break or curve on the ball to make it harder to hit solidly. They also tried changing arm angles to see with how much they could get away.

In 1883, a rule was instituted that said no pitch could be thrown above shoulder height. Ultimately, that rule was more and more ignored, resulting in overhand pitching. In 1884, overhand pitching was allowed, but it resulted in much less offense, so the rule not allowing any pitch above side arm was reinstituted for 1885. The return to the overhand ban did not last long because it was too hard to enforce. By a month into the 1885 season, the National League allowed any delivery again, and it remains that way to this day.

Ironically, even with the move from underhand to sidearm to fully overhand, some veteran star pitchers continued to use the softball style. Tim Keefe stayed "down under" and had successive seasons with thirty- two, forty-two, thirty-five, thirty-five, and twenty-eight wins between 1885 and 1890. In 1887, batters could no longer call for a high or low pitch.

Current Pitchers' Distance and Mound Debut in 1893

Now the game had swung in the other direction: Pitchers started to dominate. To counter the rules, makers moved the pitchers' area. It was originally a pitcher's six by six foot box that had its front edge move from 45' to 50' in 1881 and to 60' 6" off a pitching rubber in 1893. Hurlers who succeeded through some of the changes included two of the very best. Pud Galvin was the first pitcher ever to win 300 games as he totaled 361, with all of them coming before the mound at 60' 6" . But he had to handle the move from 45' with hitters requesting location to the move to 50' . He started when he could only throw underhanded and finished when that was no longer required.

Cy Young was another who bridged two eras. He started as a hard thrower from a 50' pitcher's box and kept rolling from an elevated 60' 6" pitcher's rubber. The rubber was placed exactly ten feet farther than the farthest point in the old five and a half foot deep pitcher's box. Young had thirty-six wins in 1892, the last year of the pitcher's box, and still won thirty-four the first year of the 60' 6" pitching rubber. His earned run average jumped from 1.93 to 3.36 but he made the adjustment.

A lot of pitchers did not adjust. Bumpus Jones was the last pitcher to win a game under the old rules and pitched a no-hitter on October 15, 1892. With the new 60' 6" pitcher's rubber, he could not adjust the next season. After just seven games in 1893, his record was 1 and 4, and his earned run average was 10.19. He was released.

It was not an easy adjustment for many hurlers. In 1892, all National League teams hit .245 with 417 HR and pitchers fanned 5,955. The next season, with the change to longer-distanced pitching, the teams hit .279 with 417, and pitchers fanned only 3,339.

Since 1893, pitchers have worked from the same distance. However, defining the exact strike zone has been another story. That rule has been tinkered with many times. The biggest advantage pitchers might have received from rule-makers once the 60′ 6″ mound became standard was in 1900, when home plate was changed from a 12″ square to a five-sided figure with a 17″ -wide front. It provided a better, larger target and was easier for both pitchers and umpires. An attempt to standardize the strike zone would now be possible, but that was another long developing story of the game.

Hit The Ball—Please!

The game was originally constructed to allow the hitters to put the ball in play. As the sport evolved over the years, it was necessary to consider some new rules. At first, there was no such thing as a strike zone, or balls and strikes for that matter. If a batter needed to wait for twenty-five pitches until he saw one he wanted to strike at, he could. Hitters could even request where they would like the ball pitched. That rule continued into the 1887 season, but as early as the 1860s, the concept of balls and strikes was being formed. It took a while to decide the best number for both and how to use them.

In 1866, the introduction of called balls began. At first, only three balls were needed for a hitter to be awarded first base. Those would not be the only three pitches out of the hitting area. Usually, they had to be extremely outside. Strikes had been introduced in 1860, but the umpire needed to warn the batter before he called the first one. When the National Association started major league baseball in 1871, the rules were three strikes and three balls, but many warnings and "non-pitches" were part of the game.

Originally, it could take as many as nine balls for a walk. In 1880, the number was lowered to eight. In 1882, it took seven balls for a walk; then it was changed to six balls in 1883, back up to seven in 1886. By 1887, they were close to getting it right by dropping a walk to five balls, but a strikeout went up to needing four strikes from three.

Finally, in 1888, the rules-makers settled on three strikes and, the next year, four balls. It has not changed since.

But What Was a Strike or Ball?

Since 1889, it has taken four balls for a walk and three strikes for a strikeout. Deciding what constitutes each is still an open question. Much is based on an umpire's judgment, and that judgment has had to be made from a number of different rulebook standards. For a while, fouls of any kind were not strikes or balls. That didn't come about until 1901 in the National League and 1903 in the American League, although foul bunts and foul tips had both been considered strikes by 1895.

In 1887, when hitters could no longer request where the pitcher threw the ball, the strike zone had boundaries. The top of the shoulder to the bottom of the knee and over the plate was the first boundary. It remained the strike zone until 1950, when it was defined as from the batter's armpits to top of the knee and over the plate. In 1963, the zone reverted back to the pre-1950 dimensions: Top of shoulder to bottom of the knee were the upper and lower limits.

After 1968, when pitchers had dominated, the height of the pitcher's mound was lowered to 10 inches and the strike zone shrunk again, back to armpit to top of knee. The American League started examining the idea of the designated hitter, which the International League would test in 1969.

By the 1980s, after many complaints that umpires were using their own strike zones, not always within the rule, the rule was re-written again. In 1987, the description said the upper level was along

159

an imaginary horizontal line at a midpoint between the top of the shoulders and the beltline. The lower level was at the top of the knees. All zones were to be determined based on individual's normal batting stances.

A move to raise the upper limit later was effective for some umpires for some time, but the zone ultimately has reverted mostly to the 1987 rule. Efforts to make umpiring more consistent in the 1990s and 2000s included video reviews from triangulated cameras. The questionable allowed margin for error led to questionable results. However, in general, the players did not complain and adjusted to whatever zone was normal in a particular game.

Pitching Stories Not in the Record Books

Sometimes unfortunate pitching stories are a result of tough luck and other times they are caused by injury, but a number of stories from baseball's past should be remembered if only for their uniqueness.

Sitting Down on the Job

Civil disobedience was costly for Boston Braves pitcher Don Rudolph and his team on July 6, 1918. So incensed with what he thought were horrible calls by the home plate umpire, Rudolph went on a sit down strike. He plopped himself right down on the pitcher's mound in protest. Needless to say, this act resulted in Rudolph's ejection from the game. And that really was the ballgame since his replacement, Hugh Canavan, was quite ineffective. He pitched two and two-thirds innings and allowed thirteen runs!

Wiltse's Loss of Perfect Game

On July 4, 1908, Hooks Wiltse was pitching a perfect game. No batter had reached base, and Wiltse needed only one more out in the ninth inning.

Then he hit a batter with a pitch. And the batter, George McQuillan, was the opposing pitcher. What was worse was that after the game, home plate umpire Cy Rigler admitted that he had missed the previous pitch. It would have struck McQuillan out.

Wiltse's next pitch was wild and hit McQuillan, which ended Hooks' shot at immortality. He got the next hitter and took a no-hitter to the tenth. He won it there, but without the perfect game that was within his reach. He had to settle for a no-hit 1 to 0 win in ten innings. By the way, his nickname, "Hooks," came from his defensive skill at hooking ground balls hit up the middle and not from his ability to throw a curve.

Joe Nuxhall Was Youngest

World War II took many star players away from Major League Baseball, so fill-ins had to be found. One of them was Joe Nuxhall, who was the youngest player ever to appear in a major league game. Joe was just fifteen years, ten months, and eleven days old when he came in to pitch relief for the Cincinnati Reds against the St. Louis Cardinals on June 10, 1944.

The event was memorable if Joe's work was not. He pitched two thirds of the ninth inning in an 18 to 0 loss to the Cards. During his time on the mound, he walked five and gave up two hits before being pulled after uncorking a wild pitch.

Nuxhall would return to the majors again, but it would take seven years. He pitched for fifteen seasons and finished with a 135 and 117 record to go with a 3.90 earned run averaged. He then became a longtime radio announcer for the Reds.

Don't Forget Jim Derrington

Nuxhall got his feet wet in relief. Jim Derringer did him better. He was only one year older at sixteen years and ten months old when he started a game in the major leagues. He was a bonus player with the Chicago White Sox who got the start on September 30, 1956.

Facing the Kansas City A's, he went six innings allowing nine hits and six runs to become the youngest pitcher to start a game in major league history. Derrington got a hit in his one game and is the youngest player to have a hit in modern major league baseball.

Unlike Nuxhall, however, his career was short. His last appearance was one year later when he was only seventeen years old. He banged around in the minors for a while, but never made it back.

Was Satchel Paige the Oldest?

The oldest pitcher to appear in a major league game was Hall of Famer Satchel Paige. The problem is no one is totally sure how old he was. The record books say his three innings for the 1965 Kansas City Athletics came when he was fifty-nine years old. It may have been partly a publicity stunt, but Paige threw three straight scoreless innings and he had been pitching regularly in the minor leagues well into his fifties.

Chapter X

SOME NOT-SO-GREAT AND SHORT-TIMERS

I get on base by making good contact with the ball. But whenever I hit a home run, I'm as surprised as everybody else.

Amos Otis
Former Royals outfielder

Archibald "Moonlight" Graham with his 1900 Baseball Team

CHAPTER 10: SOME NOT-SO-GREAT AND SHORT-TIMERS

Worst Overall Shortstop Ever?

The shortstop position is arguable the toughest defensive position in baseball. The position requires good hands, strong arms, and top-level baseball instincts. If a shortstop can hit, that is a bonus. Defensive skill is paramount. So can anyone explain why John Gochnauer was the regular shortstop for Cleveland in 1902 and 1903? He most certainly was the worst shortstop of all time, but maybe even the worst player.

Gochnauer could not field. And he couldn't hit either! In both years, he hit just .185. Oh yes, he also made 146 errors, with ninety-eight of them in 1902. Toss in that he also reportedly had very little range, and one wonders, maybe the Cleveland folks were fooled by his resume.

In 1901, he had played for Brooklyn and was four for twelve and made no errors. As a minor leaguer, he had been a decent hitter and at least an average infield defender. He just totally flopped when given a regular major league spot. It cannot be said that John did not get a chance. He played 127 and 134 games respectively for Cleveland and had more than 500 at-bats both seasons. Strangely enough, he does hold a major league record, only partly as a result of ineptitude. In his final season in 1903, he drove in forty- eight runs while hitting .185. That was major league baseball's record for most RBIs by a player with a batting average under .200 for years. The current record was established by Chris Davis of the Baltimore Orioles in 2014 with 72 RBIs while hitting only .196.

Billy Shindle Was Worse—With the Glove Only

No one has ever made more errors in a season than Billy Shindle of the Philadelphia Quakers. Because his weak fielding was in the short-lived Players' League, it may not be recognized. But the Players' League actually consisted of many of the name stars from the National League who banded together in protest of the methods of N.L. owners in controlling players and contracts.

One hundred nineteen errors is a lot in any league. Billy was the regular shortstop for the Quakers and appeared in 130 games. His fielding percentage was just .887. But, unlike Gochnauer, Billy was a much better hitter. His career mark for a thirteen-year major league career was .269. The year he made those 119 errors, he also hit .324 and led the Player's League with 282 total bases, thanks to twenty-one doubles, twenty-one triples, and ten home runs. He also drove in ninety runs.

What did it prove? It proved that if you can hit, you can play, even if your position is shortstop and you aren't the best at handling it with the glove.

Henry Long Was Another Clanking Glove at SS

So, while the ninety-eight errors by John Gochnauer in 1903 were horrid, they were not the most or even second-most errors committed by a shortstop. Henry Long, who played sixteen seasons in the major leagues, committed a whopping 117 errors during his rookie season with Kansas City in the American Association in 1889. His fielding percentage that year was only .874.

Even so, that was not his worst percentage season. He fielded less than .900 eight times. He committed ninety-nine errors in 1892 and ninety-eight in 1893 while playing for Brooklyn. But, unlike Gochnauer, he could hit adequately. His career .277 was not spectacular, but he hit over .300 four straight seasons between 1894 and 1897 with a high of .345 in 1896. He even hit twelve home runs twice, leading the National League with that total in 1900.

Short "Stops" in the Major Leagues

Fans were introduced to Archibald "Moonlight" Graham and his lone appearance in the major leagues in the movie, *Field of Dreams.*

But while Graham's story of giving up a baseball dream to pursue a higher calling in medicine was notable, he was hardly the only player with a very short taste of the majors.

Would it be surprising to know that as of 2013, between 975 and 1,000 players have had only one appearance in a major league game out of over 18,000 who have played in the majors? When one considers all the late season call-ups that have been the norm, it actually stands to reason that there might be some short careers, but only one appearance?

Of the rather large total, there are some stories that deserve special mention. In David Nemec's book, *The Great Encyclopedia of 19th Century Major League Baseball,* he found many one-game players. Perhaps most impressive are six starting pitchers who appeared between 1882 and 1890 and all pitched complete games with earned run averages no more than 3.00 but never appeared again.

George Snyder tops that list. On September 30, 1882, pitching for Philadelphia in the American Association, he threw nine innings of shutout ball, allowing only four hits. Yet, he never pitched again.

Al Travers: Worst Pitcher Ever?

It wasn't his fault, and he didn't exactly seek it out, but a check of baseball records will find the name Al Travers as possibly the worst pitcher ever. And next to that name will be his stats, which were very ugly. In one major league appearance, Al pitched eight innings, a complete game, while allowing twenty-six hits, twenty-four runs, fourteen earned runs, seven walks, and one strikeout. His earned run average was 15.75.

However, there is far more to his story. In the first place, he was selected to be part of a Detroit Tiger team to face the Philadelphia A's after the Tiger's regular players elected to strike in opposition of an American League edict that suspended their star Ty Cobb after he had physically attacked a fan for verbal abuse.

To avoid a forfeit and a $5,000 fine, manager Hughie Jennings hit the Philadelphia streets to find replacements. Travers was a junior at St. Joseph's College. He was a violinist in the student orchestra who had tried out but failed to make the school's varsity baseball team and had not pitched a game in his life. He knew baseball from serving as a student manager and writing game summaries for the school. He volunteered for the role of pitcher in this game because it paid the most. He got $50 and immortality in baseball record books for his work.

The temporary Tigers included manager Jennings and two coaches along with some of Travers fellow students. The A's won the game 24 to 2.

Travers name went down in history for having a long and infamous afternoon, but he bounced back. He finished his studies at St. Josephs and became a Catholic priest for the rest of his life.

Another interesting note came from the game. One player spelled his name backward to presumably preserve his amateur status. If one sees the name of Billy Maharg in one of those baseball record books, it was really should have read Billy Graham. No, not that Billy Graham, though.

Quitting on Top

Brownsville, Texas, native Henry Schmidt was on top of the baseball world in 1903. He won 22 games pitching for the Brooklyn Superbas. But he never won another major league game, and he had no physical problems, either from pitching or from off the field. Henry just didn't like living in the East where all the major league clubs were located at the time. His career didn't end yet. He pitched in the Pacific Coast and other leagues for another five seasons, but after 1909 he was through.

CHAPTER 10: SOME NOT-SO-GREAT AND SHORT-TIMERS

While quitting the major leagues after winning twenty-two games in one season was strange, the numbers indicate Schmidt may have had a lot of luck during his lone season. While he was 22 and 13, his earned run average was a high 3.83, and the league average was only 3.27. Furthermore, he gave up thirty-nine unearned runs and walked 120 batters while striking out just ninety-six in 301 innings. Duplicating his won-loss record in 1904 might have been impossible.

Jocko Flynn: Best One-Season Pitcher Ever

As good as Henry Schmidt was in his lone major league season, Jocko Flynn was unfortunate to do him better. In 1886, Flynn was 23 and 6 with a superb 2.24 earned run average for the Chicago White Stockings of the National League. Although he was only twenty-two years old, he never pitched in another major league game. Flynn was injured during the postseason series between the White Stockings and the American Association St. Louis Browns. He did not appear in any of the games, and St. Louis won the series four games to two. Flynn appeared in one game in 1887 as an outfielder. His pitching career was over.

Larry Yount in Box Score Only

On September 15, 1971, the Houston Astro rookie was called in to pitch in relief for the ninth inning in a game in which the Astros trailed the Atlanta Braves 4 to 1. While in the bullpen, his elbow started to stiffen. He went to the mound, hoping it would work its way out. After a couple of tosses from the middle of the field, he knew it was hopeless. He had been announced as being in the game, but never threw a pitch. He also never made another appearance in the major leagues. His brother, Robin, did okay, though. The longtime Milwaukee Brewer shortstop and outfielder was elected to the Hall of Fame in 1999.

Bill Sharman Never Got That Close

Hall of Fame basketball star Bill Sharman wore a Brooklyn Dodger uniform once. You won't find his name in any major league record book because he never got into a game. But he was once thrown out of one!

On September 27, 1951, he was a late season call-up by the Dodgers after a strong minor league season in Fort Worth. After a close call at home plate in the game that day and ensuing complaints from the Dodger bench, home plate umpire Frank Dascoli cleared everyone off the bench. Technically, Sharman was not ejected from potential use in the game, but was banned to the clubhouse until he might be needed. He never was. The next season back in the minors, his career started to trail off and the NBA looked like a better option. He never played in a major league game.

Ever Hear of Ralph Gagliano?

Certainly few baseball fans have heard of him. He had one appearance in the majors as a pinch runner for the Indians' Larry Brown at Yankee Stadium. The batter, Rich Schienblum, grounded to Bobby Richardson at second, who tossed to shortstop Bobby Murcer for the force-out. Ralph was the player forced. That was it for Ralph Gagliano. September 21, 1965, was his first and only appearance and, like Graham, never got to bat, but unlike Yount, he at least got into the game.

Buddy Hancken Got into One Game

Like Moonlight Graham, though, he never got to bat. Buddy was a catcher with the Philadelphia A's when on May 14, 1940 manager Connie Mack sent him into the game to catch the ninth inning. He was credited with a put out, but never got an at bat.

Hancken had a major league career, however. He served as a coach with the Houston Astros from 1968 through 1972 after serving as a minor league manager and baseball scout after World War II.

Walt Alston Not Much of a Player

As a major league player, Walt Alston, the longtime Brooklyn and Los Angeles Dodger manager, was not much. His major league career consisted of just three innings and one at-bat with the St. Louis Cardinals on September 27, 1936. Cardinal manager Frankie Frisch called on Alston to hit after regular first baseman Johnny Mize had been ejected. Facing Cubs hurler Lon Warneke, Alston struck out on three pitches. He did play defense for three innings and made an error in two chances.

Alston made up for his inabilities as a major league player with a twenty- three year Dodger managerial career that included over 2,000 wins, seven pennants, and four World Series Championships. As a manager, he was elected to the Baseball Hall of Fame.

Bill Schlesinger Didn't Expect It

In 1965, eighteen-year-old Bill Schlesinger was on the Boston Red Sox roster but did not expect to see any action. He was a bonus baby who had to be kept on the major league roster under the rules of the time. He thought his future was ahead of him. However, we know from a story related to writer Rick Paulas that would soon change.

One day manager Billy Herman called upon Schlesinger to pinch hit. He wasn't ready. His bats were still in the clubhouse, so he had the equipment manager bring one of them out. While Schlesinger tried to get ready in a hurry, he jammed the warm-up weighted donut so firmly on his bat that he struggled to pry it loose. Then when he reached the plate, both the umpire and catcher made it plain they just wanted to get the game over. The umpire told him to be aggressive; the catcher told him he would be getting fastballs.

Schlesinger hit a routine tapper back to the pitcher. The game was over and so, as it turned out, was Schlesinger's major league career. A beaning later during a five-year minor league career affected his vision and the one- time prize prospect never made it back to the majors.

Jeff Banister Achieved Anyway

Like Walter Alston and Buddy Hancken, Jeff Bannister built a solid baseball career, even if the major league playing portion of it was short. To be able to be in the one game he did play was almost a miracle.

Banister was diagnosed with bone cancer in an ankle during high school. Amputation was considered, but multiple surgeries were conducted instead. He recovered well enough to play collegiately as a catcher. A play at the plate resulted in a collision that shattered three vertebrae. Despite all of the physical set-backs, Banister was good enough to be drafted by the Pittsburgh Pirates in the twenty-fifth round of 1986.

He was called to the Pirates from Triple A Buffalo July 23, 1991, when Don Slaught was hurt. He got an infield single in his only big league at-bat and had been available in a second game when pitcher Bob Walk was injured running the bases. Banister was sent back down to the minors so the Pirates could make some moves to cover for the loss of Walk.

Banister never got another chance to play in the majors again. Yet, he never left the Pittsburgh family. He spent more than twenty-five years with the organization, ultimately moving into coaching. In 2010, he was named bench coach for the Pirates and was back in the major leagues.

CHAPTER 10: SOME NOT-SO-GREAT AND SHORT-TIMERS

Paciorek Greatest One Gamer Ever

While Jeff Banister's one for one game left him with a lifetime major league average of 1.000, his single day in the majors can be topped. John Paciorek, playing for the Houston Colt 45s, had a three for three game in his only major league appearance. It occurred on September 29, 1963, against the New York Mets. Paciorek, the older brother of Tom Paciorek who had a long major league career, went to the plate five times and reached base on all of them. He had three singles and two walks. He scored four runs and drove in three. His on-base plus slugging was 2.000! John was only eighteen years old in 1963 but would never appear in another major league game. A back injury cut short his career. He tried to come back and played in the minor leagues through 1969. At twenty-four his career was over. Yet, it is unlikely no player will ever have as an impressive stat line for a one- game career.

The Little Fellow Will be Remembered

The John Paciorek story won't be forgotten, but neither will the appearance of Eddie Gaedel. Unlike Paciorek or any of the other players listed in this category, Gaedel had no dreams of playing baseball. Bill Veeck is who put him in the baseball record books.

Record books and Baseball-reference.com list Gaedel as a pinch hitter who batted right and threw left. Whoever knew he threw left is somewhat amazing because he never threw a ball and never had a glove!

It is noted that Eddie was 3'7 and sixty-five pounds. Eddie was a little person in today's terminology. On August 19, 1951, he was called a midget. He was the player that St. Louis Browns' owner Veeck signed to pinch-hit against the Detroit Tigers as a publicity stunt.

For the record, Gaedel's, pinch-hitting for leadoff man Frank Saucier drew a walk from pitcher Bob Cain, with Bob Swift catching. Eddie had been instructed implicitly by Veeck not to swing the bat. Once four pitches missed the plate, Gaedel ran down to first base in his "number 1/8" uniform and was replaced by pinch-runner Jim Delsing.

Prior to the at-bat, Veeck made sure his manager, Zach Taylor, had a copy of the signed contract in his possession to show the umpire if necessary. It was necessary, and after home plate umpire Ed Hurley took a look, he signaled for Gaedel to get into the batter's box. Following the stunt, the rules of baseball were amended to require all contracts to be approved by the Commissioner's office before going into effect.

Donald Davidson Almost First

Donald Davidson worked in major league baseball for more than forty years. He rose from batboy to club executive with the Red Sox, Braves, and Astros despite being a "little person" only four feet tall. He was never a player, but he almost was in 1938.

Although he was just a bat boy and not on the roster of the Boston Red Sox, the manager of the team, Joe Cronin, told him to grab a bat and hit for catcher Moe Berg. However, he was cut short of a major league debut when home plate umpire Bill Summers would not allow the substitution. It was the "almost-at-bat" by Davidson that reportedly gave Bill Veeck the idea to actually sign little person Eddie Gaedel fourteen years later.

Chapter XI

PLAYS THAT SHOULD
NOT BE FORGOTTEN

Never let the fear of striking out get in your way.

Babe Ruth
Hall of Famer

Greg Lucas, Lance Berkman, David "Wave" Robinson, 2010

There is no way to actually have a record of all of the best plays of all time—there have been far too many over far too many years. Now, with television coverage of every game and Major League Baseball so involved with its web sites and television network, nothing escapes being saved for posterity. For most of baseball's years, only word of mouth served as the record.

I remember the greatest catch I've ever seen. I daresay few others remember it. I mentioned earlier in the book that my Grandfather Small took me to my first major league game. Well, it was my other grandfather, George Lucas, who took me to the game where I saw the greatest catch.

It was in either 1965 or 1966, in only a pre-season exhibition game at old Bush Stadium in Indianapolis. The Chicago White Sox were taking on the Cincinnati Reds a day or two before the season began. The Reds had a long ball-hitting outfielder named Art Shamsky, who would later spend time with the New York Mets and was a member of their 1969 World Champions, hit the ball that resulted in the greatest catch I've ever seen. Ironically, the man who made the catch, Tommy Agee, would also be a member of the champion Mets team.

In this game, Shamsky drove a ball to deep center field. At that time, Bush Stadium did not have an inner fence in center. The left and right field brick walls came to a point in deep center well more than 450 feet from home plate.

Agee took off on the crack of the bat. With his back turned to the infield, he seemed to run forever for the deep high drive. Shamsky was running hard himself, since he knew he wouldn't be able to clear the fence but would surely have a triple or maybe even an inside-the-park home run. Shamsky's hustle turned out to be a wasted effort.

With Agee and the ball no more than ten feet from the high brick wall, the two converged. Agee made the greatest catch after the longest run I've ever seen in my years in baseball. If the catch had been captured by television and had been in an important regular season or World Series game, it would have ranked right there with or above Willie Mays' famed catch in the Polo Grounds off Vic Wertz in the 1954 World Series. I have seen the Mays' catch many times, thanks to old films, but I would still personally rank Agee's grab of Shamsky's bomb in a preseason exhibition game the greatest I have ever seen.

In this chapter, we will remember a few plays that may have not been as spectacular as what Agee's or Mays' feat but remain unforgettable to those who witnessed them. Most are not defensive plays but are still very memorable.

First Real Inside-the-park Home Run

Physically, only one batter has truly hit an inside-the-park home run. Fred Luderus hit a long drive to the wall in Philadelphia's Baker Bowl in 1914. The ball lodged in a gap between the bricks and could not be pulled out by the outfielder. It was literally "inside the park!" Fred could hit them out of the park, too. On July 15, 1911, he was the first Phillie ever to homer twice over the fence in one game. He also hit the team's first home run in a World Series in 1915 versus the Boston Red Sox.

Grover Land Hit an Inside-the-Infield Homer

While playing in the Federal League for Brooklyn in 1914, Grover Land reportedly did something that will never happen again. He hit a home run that never left the infield, and how he did it is why it will never happen again.

Umpire Tom Brennan, who was on duty by himself, elected to call balls and strikes from a spot behind the pitcher's mound. To avoid moving around too much, he had a pile of baseballs nearby to use when the game ball was fouled off. It was a hot day as the Brooklyn Tip Tops met the Chicago Whales. Brennan apparently had things well in hand until Land hit a liner in exactly the wrong spot.

Land accidently targeted Umpire Brennan's extra ball pile with a sharply hit liner. The balls flew all over the infield. Land started running and was tagged out multiple times. But since umpire Brennan wasn't sure which ball was actually in play, he let Land round the bases for a home run. Needless to say, the decision was protested and would have been upheld later if the game had any bearing in the pennant race. It didn't, so Grover Land's inside-the-infield home run has stood as the only one ever in baseball history.

Another Weird Home Run

Cap Anson, the first hitter to 3,000 hits, was involved in one of the strangest home runs ever. In 1891, he hit a ball to deep center field. He hit it right into the opened door of a dog house. Outfielder Ed Delahanty stuck his head in the opening to get the ball out, but he didn't fit. He got stuck. Meanwhile, Anson circled the bases for an inside-the-park home run, or more precisely, an inside-the-dog-house home run.

Cap Anson

Zack Wheat's Long-Lasting Home Run

Zack Wheat was not a huge power hitter. In nineteen years, he hit just 132 home runs. But he was a good hitter with a lifetime .317 average and a National League batting title with a .335 mark in 1918. In 1926, he hit one of his relatively rare home runs at Ebbets Field in the ninth inning to win the game for the Dodgers. This was a very long home run, not because of the distance, but because of the length of time it took Wheat to get around the bases.

When he got to second base, he had pulled muscles in both legs. He couldn't move. So, he sat down on the bag and started to massage his legs. He worked on them for five minutes. Just as his manager, Wilbert Robinson, was about to call for a pinch runner, Wheat thought he could give the final 180 feet a try. He got up and limped the rest of the way home.

Wheat was also involved in a strange home run while on defense. He misjudged a fly once that had hit his foot and that he kicked over the wall.

Ruth and Aaron Both Lost Homers

For years, Babe Ruth held the major league record with 714 career home runs. Then, in 1974, Hank Aaron topped that total with his famed home run off Al Downing in Atlanta. But it could have been Aaron's 716th homer to best Ruth's 715.

You see, during a portion of Ruth's career, a home run that won a game wasn't always credited as a home run. If the winning run was on base, once the run scored, the game was over and the hitter who drove it in only got credit for the bases needed to drive it in. For example, if the winning run was on third base, the batter would be credited only with a single even if he had hit the ball over the wall! During his career, Ruth lost one home run to that rule. So, his final career total could have been 715 home runs.

But Aaron also lost a home run, too. It happened at old Busch Stadium, formerly known as Sportsman's Park, in St. Louis in 1965. Hitting against Cardinal lefty Curt Simmons, who was featuring an almost blooper changeup to Aaron, the Braves outfielder decided to try and time one and go to right field.

He caught hold of one of Simmons' slow balls and drove it onto the roof of the right field pavilion. This author was in the stands and remembers the majesty of the high drive to the opposite field. Also remembered is the commotion at home plate. Umpire Chris Pelokoudas was raising his right fist in the air, signaling an out and then pointing toward home plate. Pelokoudas had called Aaron out, nullifying the home run, because to hit the floater, Hank had stepped on or across home plate. That was the night of the "homer that never was" and never forgotten during all the time Aaron was chasing Ruth's record.

Canseco Used His Head

Baseball history records many instances when players have hit home runs after the ball glanced off a leaping player's glove, but only one is recorded to have glanced off an outfielder's head. The outfielder was Jose Canseco of the Texas Rangers, and the hitter was Carlos Martinez. The place was Municipal Stadium in Cleveland. The date was Wednesday, May 26, 1993.

In the bottom of the fourth inning, with the Rangers leading 3 to 1, Martinez led off against Texas starter Kenny Rogers. He hit a high fly ball that kept drifting toward deep right field. Canseco seemed to have a bead on it, and he averted his eyes once he felt the warning track under his feet to check his position in relation to the fence.

When he looked back up, he couldn't find the ball. The ball found him. More precisely, the ball found the front of the top of his head as he was reaching up. With one bound, it hopped from his head directly over the fence. Martinez had his fourth home run of the season. And the prophecy that came from this author's lips while calling the play for Ranger's television proved true: "Jose, you have done some great things in your career, but this will live forever."

179

Chapter XII

WHEN BASEBALL BECAME A BUSINESS

These days baseball is different. You come to spring training. You get your legs ready, your arms loose, your agents ready, and your lawyer lined up.

Dave Winfield
Hall of Famer

Concession Yankee Stadium

BASEBALL: IT'S MORE THAN JUST A GAME

Early On, Amateurism was Foremost

When baseball was first played in the United States, it was between men who played only for fun and never considered making money in playing a game. That changed, however, when the will to win drove teams to consider making under-the-table payments to entice better players to change loyalties.

Well before the 1869 Cincinnati Red Stockings started importing and paying all players, a large number of individual players received money from the game. The first game in which an admission was charged was on July 20, 1858, on Long Island, New York. But it wasn't until 1862 when William Cammeyer in Brooklyn built the first totally enclosed ballpark that regular admission would be charged. Most of that money went to the ballpark owner, but that would soon change.

In 1868, the National Association of Base Ball Players officially recognized professional players for the first time, although they had been interspersed with amateurs on many of the top teams for years. Do not credit the NABBP as being forward-thinking, however. One year earlier they had officially banned black players on "political grounds."

In 1871, major league professional baseball was born with the establishment of the National Association. The players were not paid much, but they did make money for their skills.

How Much?

With no player unions for the first eighty or ninety years of major league baseball, salaries were not excessively higher than what an average, well-paid citizen might earn. As early as 1892, the average salary in the National League was $3,054. The average salary for a working man was $479 per year. Today that $3054 might not seem like much, but it was six and a half times more than the average worker. In today's baseball, with the average salary about

$4 million in 2013 and the average salary for other workers at about $60,000, the difference is about sixty-seven times more.

Ticket prices and some ballpark advertising were the only ways for early clubs to pay those salaries. There was no radio or television. Tickets took a good bit of the average working man's salary, even when priced at just fifty cents. Fortunately for early fans, a twenty-five cent charge was more common for a number of years.

While ticket prices rose gradually, the highest-priced ticket in the ballpark did not exceed $4 until the 1970s. By the early twenty-first century, the average ticket price had passed $25 by a large margin in some locales. At the same time, baseball even with more competition from other sports and sources for the viewing public's dollars, has seen attendance and revenues rise. Broadcasting and television is behind the rise in both.

Baseball Reporting Led to New Revenue Sources

When baseball began, they just played the games, started charging admission eventually, and had game stories appear in newspapers. But it didn't take too long for owners to realize they had something in the sport that could use media attention for more than just free publicity to lure fans to attend games. The publicizers themselves might become a source of revenue.

It Started with the Telegraph

As far back as 1897, major league baseball teams received a "trade-off" deal from the media. Clubs each received $300 credit for telegrams in exchange for the right for telegraphers to transmit game information over the wires. By 1913, Western Union had upped the ante. Seventeen thousand dollars per year on a five year contract was paid to all clubs in both the American and National League for the same rights. Two years earlier, the two leagues negotiated a $3,500 deal with the movie industry for the rights to film game highlights.

Then Came Radio

When radio came on the entertainment scene, baseball owners were not sure how to use it. Some saw it as a way to promote the game. Others saw it as a threat to attendance. None saw it as a major revenue source directly.

History records the first broadcast aired on KDKA in Pittsburgh on August 5, 1921. The announcer was Harold Arlin, who sat in a ground level box seat at Forbes Field. Arlin would also be the first to broadcast a tennis match. He did that on the day after his baseball debut. In the fall, he introduced football on the air with West Virgina at Pittsburgh. Nothing Arlin did had a precedent for him. He admitted later in life that things did not always go smoothly. He would make mistakes in identification, and his broadcast equipment, including the station transmitter, often would go down. But he was the first.

Two Months Later, the World Series on the Air

By the fall of 1921, the baseball World Series was on radio for the first time. Calling the action was noted sportswriter Grantland Rice. It was not exactly a national broadcast, but it was on several stations in the East. The Yankees played the Giants. The Giants won the series, but radio was not on hand for the final two games. No sponsors could be found.

Graham McNamee: First Famous Voice

While baseball announcing was not Graham McNamee's major responsibility during his career, he was the first announcer to gain fame for doing it. Rice had done the World Series in both 1921 and 1922, but McNamee, who had only begun a staff announcing career with WEAF in May 1923, was added as a color announcer to work with Rice for the World Series in 1923. By the fourth inning of game three, Rice was beginning to tire and turned things over the McNamee. He became a star.

What made McNamee stand apart was his ability to fully describe the scene. Rice had handled the job with a reporter's eye—just the facts and little else. He had also been dry and boring. In contrast, McNamee added some show business appeal. The listeners loved it, even if some news reporters wondered at times if they and McNamee were watching the same game.

How to Use Radio

The real story of radio and baseball was not the development of a style of announcing but how radio could help spread the game and entice more fans to offset those that might be happy just listening. At first, having stations pay fees for rights was not considered. In fact, for years and in a number of cities, more than one station might broadcast games. Not all would do all games, and no one broadcast road games.

The first teams to cover their team's action when out of town used a method invented for and only used extensively for radio.

The Radio Baseball Re-creation

Baseball had been doing a form of re-creation for years during the World Series. In many cities, newspapers would erect large scoreboards outside their buildings. Many had lineups posted with baseball diamonds in the middle. Figures of players could be moved from base to base as needed. The ball and strike counts might be shown, and other information was available. Some papers had men with megaphones who would announce what just happened. The information came from teletype reports from the game.

During the 1921 World Series—the first series with live radio coverage—some stations that were not of the network that could receive the Grantland Rice broadcast did on-air re-creations for the first time. A reporter from a Newark, New Jersey, newspaper did not relay information by teletype but rather used a telephone to directly connect with announcer Tommy Cowan.

Cowan would repeat what he heard, add whatever he could, and the result was heard over stations in both Newark and Springfield, Massachusetts. The fans in Springfield could hear Rice on one station and Cowan on another.

Baseball is by far the best sport for re-creations on radio. Major League Baseball featured re-created games into the 1960s when all teams finally started sending their announcers nationwide. For four years after the Giants moved from New York to San Francisco, Les Keiter of WINS radio convinced his boss he could re-create Giants games for their fans left in the city. The broadcasts were often far more entertaining than the real thing, even though Keiter was as many as 3,000 miles away. He used bare-bones information transmitted over a Western Union wire. At times, the wire would go down, and Keiter would have to cover delays that could include anything from extra foul balls to rain storms.

Former President Ronald Reagan had re-created Chicago Cubs games for WHO radio in Des Moines in the 1930s. One of his accounts of a record-breaking number of foul balls hit in one of his broadcasts was a regular part of his chats whenever the topic turned to baseball.

Even today, some minor league games can be found being re-created. Some of the minor league practitioners of the art became very skilled at making the game sound almost as it would have coming from the game site. That was a Les Keiter trademark in New York and, later, when he wound down his career in Honolulu. This included acquiring audio tape of typical sounds from the road ballparks, including scheduled trains, the sounds of the actual public address announcer, and mid-game festivities.

Red Barber Would Have None of That

Hall of Fame radio broadcaster Red Barber, who was one of the first and best baseball announcers of all time, did a lot of re-creations during his years with the Reds, Dodgers and Yankees. But he would never put on an act. If he was re-creating a game, he

185

never tried to hide it. Instead of crowd noise, the background of his broadcasts might feature the teletype ticker where he was getting his information or dead air. He would not describe the action as if he was seeing it, but simply report what was happening. That method was very dull and boring, but Barber did not care. He felt he was a baseball reporter and not a baseball showman.

Early On, Making Money Was Not a Big Factor

While the ball clubs were not generating much, if any, revenue when radio broadcasting was new, the stations were making some. If they didn't, they did not air the games, as was the case in those last two games of the 1922 Series.

In Chicago, there were five teams carrying baseball. A broadcast license and equipment was all that was needed. There was no such thing as either exclusivity or rights fees. The Cubs wanted them all. They wanted to control baseball in Chicago. Other teams took note. Soon, at least one station was airing home games in Philadelphia, St. Louis, Cincinnati, Boston, and Cleveland. Radio was an advertising medium. The stations made some off commercials within the broadcasts. The teams were advertising their product by having it on the air. Even so, it would not be until 1939 that all teams were broadcasting most, if not all, of their home games.

First National Radio Network

While the World Series and All Star games had been on network radio for years and the money paid for the rights by a single network had gradually gone up, it was still not a windfall for the teams. The first regular season broadcasts of regular season games on a national basis that generated income for all teams was in 1950, though they didn't receive much.

The Liberty Network was the first. They received access to game details from Western Union for $27.50 per game. The Dallas-based network, which used re-creations extensively, did not last long, but all clubs shared the revenue paid. Stations who carried the games paid Liberty $10 per game. To protect local radio stations, Liberty was edged out in most major league cities. But the network provided baseball a great service by taking major league baseball, then mostly a northeastern and mid-western-based sport, into the whole country. Network radio would be revived when Mutual started a "Game of the Day" and CBS radio aired regular season games. Later, ESPN Radio would take over in the role, primarily of postseason games.

Baseball First Seen Collegiately on TV

On May 17, 1939, Princeton beat Columbia 2 to 1 in baseball. The game was played at Baker Field on Columbia's upper west side campus in New York. But the game was far more important than the score. It was the first game ever put on television.

Station W2XBS, later to become WNBC-TV, carried the game with veteran Bill Stern, the lone announcer. It was shot with one camera that was mounted on a platform above and behind the third base on deck circle. It was available to only about 400 television sets in the New York area. The telecast costs for W2XBS ran to about $3,000. That first game was actually the second game of a doubleheader and scheduled for seven innings, but it tied at 1 to 1 and eventually went ten innings. Columbia shortstop Sid Luckman—yes, the same Sid Luckman who played quarterback and became a star with the Chicago Bears—was unable to make a key play in the tenth, which led to Princeton's game-winning run.

The ball wasn't easy to follow and it was hard to capture fast-moving plays the first time out. However, things went smoothly enough that the same station elected to try to air the first major league game in a few weeks with a few modifications.

Red Barber and the First TV of MLB

After the Princeton-Columbia telecast, the television folks were ready to give the major leagues a try. The Brooklyn Dodgers, with innovative owner Larry MacPhail, were picked to be the hosts. But MacPhail wasn't just going to give away his telecast: He wanted a rights fee. And thus, the connection between television, baseball, and money was born.

MacPhail did get a small remuneration as well as television sets in several locations so the game could be watched by team executives. The station also decided to reposition and add another camera. One was set up on the first base side on the outfield end of the dugout to pick up plays at first base. The main camera was moved up and behind home plate. On August 26, 1939, Dodger announcer Red Barber called the game solo and without the benefit of monitors. His call was mostly radio on television. The telecast was, like the game at Columbia, the second game of a doubleheader. The Cincinnati Reds had won the first game 5 to 2, but the Dodgers won the MLB TV debut 6 to 1.

World War II curtailed the development of television in general, and it was not until 1946 that the product would start to be developed. Major League Baseball jumped right, and leading the way was a team that had been reluctant to get on the radio bandwagon.

Local Television Started in New York

In 1946, the New York Yankees, which was one of the last teams to embrace regular radio broadcasts, became the first team with a local television contract. The club was paid $75,000. Chicago was next, with both the Cubs and White Sox contracted to WGN-TV. By 1955, every team in baseball had at least a few games on local television.

The rights fees for those telecasts varied widely based on market size and number of game contracted.

National Television History

The World Series first appeared on national television in 1947, and it has never left. Television rights fees for 1947 were only $175,000. Radio paid $65,000. Compared to what national networks pay now, those fees are ludicrous. But remember, everything was far less expensive than now. National television was a misnomer since few stations actually carried the games before the coaxial cable and because few homes had television sets.

The national baseball "Game of the Week" concept on television began in the early and mid1950s. It was not exactly a true national game since major league cities were not on the network. They also featured game telecasts for some, but not all clubs as contracts were negotiated with individual teams. The games were to promote the game in areas that did not have major league baseball. Dizzy Dean and Buddy Blattner were the first announcers of note on CBS. Later, Pee Wee Reese would replace Blattner. On NBC, another "Game of the Week" would emerge in the 1950s with Lindsay Nelson and Leo Durocher and, later, Fred Haney handling the game telecasts. They aired games for different teams than did CBS.

Ultimately, ABC would also join the fray, and at one point, all three networks were televising major league games on weekends. The economics of carrying baseball on a weekly basis was not the best since most fans preferred to watch their own teams than a national selection. Ratings improved but were not outstanding, even after restrictions were lifted to allow the national games to go into major league markets. Attempts to at least regionalize the weekend games by using multiple telecasts were introduced, which helped cumulative ratings somewhat but never solved baseball's network television problem as the rights moved from CBS, NBC, ABC, and later FOX. Fans wanted to watch their teams, but the networks needed the rights for the All Star Game and World Series, and baseball wanted the money the networks could provide as well as weekly national exposure.

189

Then Came the Fall

During the late 1960s to mid1970s, baseball was losing ground to football as the nation's most popular sport. Because football's schedule was much shorter and mostly limited to Sundays, the sport was perfect for television. It could be regionalized so home fans always saw their team. With so many teams and games, network televised baseball could not compete. Ratings fell. That meant that other than for the All-Star Game and World Series, the networks had lost some interest. In 1969, for the first time, a national Harris poll placed football above baseball as the favorite sport of the most Americans. The game was judged too slow. But it may really have been that a weekly football game is more precious for fans than a game that is played daily. Baseball tried to make itself more attractive.

Major League Baseball instituted some rule changes to put more offense into the game. The designated hitter was added to the rules in the American League. But it was a single World Series that brought baseball back. And television had a lot to do with it.

Reds-Red Sox Peaked Interest

The Reds' thrilling win over the Red Sox would not be enough to solidify baseball's increased revenue hopes, but it was a start. The game now had more power to require larger financial considerations from those that carried their games. Radio was pretty much limited by market size. Television was also under the current "over-the-air" restrictions. Could network television generate enough revenue in the era of free agency that began shortly after the classic series? Would the ratings justify a boost?

There were many questions, including acquiring air time and a number of restrictions that had to be worked around those restrictions. Local television and local fans wanted to see more of their teams and not so much of the others. The question over local versus national television was getting harder to answer.

Baseball needed the revenue from a good national network package of games, but with network weekend games calling for priority over any local telecasts, that meant some of the prime spots for local telecasts were gone. Showing games only during weekdays or nights was hardly the best. Weeknights resulted in conflicts with the major network programming and much competition for viewers. Plus, network affiliated stations that had been carrying baseball could not afford to pre-empt regular network programming, no matter how popular the local baseball team might be.

Then there was the problem of rights fees. Network affiliates had more financial resources to meet team demands but less air time. Local independent stations had more time but less money. Because local television was growing, the importance for baseball to be aired on a national network for exposure was diluted. But baseball still needed the money. They would get some of it from a new source.

Enter Cable Television

Although now what we generically call "cable" really also includes satellite, internet, and telephone company providers, it was actual cable television that opened the door for more games on the air and more revenue for the teams.

When cable television began it was often primarily a relay system for existing television signals that could not be brought in well by antennas. There was no real programming other than perhaps some local low cost and low quality production on one of the system's access channels.

But then a number of entrepreneurs got some ideas. They considered creating programming especially for cable television. Programs for which there was no room on established "over-the-air" television would fit the bill. The programs would offer cable operators more options to provide for potential subscribers, thus driving up the number of subscribers.

Nationally, such networks as ESPN and CNN led the way. Some "over- the-air" operators thought that having their channels re-broadcast nationally might be profitable. So WGN-TV in Chicago, WTBS-TV in Atlanta, and WOR-TV in New York put their programming on satellite where it could be picked up and rebroadcast by cable systems across America. The fact that those stations in Chicago, Atlanta, and New York had major league baseball as part of their programming took the game to new places. In the meantime, the national broadcast networks were tossing Major League Baseball around like a hot potato. Did they want an obligation to carry a low rated "Game of the Week" just to obtain rights to the World Series? Ultimately, the answer was "yes," as the Fox Television Network—a newcomer to the national scene— elected to use the NFL and MLB as its ticket to legitimacy. Later, combined with packages by the now grownup ESPN and other national cable networks, baseball had more games on national television than any other sport, while continuing to expand local coverage to new heights as well.

The Regional Sports Networks

It took a few years for the national and regional cable networks to become players. At first, due to the cost, ESPN began telecasting with few high- impact sporting events. There was no NFL, no MLB, no NBA, and no NHL. Rights for distribution were either too high, or one of the "over-the- air" networks already had them. But local rights to local teams were not tied up. If teams had contracts with stations, few were for the full schedule of games. The reason for the birth of the regional sports network was at hand. The names and ownerships have changed over the years, but some of the sports pioneers were known as SportsChannel, Home Sports Entertainment (HSE), Madison Square Garden Network (MSG), and SportsTime. They all went after and got large portions of local baseball television that was being un-aired by local stations.

In most cases, the cable nets picked up the home games while the television partner carried the road telecasts. Sometimes they had the same announcers and crews. Sometimes they did not. The advantages that these cable programmers had was they could receive a fee per subscriber from the cable systems, and later satellite systems, that agreed to carry their programming, while also selling commercial time within the games. Standard televisions stations do not have built-in subscriber payments.

A change started to occur in the 1990s when some clubs decided to increase the value of their holdings by adding their cable operations to the team's holdings. The Boston Red Sox have long held a major interest in the New England Sports Network. The Yankees were the original primary owners of YES, the Yankees Entertainment and Sports Network. Other teams have teamed up with producing companies with ties directly to or ownership of cable or satellite companies like Comcast, Time Warner, and DirecTV. The clubs have an equity stake in their network or, in the case of the Atlanta Braves, are owned by the same company that owns DirecTV).

In many cases, instead of taking rights fees with the obligation on the production company like Fox Sports Net or other systems to generate all the revenue to pay those rights, clubs are now gambling they can make more money through the partnership. All the money may not be guaranteed but is tied into subscriber fees and advertising, which can fluctuate with the success or popularity of the team. As long as there is competition to telecast the games, the financial gamble is minimal. Selling full rights to a production company guaranteed the negotiated price but limited growth within the contract years.

The gamble was with distribution. If a team could not get distribution to generate that extra revenue, its investment lost value. The money would no longer be guaranteed by a contract from a production company.

Start Was Like Radio

The reason the home games were okay for cable was that not everyone had cable at the time. The telecasts were deemed as less of a risk to harm attendance. History would prove that to be another unfounded fear as baseball revenues continued to rise, as more and more games were available and more and more homes were wired.

Where Does it Go?

If the universe is endless, then perhaps ticket prices, player salaries, and cable and satellite costs can continue to rise to infinity as well. For team owners and players unions, that may be a goal. If it is unrealistic, it will be tested when stations, cable, and satellite companies refuse to raise commercial or subscriber rates to pay for major league baseball and other sports. If they have no competitive reason to be forced to do it, the "Golden Goose" may start to lose some feathers.

Money Rolling In

Broadcasting—mostly television and cable/satellite—revenue has been increasing at almost shocking rates since the 1980s. A few teams have a chance to earn $100 million per year off local rights alone. When added to the national television revenue share, selling actual tickets will be almost secondary income. As has been the case with the National Football League for years, an owner will have no concern of ever losing money. How much he wants to spend will be the question.

This question, however, will never apply to all teams. As average salaries for lawyers differ from city to city, so do potential revenue levels in baseball. Having many different teams be competitive has not been a major problem. Some have had long dry spells but have been able to rebuild. Others have been and will be near the top every season. The finances will never be on a level playing field. But they really never were.

Other Media Resources

Since the advent of the computer and all that has followed, baseball fans are in the information age. With a few keystrokes, the latest stats for any player are available from the basic to the most esoteric. Careers or stories of players from the past are only a few more key strokes away. At the same time, Major League Baseball and its teams have learned how to increase revenues by offering some items to fans for a fee.

One way to increase revenue includes access to radio or televised games over the internet. While the objective is still to protect teams' local broadcast rights, it has been possible to watch teams from other regions or listen to their radio broadcasts. Major League Baseball controls those rights with revenue shared by all the clubs. MLB has also created its own network available on cable and satellite systems that offer programming twenty-four hours a day, 365 days a year. Baseball fans don't have to wait until spring anymore. The game may still trail football in polls of favorite sports for Americans, but it is a very strong number two and it has proven there is room for both and more in this modern sports era.

Chapter XIII

BASEBALL AND THE PRESIDENTS

I honestly feel that it would be best for the country to keep baseball going.

Franklin Delano Roosevelt
Former President of the United States

Franklin Delano Roosevelt, Washington, D.C., 1936

I am a lucky man. I have met two Presidents, who also knew who I am, without being a news reporter. I have even announced a major league baseball with one of them before he entered the White House. But baseball and the U.S. Presidents have been associated for years.

Presidential Support

From the days of George Washington throughout the history of the United States, presidents have had a connection to baseball. Washington, for instance, was mentioned in an unidentified soldier's letter home. The soldier wrote, "Washington sometimes throws and catches a ball for hours with his aide-de-camp."

Other presidents are linked to the sport in writing. In listing the many sports available, John Adams included "bat and ball." Thomas Jefferson was rather unkind when he wrote, "Games played with the ball and others of their nature are too violent for the body and stamp no character of the mind." Maybe he was writing of soccer or football?

Abraham Lincoln both played and watched baseball. Although it has been reported he was playing the game when notified he had won the Republican presidential nomination in 1860, that story is not true.

His successor, Andrew Johnson, was a true fan. He was so excited about watching two games, one between the Washington Nationals and Philadelphia Athletics and another between the Nats and Brooklyn Atlantics, that he gave government clerks and employees time off to watch and even had chairs set along the first base line for himself and a White House group.

Grover Cleveland once had his hand shaken so hard by a number of ballplayers that it became swollen. According to player King Kelly, "The president's hand was fat and soft. I squeezed it so hard, he winced."

Benjamin Harrison attended at least two National League games in Washington in 1892. William McKinley, however, was a no-show in 1897 when he was scheduled to be the first president to throw out the first ball on Opening Day.

Theodore Roosevelt regarded baseball as a "mollycoddle game." He preferred football, lacrosse, and boxing. He also was not much on professional sports in general, and was referring mostly to baseball when he said, "When money comes in at the gate, sport flies out the window." Even so, Theodore Roosevelt was the first U.S. President awarded a lifetime pass. It was made of 14k gold and is now on display at the Library of Congress.

It was not until April 14, 1910, that a president threw out the first pitch to begin the baseball season. William Howard Taft did it that day and again in 1911. He missed 1912 due to the Titanic disaster. He attended at least fourteen games while in office, including games at Pittsburgh, St. Louis, Cincinnati, and Chicago, along with Washington.

His first Opening Day toss in 1910 was only one of a few stories that day. Vice President James Sherman was also on hand. During the game, Sherman was knocked unconscious by a foul ball. Also, although he was given credit for it, Taft probably did not originate the "seventh inning stretch," but he did certainly participate. Taft was added to the "Racing Presidents" at Nationals Park in D.C. starting with the 2013 season, which is fitting for his love of the game.

Woodrow Wilson played baseball during his first year at Davidson College. During World War I, he missed two openers and had Vice President Marshall and Navy Secretary Franklin Roosevelt fill in.

Warren Harding was visited at the White House by Babe Ruth on seven occasions during his term. He also was the only president injured in office while playing the game. He injured a finger when he caught a hard-hit ball in a charity game at his hometown in 1920.

Calvin Coolidge was not a fan, but he attended ten games and threw out first pitches for three opening games and two World Series games. Herbert Hoover, however, was a fan and had played shortstop as a child.

Franklin D. Roosevelt gave baseball the "green light" to continue playing during World War II and threw out the first pitch of all eleven games he attended during his White House years, in addition to the one he threw for Woodrow Wilson years before.

Harry Truman was the first lefthander to toss a first presidential pitch. He attended sixteen games while in office.

Dwight Eisenhower let Vice-President Richard Nixon sub for him on Opening Day duties in 1959. Ike played baseball in high school and junior varsity baseball at Army.

John Kennedy attended just four games during his shortened presidency but was the first president to watch every inning of every game. He threw out the first pitch ever at the stadium in Washington that would one day be named after his brother—RFK Stadium.

Lyndon B. Johnson was on hand for the opening of the Astrodome in Houston, but attended only three games in Washington.

Richard Nixon was a huge fan. "I never leave a game before the last pitch, because in baseball, like politics, you never know what might happen," he said. Nixon was offered the job as head of the MLB Players union before Marvin Miller.

Gerald Ford was the first "switch-thrower" in presidential annals. He threw righty to Johnny Bench and lefty to Carlton Fisk prior to the 1976 All Star Game. He was in the stands prior to his presidency to see Hank Aaron's 714th home run.

Jimmy Carter attended one game as president, the last game of the 1979 World Series in Baltimore. He would later attend a number of Atlanta Braves games after he left office.

Ronald Reagan was the only president who announced baseball games on the radio. As an actor, he was Grover Cleveland Alexander in a film. With no team in Washington, he attended four games in Baltimore and one in Chicago. During the latter, he announced one and a half innings.

George Bush was a college baseball player at Yale and played in the College World Series. He threw out the first pitch eight times, including once in Arlington, Texas, when his son George W. Bush was part owner of the Texas Rangers. After George Bush, the forty-first president, left office and retired in Houston he and his wife Barbara were regulars at Astros games.

Bill Clinton has the distinction of being the first president to make his opening pitch from the mound to the catcher. That was in Baltimore in 1993.

George W. Bush was the first president that was formerly co-owner of a major league baseball team, the Texas Rangers major league baseball team. During that time before he began his political career, he often stopped by the television booth and provided commentary, especially during Nolan Ryan starts. Years later as President, he also threw three opening pitches at six different ballparks. George W. Bush was also the first former Little League player to be elected president.

Barack Obama once caught some heat from fans for wearing Chicago White Sox gear when throwing out a first pitch not in Chicago. Coming from the Chicago south side, he had long been a White Sox fan.

Woodrow Wilson, 1916

Chapter XIV

MINOR LEAGUES HAD SOME GREAT PLAYERS

One of the beautiful things about baseball is that every once in a while, you come into a situation where you want to, and where you have to, reach down and prove something.

Nolan Ryan
Hall of Famer

Buzz Arlett

Chapter 14: Minor Leagues Had Some Great Players

My first chance to watch and, later, broadcast professional baseball came in the minor leagues. I had been watching Orlando "Zippo" Cepeda and, later, Tommy Davis in Kokomo, Indiana, before and shortly after my granddad and I made that first trip to Cincinnati. And I announced minor league baseball in Buffalo, New York, before working games for the Texas Rangers and Houston Astros in MLB. I remember names like Don Miles, Paul Abraham, Emmy Unzicker, Duke Durden, Eddie Serrano, Bruce Crenshaw, Napoleon Savinon, Dale Reichert, Gus Sancimino, Rick Lancellotti, Tom McMillan, and Chick Valley. None of those players made big names for themselves in the major leagues. In most cases, they never played there at all. But I remember them from what they did in the minors.

Minor League Legends

Some of the great players of all time, unlike African American players, had a chance to play in the major leagues but couldn't succeed. Those were the greats from the minor leagues, and there were a number of them.

Unlike today, when the minor leagues are training grounds for potential major league players, that was not totally always the case. There were far more minor leagues at one time, and many of the players knew they would never play in the majors. They just liked to play. Some became local heroes, like Joe Bauman of Roswell, New Mexico. He ran a filling station but also played for the Roswell Rockets.

Joe Bauman: Home Run King

It is possible that Joe Bauman might have made it to the major leagues. But if he had, the odds are great that he would just be named in the record books and not a legend. He also might have been totally out of baseball before the one season that made his name legendary. Because he did not make the "show," his memory may last as long as baseball is played.

Joe Bauman once hit seventy-two home runs in a 138-game minor league season. No one has come close to his home run frequency, even though Barry Bonds hit seventy-three home runs for the National League San Francisco Giants in 2001.

Bauman also hit .400 and drove in a whopping 224 runs during that 1954 season in the Class C Longhorn League. But when he did, his career was nearing an end. Joe was thirty-two years old and a long way from the majors. During his peak years, he was not available. When World War II broke out, he played semiprofessional ball in 1942, waiting for the call to serve. He got it and was in the service from 1943 through 1945. He returned to baseball at only twenty-three years old but had missed four seasons, and it was not determined yet whether he was a pitcher or a first baseman. Before the war, he had done both, although not very successfully.

In 1941, he had played for both Newport and Little Rock and was 0 and 10 as a pitcher while hitting only .215.

Bauman rose as high as triple A with the Milwaukee Brewers in 1948 after he had hit forty-eight and thirty-eight homers in successive seasons for Amarillo of the West Texas-New Mexico League the previous two seasons. He got only one at-bat. He retired after playing at Hartford in the Eastern League most of the season, with a pedestrian .275 batting average and ten home runs in ninety-eight games. From 1949 through 1951, he did not play. But in 1950, he signed on to play for Artesia in the Longhorn League. He then had a three-season run never matched in professional baseball.

In 1952, Joe hit .357 with fifty homers and 157 runs batted in, followed by a .371-53-141 season the next year. That was followed by the biggest of all—his 1954 colossal season.

Bauman hung it up for good after the 1956 season. His final minor league numbers showed a .337 average, 337 home runs, and 1,057 runs batted in over ten seasons. He had one of the best minor league careers ever.

Others May Have Been Better—Like Buzz Arlett

While Bauman's home run and hitting feats are impressive, there have been a number of mostly career minor leaguers who were even more impressive. None of them hit seventy-two home runs in a season, but some were more versatile.

Buzz Arlett played most of his minor league career on a higher level than Bauman. In fact, other than a brief stint with Birmingham in 1934 and the National League Philadelphia Phillies in 1931, his twenty-year career was in triple A or the equivalent.

He played 1918 through 1930 in the Pacific Coast League and also had stints in both the American Association and International League.

Arlett compiled a .341 lifetime minor league average. He also hit 432 homers, drove in 1,786 runs, and stole 200 bases.

If that is not enough, Arlett also pitched. From 1918 through 1930—all with Oakland—he won 108 games with an earned run average of 3.42. His main use as a pitcher ended in 1923, but before then, he had won twenty or more games three times with a high of twenty-nine in 1920. It must be noted, however, that the Pacific Coast League played a longer schedule than any other pro league. In 1929, Arlett is recorded as having played in 200 games with 722 at-bats. That explains why he was able to hit seventy doubles.

Arlett was a switch hitter who hit four home runs in a game twice in the same 1932 season with Baltimore of the International League. That year, he set a personal career high with fifty-four homers. Because of his pitching background and his power hitting, Buzz was often called "The Babe Ruth of the Minors."

Buzz saw major league action in 1931 for the Phillies and hit .313 to go with eighteen home runs and seventy-two runs batted in. Why did he not make it in the majors? It was his lack of defensive ability. Over the years, Arlett had gained a lot of weight. Until 1930, he had been a good base- stealer with a high of twenty-six steals in successive seasons. But he had weighed only about 185 pounds then. By 1931, he was over 230 pounds and very sluggish defensively. In fact, during that one season with the Phillies, he was relegated to pinch-hitting much of the second half of the year.

Smead Jolley Was Similar—As a Hitter

Another player with defensive shortcomings but a good bat was Smead Jolley. Jolley played professionally from 1922 through 1941 and had a .366 lifetime minor league batting average. He also hit 336 home runs with a high of forty-five in 1928 with the Pacific Coast League San Francisco Seals. That season, his batting average was .404, and he also drove in 188 runs in 191 games. Unlike Buzz Arlett, he did get a decent shot in the major leagues. He spent 1930 thru 1933 in the majors with the White Sox and Red Sox.

Jolley hit, too. He compiled a .305 batting average in 473 major league games. However, he was a horrid outfielder. He made forty-four errors in 778 chances for an awful outfielder's percentage of .944.

While his major league career did not match what he did in the minors, he wasn't flustered when he went back down. He continued to hit. At thirty-eight years old with Spokane of the Western International league in 1940, he hit .373 with 181 runs batted in, in just 145 games. The next year he retired, but not until he hit .345 with twenty-four homers and 128 runs batted in.

Ike Boone Best Career Average

Ty Cobb had the highest lifetime batting average in major league baseball history at .366. Ike Boone's was higher but on the minor league level. The outfielder, who did get into 356 games and hit .321 as a major leaguer, hit a whopping .370 in 1,857 games during his

minor league career. His best season was with the Mission team of
the Pacific Coast League in 1929 when he hit .407 with fifty-five
home runs and 218 runs batted in over 198 games.

More Memorable Minor Leaguers

How about Moose Clabaugh? He hit .339 in 2,098 minor league
games with 346 homers, including sixty-two for Tyler of the East
Texas League in 1926. Consider Joe Hauser, who hit sixty-three
homers for Baltimore in 1930 and sixty-nine for Minneapolis in
1933. Joe hit 399 in the minors and another seventy-nine for the
Philadelphia A's of the American League.

Bob Crues set the record for organized baseball runs batted
in for Amarillo of the West Texas-New Mexico League in 1948. He
drove in 254 along with sixty-nine home runs in just 140 games.
He also hit .404. His minor league lifetime record was .337.

In addition, Ox Eckert had a lifetime minor league average of
.367 and won five minor league batting titles.

Hector Espino Deserves Special Mention

Hector Espino never played a game for a team outside his native
Mexico. In a career that lasted from 1960 through 1984, the 5'11,
185-pound catcher hit 484 home runs, which is the minor league
record. His career batting average was .337. He won five Mexican
League batting titles and led the league in home runs four times.

Some Pitchers Did Big Things

There have been pitchers in the minor leagues who have won 300
games. The first was Willard Mains who was 318 and 181 in a career
that ran from 1887 to 1906. Admittedly, the game was different
then. "Grasshopper" Mains started as many as forty-nine games
one season. He won twenty or more on seven different occasions
with a high of thirty-eight in 1889. Since his career included a major
rule change in 1893, he had to make some adjustments. Six of

his twenty-win seasons came after the 60' 6" mound rule, but it took him two seasons to get straightened out.

William Thomas was 383 and 347: Tops in Wins and Losses

William Thomas was once suspended for two and a half seasons in 1947 and 1948 after having skipped a whole season back in 1930. Yet he still won a minor league record 383 games in a career that started in 1925 and ended in 1952. He was a curveballer with outstanding control. He would also easily have been a 400-game winner except for his absences from the game. His suspension during the late 1940s was as a result of allegations of having gambling connections, which he denied. Thomas also had 347 losses, the minor league record for most games lost.

The minor leaguer with the second most wins of them all was Alexander "Red" McColl. He won 332 games and also lost 263. McColl pitched between 1915 and 1941. His was a pure case of longevity since only seventeen of his twenty-five seasons featured double-figure wins, and only four times did he win twenty or more in a season. He won twenty-one games on three occasions for his season best.

Several other minor leaguers of note include Frank Shellenback, who won 315 games, and Spider Baum and Tony Freitas, who both won twenty or more games nine times. Add to that list George Brunet, who struck out 3,175 batters. There were some pitchers that made their reputation in the minor leagues, even if their visit to the majors may have only been long enough for their cup of coffee to get cold.

Chapter XV

STORIES FROM TV'S "TALES OF THE GAME"

I knew when my career was over. In 1965, my baseball card came out with no picture.

Bob Uecker
Broadcaster and former catcher

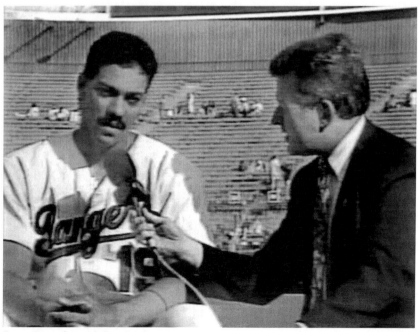

Juan Gonzalez and Greg Lucas, 1991

From the Archives of "Tales of the Game"

For more than twenty-seven seasons of major league baseball, I researched, wrote, and hosted a series of baseball vignettes originally called "Tales of the Game," which were part of Texas Ranger and Houston Astro telecasts and special shows. Some of those stories have already been integrated into the historical portions of this book in which they fit.

However, we have only touched the surface of baseball's long, grand past— there are lot more tales where these came from. Here are more strange and anecdotal stories from baseball.

Frank Lane Never Saw a Trade He Wouldn't Make

Frank Lane was a longtime major league general manager. If you were a player and he was your GM, he believed it was always better to rent than buy. He had the nickname "Trader" Lane for a reason: No player was too big to be untouchable. He once dealt the reigning American League home run champ, Rockie Colovito, who was also a very popular player in Cleveland, for the reigning A.L. batting champion, Harvey Kuenn of Detroit. While in St. Louis on one of his five stops as a G.M., he proposed a deal that would send Stan Musial to the Yankees in exchange for St. Louis native Yogi Berra. His owner, Gussie Busch, quashed that deal and soon after, Lane was seeking a job. Lane landed in Cleveland, where he made the Colovito-Kuenn trade.

He then came up with the only trade of its kind in baseball history. In mid-season 1960, he traded with Detroit again. This time, he sent his manager, Joe Gordon, to the Tigers for the Detroit skipper Jimmy Dykes. Never before and never since has something like this been attempted.

In large part because of all his maneuvers, and in larger part due to his abrasive personality, Lane was not popular within the baseball community. When he died at age eighty-four in 1981, only one representative of baseball would attend his funeral in Dallas, and Bobby Bragan had been specifically requested by Commissioner Bowie Kuhn to be on hand.

Switch-Pitching Just Never Caught On

While Bob Ferguson was the first of what would be many switch-hitters in baseball, the first known switch-pitcher was Elton "Icebox" Chamberlain. He played before the turn of the century and was even listed on roster sheets as a switch pitcher, although he reportedly only used both arms twice. He played ten years starting in 1886 and won 157 games, including thirty-two in 1889. While a natural righty, he made his last appearance on May 9, 1888, pitching two scoreless innings as a lefty for Louisville against Kansas City.

ROBERT FERGUSON, VETERAN MANAGER, CAPTAIN, AND UMPIRE.

Bob Ferguson

One of Chamberlain's worst outings was also a history maker. Pitching on May 30, 1894, for Cincinnati against Boston, he was beaten 20 to 11 and gave up all the runs, including four home runs by Bobby Lowe, who became the first player in major league history to hit four home runs in a game.

Prior to Chamberlain, Tony Mullane had made two appearances as a switch-pitcher on July 18, 1882, and July 14, 1883. Mullane was normally a right-hander, but he learned to pitch with his left arm when injured. In addition, Larry Corcoran had done it on June 10, 1884.

Mullane is linked to the start of "Ladies Day" in baseball, but it had nothing to do with his ability to throw with either arm. Mullane was quite handsome and drew attention from the female set. In fact, one of his nicknames was "Apollo of the pitcher's box." He was so popular while with Cincinnati that the club would make sure he pitched every Monday home game and designated the normally low-attended Monday games as "Ladies Day." The promotion was a staple by teams in major league baseball for years.

After Chamberlain, a pitcher would not work with both arms in a game until September 28, 1995. Greg Harris of the Montreal Expos faced two batters with each arm. He retired the Reds' Reggie Sanders with his right, and then used his left and walked Hal Morris. Staying with the left, he retired Ed Taubensee on a ground out. Moving back to the right arm, he retired Brett Boone on another ground out. There have been other switch- pitchers in high school, college, and even professional baseball on the minor league level. But no one since Harris has tried it in a major league game.

Wrong-Armed Players

Thanks to the geography of the baseball diamond and the direction bases are run, it has always been more advantageous for players who threw with their right hand. Some positions, including most on the infield and catcher, are not suited for the lefties.

But some players have spent time at those "forbidden" positions. In baseball's early days, before the fielders wore gloves, being able to throw with either hand was an advantage. Jeremiah Denny was a noted third baseman who could and was one of the most wide-ranging third sackers of all time. Generally, though, a lefty would not play anywhere on the infield except first base. There have been many lefties who have filled in at other spots, including catcher, but the last regular left- handed catcher played between 1884 and 1890. His name was Jack Clements. Clements caught

1,073 games, about four times more than any other lefty catcher in baseball history. He was the first player to catch 1,000 games. His career started in Philadelphia and included stops in St. Louis, Cleveland, and Boston. He managed the Phillies in 1890. Although highly regarded as a player during the bulk of his career, he was ignomiously released by the Cleveland Spiders after playing only four games in 1899. The Spiders were the worst team in the history of baseball.

OLD JUDGE CIGARETTES

Jeremiah Denny

How Bad Were Those Spiders?

Speaking of the 1899 Cleveland Spiders, no one has done it worse. The team was 20 and 134 and was so bad they couldn't set foot at home for much of the second half of the season. It wasn't the players' fault. It was directly the result of their owner taking his best players to the other team he owned in St. Louis.

After Frank and Stanley Robison bought the Browns during the off season while still owning the Spiders, some transfers of major player proved a statement attributed to Stanley Robison that the Browns would get most of his attention and the Spiders would be a side show.

Cy Young, Jess Burkett, Bobby Wallace, and even manager Patsy Tebeau were moved from Cleveland to St. Louis. Lefty catcher Jack Clements, whose career would prove to be almost over, had the misfortune of being sacrificed to the Spiders.

During the Spiders' first sixteen games in 1899, they were averaging fewer than 200 fans per game. Before long, since visiting teams took a share of the gate to pay expenses, those teams wanted to skip going to Cleveland. The Spiders played only eight games at home after July 1 and only a total of forty-two for the whole year.

They lost 101 road games, which will never be equaled since teams no team in history has ever or will ever play that many. The Spiders finished eighty-four games off the lead in twelfth place, but they didn't finish that far behind the St. Louis Browns. Despite Stanley Robison's efforts, the Browns were only able to secure a fifth place finish, an 84 and 67 record, and be eighteen and a half games behind the champion Brooklyn Superpas when the season ended.

Rare Grand Slam Homers in First Major League At-Bat

There have been only three players to hit grand slam home runs in their first major league at-bats. The first was pitcher Frosty Bill Duggleby for the 1898 Philadelphia Phillies. Duggleby would hit a total of six home runs in an eight-year career. It would take 107 years for that the feat to be duplicated by Jeremy Hermida of the Florida Marlins off St. Louis Cardinal hurler Al Reyes on August 31, 2005. But just over a year later, on September 21, 2006, Cleveland Indian Kevin Kouzmanoff did something that can never be exceeded when he not only hit a grand slam homer in his first at-bat, but he did it on the very first pitch from Texas Ranger pitcher Edinson Volquez.

Hank and Hugh: Baseball's First Soldiers

Perhaps it was only fitting that the first two major league baseball players to enter both World Wars formed a battery of sorts between catcher Hank Gowdy and pitcher Hugh Mulcahy. In World War I, Red Sox Catcher Gowdy was the first baseballer to serve. He saw considerable action in France. Eddie Grant, who served after leaving the New York Giants in 1914 and 1915, was the only major leaguer to be killed in the First World War.

In World War II, the first to serve was Hugh Mulcahy. He was drafted and served on the winning side from 1941 through the end. That was a change for Mulcahy, whose nickname of "Losing

Pitcher Mulcahy" appeared in many box scores during his years with the Phillies of the 30s. He was 40 and 76 in the four years prior to being drafted and lost twenty or more games twice during that span. Mulcahy later served as a scout for many years.

First Player with a Pension

A player's union had nothing to do with the first pension, but honesty did. In 1903, none other than John McGraw introduced a gambler to Red Sox catcher Lou Criger, who offered Criger $12,000 to "lay down" in the first World Series between the Red Sox and Pirates. Criger reported the gambler and then helped the Red Sox knock off the favored Pirates. In gratitude, the American League awarded Criger a lifetime pension. In those days, no players had any post-career guarantees.

Using Yellow Baseballs

Iridescent orange and yellow golf balls can still be found in some pro shops. They are not as common as in the 1990s, but their purpose was to be easier to spot on the course. Their use has dwindled over the years, though they are especially good for novice golfers who might have to spend time in the rough and woods searching for their errant shots. However, the same concept of using colored balls has been applied to baseballs to make the sphere easier for both players and fans to follow.

Actual Games Used Them

Four National League games in 1938 and 1939 actually were played with bright yellow colored baseballs. Their use was the idea of Brooklyn Dodger general manager Larry MacPhail. In 1938, the Cardinals and Dodgers first used the yellow ball in a game at Ebbets Field. After some refinements—they were deemed a bit slick—they were pulled out again the next season and used for three games more—two against the Cards and one against the Cubs. Nothing more came of the attempt as National League teams resisted any change.

Finley Wanted Orange

The idea of using a colored baseball was not dead; it just rested for thirty- four years. In 1973, Oakland A's owner Charlie Finley, who was always looking for new ways to present baseball, thought iridescent orange was the right color. Tests had proven the human eye could see the color orange better than white. Finley used the balls in a few spring training games but could not get approval for further use. Again, the covers were a bit slicker, and the seams were much harder for hitters to see than those of white baseballs.

Home Plate Was Originally Round

Home plate was also very hard and dangerous since it was first made of stone or cast iron. By the way, the term "dish" was used originally when the plate was dish-like round. It was changed to square in 1869. In 1885, the rules called for the plate to be constructed of rubber instead of stone or iron since too many players were injured sliding across it to score runs. It was not until 1900 that it was changed to a pentagonal shape. Since the square plate was set with points facing the pitcher and catcher, the strike zone didn't change, but it was easier to call balls and strikes with a wider front.

Overcoming Physical Handicaps

Athletes need to have all their physical talents in top form to play any sport with optimal skill level. Yet baseball history records instances where players who, for one reason or another, had to overcome tremendous physical disadvantages and still were able to play.

Mordecai Brown Leads the List

Hall of Fame pitcher Mordecai "Three-Fingered" Brown really was three- fingered on his pitching hand. His index finger was only a stub. His middle finger was badly bent. His thumb, ring, and little finger were normal. Brown had lost his index finger in a farm accident with a feed chopper. His bent middle ringer resulted from a later broken bone that was badly set.

The mangled pitching hand may have actually helped him as a pitcher. He threw a sinking fast ball and a very good curve. He won 239 games and was on four pennant winners and two World Series champions in a seventeen-year career.

Jim Abbott: MLB and Olympic Star

Left-handed pitcher Jim Abbott was born without a fully formed right hand, yet he was able to pitch in the major leagues for eleven seasons between 1989 and 1999. During that time, he won eighty-seven games, including a no-hitter for the New York Yankees against the Cleveland Indians on September 4, 1993.

Before major league baseball, Abbott had already made a name for himself. He played collegiately at the University of Michigan and became the first baseball player to win the James E. Sullivan Award for being the top amateur athlete in the United States. Then he pitched the U.S.A. to the top spot in the 1988 Olympic Games, where baseball was played as a demonstration sport.

Abbott would tuck his glove against his chest while he pitched, and then after the ball left his hand, slip his hand back inside to be ready to field his position.

With most of his career in the American League, which used designated hitters, trying to hit was not a problem. Yet, as he finished his career in 1999 with the National League Milwaukee Brewers, he was able to get two hits in twenty-one at-bats.

Bud Daley's Withered Arm

Another lefty pitcher that preceded Abbott had a right arm that was not quite normal. Bud Daley had a fully developed hand, but a withered right arm. He pitched nine years in the major leagues with a large variety of pitches but no real power fast ball. He was effective, though. He won sixteen games twice for the Kansas City Athletics, then finished his career with the New York Yankees, pitching mostly out of the bullpen.

Daley said his withered right arm was a result of an accident during his birth. Forceps apparently pinched a nerve, which stunted the growth of the arm. Massage and exercise brought use back to the arm, but it was always less developed, and Daley had limited range of motion. Yet, he was still a good fielder during his major league career.

Pete Gray Had a Long Career With One Arm

Pete Gray's major league opportunity likely would not have happened if not for World War II, but the one-armed outfielder had a very successful and long minor league career. Gray had lost his right arm in a truck accident as a child. But he loved baseball and learned how to play it one-armed, and he did it well. After a solid amateur and semipro stint, he signed a minor league contract and hit .381 for the Three Rivers team in the Canadian-American League in 1942. Rising to Memphis in 1943 and 1944, he hit .333 with five home runs the latter season and, with the war taking many able-bodied players, was given a chance in 1945 by the St. Louis Browns.

While not as successful as he had been in the minors, Gray still played in seventy-seven games and hit .218 with his one-handed swing.

When the players returned from WWII, his career in the major leagues was over. But in a six-year minor league career, he hit .308. He hit five home runs, all for Memphis, in 1944.

Monte Stratton Tried with One Leg

One of the sadder stories of "what might have been" involves pitcher Monte Stratton. Until he lost his right leg in a hunting accident during the off season following the 1938 season, he was on his way to becoming one of the top pitchers in the American League. He had won fifteen games in each of his last two seasons with the Chicago White Sox. At only twenty-six years old, he seemed ready to reach his prime.

But then he fell while hunting rabbits, and a holstered pistol discharged. The bullet tore through his right leg and damaged a main artery so severely that the leg had to be amputated. Stratton would never pitch in the major leagues again. But he DID pitch again eight years later.

Using a wooden leg, Stratton learned how to pitch again. But fielding well enough with the artificial leg was the problem. There was nothing wrong with his arm, as attested by his eighteen victories for the Sherman team in the Class C East Texas League in 1946 at age thirty-four. He just could not field his position, and a dream to make it back to the majors was not to be possible. His story is remembered in the film "The Stratton Story," starring Jimmy Stewart.

War Hero Bert Shepard Did Make it Back

When Bert Shepard broke into the major leagues on August 4, 1945, at age twenty-five, his odds to ever getting there were perhaps the longest in baseball history. Bert had been in pro-ball since signing as a twenty-year-old out of Dana, Indiana, in 1940. His career had been nondescript. After three seasons, he had been still in Class D and coming off a 9 and 13 season for LaCrosse in the Wisconsin State League. Then came World War II, and everything changed for Shepard.

He became a fighter pilot for the Army Air Corps but was shot down in Germany. He crashed into a field, injured badly by shells that had penetrated the cockpit. When a German Luftwaffe physician got to the scene, he rescued the U.S. Army pilot and took charge so he could be treated. The treatment required that Shepard's right leg had to be amputated. He was then sent to a prisoner-of-war camp. While there, a fellow prisoner who was a Canadian medic fashioned an artificial leg. As soon as he could, Shepard was playing catch. Bert was returned to the United States in February, 1945, as part of a prisoner exchange. After returning, he made it clear he wanted to pitch again.

The Washington Senators gave him a tryout. He pitched some batting practice and four innings in a War Relief Fund game on July 10 against Brooklyn. A little less than a month later, on August 5, 1945, Shepard got into a real major league game.

The Boston Red Sox were thumping the Senators 14 to 2 when Shepard entered the game in the fourth inning. He struck out the first man he faced, George Metcovich. He also finished the game by pitching five and a third innings. He allowed just three hits and one run. He never pitched in the major leagues again but hung around the minors till 1954.

Baseball on Ice

In the early days of the sport someone came up with the idea that if baseball was good on grass and dirt, it might be even better on ice. On February 4, 1861, on Litchfield's Pond in South Brooklyn, the Atlantics beat the Charter Oak Club 36 to 27 on ice.

219

But that wasn't the end of it. In 1875 at New York's Prospect Park, a team managed by Billy Barnie beat a team managed by fellow National Association player George Crawford on ice, 20 to 7. The game went only five innings and used two outs per half inning. Then in Chicago, during the winter of 1881, a series of regular Tuesday games on ice were played, featuring professional and amateur baseball players.

If one wonders why baseball and not hockey players were involved, it was not because hockey had not been invented. The history of hockey is similar to baseball in that it was a sport that evolved from a game on ice played in Europe. It had been played in North America after French explorers saw Iroquois Indians batting a ball around on a pond and yelling "Ho-gee," which translated to "It hurts!" It became "hockey," or at least so says the legend. If for no other reason than the colorful history of the name of the game, "Baseball on Ice" just could not compete with hockey!

Best Advice Bobby Bragan Ever Got

Bobby Bragan was a major league player and later a manager. He played for the Phillies and Dodgers and later managed the Pirates, Indians, and Braves.

As a manager, he was the last for the Milwaukee Braves and the first for the Atlanta Braves when the franchise changed cities. He was later also a baseball executive.

But he may be best remembered for the advice he received from Birdie Tebbetts, whom he replaced as manager in Milwaukee. As Bobby put in in his book, *You Can't Hit the Ball With the Bat on Your Shoulder*, "When I moved into Birdies' old office, there was a note on the manager's desk with two envelopes, number one and two. The note instructed me to open the envelopes only in the case of a crisis. I promptly put them both in a desk drawer. Later on in the season, when we were in the throes of a losing streak,

I opened envelope number one. The note inside said, 'Blame everything on me.' So I called a press conference and informed the media covering the Braves that Birdie Tebbetts had left me a team primarily of players on the decline. I said I couldn't do anything about that. That got me by for a while.

"Later, when we weren't playing that well and word got out the team would be moved and the fans started to boo, I felt it was time to open envelope number two. The message inside that one said, 'Prepare two more envelopes.'"

Weird Injuries

Injuries are part of sports. They are never planned but sometimes just happen. Baseball history has recorded some of the weirdest reasons for players to be sidelined, even with many of them off the field. The following pages include incidents from the early days to the present. It is a list that will keep growing as more and more strange things happen.

Sneezes Have Been Dangerous

Big sneezes has been known to sideline major league players. In 1985, Goose Gossage missed some time because of it; so did Mark Valdez in 1995. Former Angel pitcher Don Aase actually separated cartilage in his rib cage after sneezing. Russ Springer hurt himself with a big "Ah-Choo!" While with the Cubs, Sammy Sosa sneezed too hard once. Mat Latos tried to stifle a sneeze, which turned out to be a mistake: He missed time with the 2010 Padres afterwards. Juan Gonzalez was sidelined with back spasms that he attributed either to a violent sneeze of an overly soft mattress. He wasn't sure which.

Furniture can be a Culprit

Whether it was Gonzalez's sneeze or his bed that sidelined him may still be an open question, but chairs have certainly been a dangerous piece of furniture for some players. When Fred Fitzsimmons fell asleep in a rocking chair and crunched his fingers under the chair, he could not pitch for a month.

More victims of run-ins with furniture include pitcher Mike Remlinger of the Cubs, who went on the disabled list with a fractured finger when he turned in a club house recliner and caught his finger between chairs.

Pitcher Dave Veres sidelined himself with a swollen tendon on his right little finger after he punched the bed headboard in his hotel room, trying to get the occupants in the next room to quiet down.

Florida reliever Ricky Bones strained his neck in 2001 while getting up from a recliner in the club house to change TV channels.

Pittsburgh Pitcher Oliver Perez broke a toe after kicking a laundry cart in 2005. Former Atlanta pitcher Jamie Easterly pulled a groin while watching television. George Brett broke his toe when he collided with furniture in a race back from his kitchen to watch Bill Buckner hit in a televised game.

In April 2005, Minnesota shortstop Jason Bartlett was hurt during a game that was snowed out. He was in his hotel room trying to get a better picture on his television set when he caught his finger and ripped off a nail.

Russell Branyan of the Mariners missed nearly a week of play after a hotel room table fell on his left big toe. Catcher Jonathan Lucroy of the Brewers broke his hand after a large trunk fell from a hotel room bed onto his hand while he was searching for a sock. He missed six weeks of play in 2012. Dennis Martinez hurt his arm after heaving luggage aboard a team bus.

Astro infielder Geoff Blum had to go on the disabled list after injuring his elbow while putting on his shirt after a game. Floating bone chips that he had been carrying around finally locked. Pitcher

Rich Harden once strained his shoulder trying to turn off an alarm clock. Tom Glavine broke a rib while vomiting up an in-flight meal in 1992. Kevin Mitchell of the Giants strained his back doing the same act. Mark Smith broke his hand after sticking it inside an air conditioner to see why it didn't work.

Keep Those Utensils and Knives Away

Furniture isn't the only household item that has posed a danger to players. Pitcher Matt Wise of the Brewers cut the middle finger of his pitching hand with salad tongs and could not throw his best pitch, a change-up. Pitcher Ian Snell burned a finger and missed a start while trying to cook a chicken breast to add to a salad. Joe Niekro missed a start after burning his fingers while trying to cook.

Catcher Mike Matheny missed the postseason with the Cardinals when he severed two tendons and a nerve with a hunting knife. In the 1950s, pitcher Curt Simmons sliced off a toe while mowing his lawn.

Slugger Jimmy Foxx lost his power late in 1932 when he was challenging Babe Ruth's sixty-home-run record. While on a step-ladder trying to change a light bulb, Foxx lost his balance, fell, and sprained his wrist. He didn't miss a game, but he lost his ability to pull the ball and finished the season two homers short of the Babe.

Pitcher Adam Eaton stabbed himself in the stomach with a knife while trying to remove the shrink wrap on a DVD.

Jason Isringhausen also stabbed himself opening a package and then hurt himself punching a trash can. Bret Barberie temporarily lost his vision after rubbing chili sauce in his eyes. Then trying to stem the pain, he ripped the contact lens on his eye.

Florida pitcher A.J. Burnett burned his pitching hand while ironing a pair of jeans. John Smoltz burned his chest when he tried to iron a shirt while he was wearing it.

And the List Grows and Grows

Wade Boggs missed a week of play when he lost his balance putting on cowboy boots and fell into a chair. Pitcher Greg Harris could not work with an injured elbow sustained from flicking sunflower seeds. Lefty Gomez smashed his ankle while trying to knock dirt off his spikes and had to be carried off the field. Jose Cardenal missed opening day in 1974 because he slept on his eye wrong. Giants' outfielder Chris Brown missed five games with the same complaint.

Pitcher Brad Bergeson of Baltimore missed part of spring training in 2010 after he injured his pitching arm while throwing hard in December during the videotaping of a promotion for season ticket sales. Vince Coleman of the Cardinals was run over by an automatic tarp and missed most of the 1985 postseason.

Dizzy Dean once missed a scheduled start versus Pittsburgh in 1937 because he was sick from downing too many very cold drinks. The type of drinks was not mentioned, only their temperature. A few years earlier, another Cardinal pitcher, Flint Rhem, missed action when he claimed he had been kidnapped by gamblers who forced him to drink whiskey for two days. He later admitted no one kidnapped him or forced the alcohol on him.

Jim Palmer missed a start due to a stiff neck because he forgot to bring his favorite pillow with him on a road trip. Denny McLain claimed he once went to bed in perfect health but woke up with four dislocated toes.

David Wells once broke his pitching hand in a street fight outside a bar after his mother's wake. Someone made a disparaging comment about her days riding with Hell's Angels.

Tampa Bay pitcher David Price had to leave a spring training start when he hurt his neck while toweling off between innings. In 1992, Rob Deer broke his wrist while striking out. In 2005, Junior Spivey of the Nationals broke his wrist while working on a batting tee. Also in 2005, Kelly Wunsch of the Dodgers broke his ankle while warming up in the bullpen. Richie Sexson strained his neck on team photo day when he tried stretching a cap on his head that was a full size smaller.

In the minor leagues, Clarence "Climax" Blethen once slid into second base and bit himself on his rear end. He had been carrying his false teeth in his back pocket.

Around the House and Kids

A player's home and family can be hazardous to his health as well. Jeremy Affeldt once cut his hand trying to pry apart some frozen hamburgers with a knife. He later suffered a knee injury hugging his four-year-old son. Ken Griffey, Jr., was injured when he broke his hand while wrestling with his son. Yankee pitcher Joba Chamberlain dislocated an ankle playing with his son on a trampoline. Pitcher Carl Pavano ruptured his spleen after he slipped and fell while shoveling snow in January 2013.

Carlos Baerga suffered a bruised and cut middle finger as he reached into his car to hand money to a cousin while pumping gas. A gust of wind had slammed the door on his hand. Kansas City outfielder Mark Quinn cracked a rib while kung-fu fighting with his brother before spring training.

J.D. Drew missed games after suffering a neck strain from swimming in a friend's pond. Nolan Ryan missed a start after being bitten by a coyote and needing a rabies shot.

Flukes

Kyle Denney was hit by a bullet from a wild gunshot that was fired into the team bus. He was hit in the right calf, but thanks to the cheerleader boots he was wearing, the bullet had been slowed. Denny was in full female cheerleader garb as part of the yearly rookie hazing.

Jerrod Washburn hurt his shoulder during pitcher's fielding practice when he stumbled and fell, trying to avoid a collision with Brendon Donnelly. Pitcher Mike Lincoln hurt his shoulder while jogging in the outfield and falling after slipping on a golf ball on the outfield warning track. Larry Yount, Robin's older brother, was called in to make his major league debut pitching for the Houston Astros in 1971. But he hurt his arm while taking his final warm up pitches on the mound and never saw action in a major league game.

Milwaukee Brewer pitcher Steve Sparks suffered a dislocated shoulder when he tried to rip a phone book in half after seeing a motivational speaker hired by the team accomplish the feat. San Diego pitcher Akinora Otsuka was struck in the face by a bat thrown by a fan who wanted him to autograph it. Otsuka said he had missed the bat when distracted by a piece of paper thrown at him by another fan.

Henry Cotto was hurt when a teammate bumped into him while he had a Q-tip in his ear. Oddibe McDowell had to start a season late when he cut his finger buttering a roll at the Texas Ranger's Welcome Home banquet. Ranger teammate Charlie Hough was sidelined when a friend gripped too hard for a hand shake.

Terry Muholland scratched his eye with a feather protruding from a hotel room pillow. He missed one day. Pitcher Goose Gossage broke his wrist after he tripped and fell over a ball bag in 1993.

Glenallen Hill, who had a deep fear of spiders, dreamt of them one night. He fell out of bed and crashed through a glass table top. He cut himself seriously by crawling through the broken glass. Astro pitcher Tom Griffin was bitten on his pitching elbow by a spider. Despite the elbow being swollen to twice its normal size, Griffin pitched a one-hitter the next day. It was the best start of his career.

Rich "Goose" Gossage and Greg Lucas, 1993

Andy Pafko muffed a ground ball during batting practice, tripped over the ball, and sprained his ankle. George Myatt ran out to his position for opening day in 1946, but tripped on the dugout steps, fell backward, and broke his ankle. Reds infielder Lonny Frey dropped the water cooler lid on his right foot and broke a bone. Darrell Porter tripped and fell in the on- deck circle and broke his ankle.

Mickey Tettleton went on the disabled list in 1987 after he developed a foot infection caused by him tying his shoe laces too tightly.

Jeff Kent missed the opening of a season with the Giants when he said he broke his wrist while washing his truck. Others suspected he fell while doing "wheelies" on his motorcycle. Similar suspicions arose when Moises Alou missed virtually all of the 1999 season for the Astros after he said he injured his knee falling off a treadmill.

Rockie Infielder Clint Barmes said he fell down the stairs while carrying packages of deer meat and broke his collarbone. He had been riding all-terrain vehicles earlier in the day. There were doubters.

Chicago Cub pitcher Carlos Zambrano had elbow pain traced to excessive time on a computer e-mailing friends and relatives in Venezuela. Joel Zumaya of the Tigers missed three games of the 2006 ALCS with wrist and forearm inflammation traced to his playing too much "Guitar Hero."

Even Winning Can Hurt

In 2012, Bryce Harper of the Nationals broke teammate Mark DeRosa's finger while high-fiving. Also in 2012, teammate Aubrey Huff was so excited to join the on-field celebration after Matt Cain of the Giants threw a perfect game against the Astros that he sprained his knee trying to jump the dugout barrier. He went to the disabled list.

On opening day in 2005, Rockie Dustan Moore tried to hop a dugout barrier to help celebrate Clint Barmes' game-winning home run. Moore didn't quite make it. He suffered a strained left calf and missed eighteen games. Terry Harper was trying to waive a runner home from the on-deck circle and dislocated his shoulder. Kendry Morales hit a game-winning home run in 2010. But when he took a big jump on home plate amidst his teammates, he landed wrong and broke his leg. His season was over.

Chris Coghlan tore the meniscus in his left knee while "pieing" Wes Helms after a game-winning triple. Coghlan jumped to place the pie and landed wrong. Larry Andersen strained a rib muscle while jumping off the bench to join an on-field brawl.

And Finally, Two Very Dumb Situations

Rickey Henderson developed a very bad case of frost bite—in August— because he left an ice bag on too long. He missed three games. And pitcher Rick Honeycut had just been ejected from the game for defacing the baseball when he wiped his forehead and opened a large and profusely bleeding cut. He still had the tack he was using to deface the ball taped to his finger.

Chapter XVI

LIES AND SCANDALS

I'd trip my mother. I'll help her up, brush her off and tell her I'm sorry...but mother, don't make it to third!

Leo Durocher
Hall of Famer

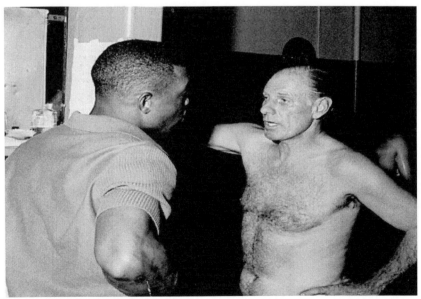

Willie Mays and Leo Durocher, 1954

Leo Durocher himself was involved in a baseball scandal. He was banned from the game for the entire 1947 season. Instead of leading the Dodgers during Jackie Robinson's rookie year, he was spending the summer in California. Leo was suspended due to repeated connections with known gamblers and suspected undesirables. One of his "buddies" was actor George Raft, who reportedly had mob friends and connections.

Leo was also accused of gambling in the clubhouse and on trains, including being involved in high stakes poker games, which he denied. Durocher denied to his final days that the suspension was justified. His case was hardly the first and certainly not the last of baseball's darker days.

Clean Up the Game

One of the tenets of the new National League when it started play in 1876 was a commitment to a cleaner game than that played under the auspices of the National Association. Gambling had been a major feature of baseball, often going on right in the ball parks. Accusations of games thrown by players who were in cahoots with some of these gamblers were rife. Many ballparks sold hard liquor and even featured regular areas for the gamblers to hang out. Drunkenness and overall rowdiness was hardly uncommon: Fights occurred regularly in the stands at ballparks. Attending a ball game was certainly not a family affair. The National League pledged to change that. It vowed to provide a better atmosphere for fans.

Yet there was still scandal in the league's second year of play. Both George Hall and Jim Devlin were ultimately banned from the National League for being involved in shady dealings with gamblers. The scandal also ultimately cost Louisville its franchise.

Banned for Gambling

Gambling and baseball has been linked far more than Pete Rose betting on his team or the Black Sox scandal during the 1919 World Series. Notables as revered as John McGraw, Tris Speaker, and even Ty Cobb were connected with shady deals but never penalized. Longtime first baseman Hal Chase was almost a joke in his willingness to deal with gamblers. He was finally banned in 1921, after having several previous run-ins. Others that were banned included Joe Devlin, George Hall, Heinie Zimmerman, Joe Gedeon, Eugene Paulette, Lee Magee, Jimmy O'Connell, Richard Higham, William B. Cox, and the eight members of the 1919 AL Champion White Sox, including Lefty Williams, Chick Gandil, Fred McMullin, Swede Risberg, Happy Felsch, Buck Weaver, Eddie Cicotte, and Joe Jackson.

A ninth Sox player, pitcher Dickie Kerr, who won two games and was not implicated in the throwing of the series—was banned in 1921 for playing exhibition games with his former teammates. The ban was rescinded in 1925.

Two names on the list of note include William B. Cox, a club owner. He had the Phillies but was banned in 1943 after betting on his team. Another name to remember was Richard Higham, a crooked umpire who was banned in 1882. He was charged with conspiring to help throw a Detroit game after the owner of the club had hired a private investigator and found out he was an associate of a known gambler.

Most Despicable Man in Baseball History

If the name Dick Higham doesn't come to mind, that is to be expected. He was an English-born baseball player from before the turn of the nineteenth century. He played in the National Association and National League, spending much of his time as a mask-less catcher. He even served as manager of the New York Mutuals for a time. During an eight-year career, he hit .307. At times he filled in as an umpire, a custom of the day, whenever the regularly scheduled umpire was not available.

In 1881, he became a full-time National League umpire. He has also been remembered as the first umpire to wear a protective mask.

In those days, umpires were assigned to teams. They would work that team's games until later, perhaps being assigned elsewhere for a time. The fact that Higham moved into this work was somewhat surprising, since some felt he may have been involved in fixing games while still a player. He was never formally charged or accused; however, while on an umpiring assignment with Detroit, several calls against the Wolverines resulted in the team owner hiring a private detective to investigate Higham. The detective turned up several letters between Higham and a well-known local gambler. The gambler and the ump had apparently devised a code, letting the gambler know which way to bet.

Dick Higham

As a result, Higham was fired and banned from baseball. He is the only umpire ever to face that sanction. It occurred more than 130 years ago.

Others Have been Fired For Ineptitude, Not Dishonesty

One of the best examples of losing control and, ultimately, a job involved Vic Delmore on June 30, 1959. He put two balls in play at the same time. To be fair to Vic, it was a confusing situation, but he was not on top of things.

Stan Musial of the Cardinals drew a walk in the game played at Wrigley Field in Chicago, but Cub catcher Sammy Taylor was enraged. He was convinced that the final pitch had ticked Stan's bat and was not a passed ball or wild pitch. Taylor didn't go back to the screen to retrieve it. Delmore was so preoccupied with responding to Taylor that he never declared the ball in play. Musial knew, so he didn't stop after he raced down to first and went on into second. Cub third baseman Alvin Dark knew what was going on, so he ran in to get the ball. But before he got there, a batboy had picked it up and tossed it to field level public address announcer Pat Pieper.

With Dark charging in, Pieper dropped the ball. Dark grabbed it and fired to second to try and get Musial. Unfortunately, Delmore didn't know any of this was going on and had given a new ball to Taylor. He had forgotten he had called ball four and a new ball was not needed. Then, pitcher Bob Anderson ran in from the mound, grabbed the ball from Taylor, and turned to throw— to second. Suddenly, two balls were headed in that direction. Musial only saw the Anderson throw, which was heading into center field. He headed to third. However, shortstop Ernie Banks had the other ball and tagged Musial. Banks had the correct ball, but it should have been dead since it was touched by both the batboy and announcer. St. Louis protested the game but won anyway.

That, however, was not the end of the story. In large part because he totally lost control, Vic Delmore was not rehired for 1960.

Twenty-Two Umps Quit and Resignations Accepted

In 1999, during a labor dispute between Major League Baseball and the Umpire's union, twenty-two umpires resigned in hopes of putting pressure on MLB. The ploy did not work, and when they all tried to rescind their resignations, MLB would not let them. Some were ultimately hired back but not until they won court cases. Others never umpired in the major leagues again.

Supervisors Got the Boot in 2010

Following the 2009 baseball postseason, three umpire supervisors were fired by Major League Baseball as a result of a number of blown calls. Retired umpires Marty Springstead, Rich Garcia, and Jim McKean were thanked for their service but put out of their jobs. None of the actual umpires who erred that postseason were let go. Of course, the supervisors no longer were members of the World Umpire's Association. The erring umps were.

Al Clark Terminated for Airline Ticket Scam

In 2001, veteran umpire Al Clark was fired for allegedly exchanging the first class airline tickets umpires are granted to travel between cities for economy seats and pocketing the price difference. Clark had been accused a few years before of profiting from the sale of autographed baseballs. Nothing came of that, but his ticket trick did him in.

Umpire Rejected Pay Offer for Post Season

They didn't have unions for umpires in 1889, but Tom Lynch staged a one- man holdout and lost his job for it. Lynch had been selected to umpire the postseason series between the National League and American Association. He was an N.L. ump and wanted $800 for handling the job. The owners balked and replaced him with Bob Ferguson.

Now persona non grata, Lynch's umpiring days were limited, so he returned to being a player. He spent the 1890 season in the minors but would play no more after that.

The reason he would play no more was because he had been shot and nearly killed on October 27 of that year. A millworker named Richard Doyle and Lynch had gotten into an argument that had escalated. Doyle pulled a gun and shot Lynch in the chest near his heart.

Miraculously, not only did Lynch survive, but after working as a spokesman for National League umpires for a while, he was named N.L. president after Harry Pulliam committed suicide. Lynch held the job from 1910 to 1913, which was pretty good for a man who had been essentially black-balled after holding out for more money to umpire in 1889.

The former umpire who had lost his job for holding out and then had been shot through the chest lived to be ninety-four years old before he died in 1955.

Ray Chapman's Death

On August 16, 1920, Cleveland Indian shortstop Ray Chapman was at the plate. Carl Mays, a submarining spitball pitcher for the Yankees, threw a high and tight fast ball that Chapman apparently never saw. The ball bore into Chapman, cracking him solidly on the head. He died twelve hours later. The result of the tragedy changed baseball. Major League Baseball introduced a rule requiring umpires to replace the ball when it became dirty and harder to see. In addition, pitches like spitballs, greaseballs, and those that required defacing the ball were banned after 1920—with a caveat.

Pitchers who used spitters as a primary pitch would be allowed to continue through the end of their careers.

Mays was a spitballer who won over 100 more games after the Chapman incident. The last legal spitballer was Burleigh Grimes, whose career ended after the 1934 season. This did not end the use of substances or other actions upon the baseball, but by making it illegal, the rule cut down the use substantially.

Once the baseball would be replaced more frequently and some pitches were outlawed, the game changed forever. The home run became the number one offensive weapon. Babe Ruth was the pied piper, and many others soon started to follow.

Cocaine and Marijuana Caused Problems in the 1970s

After the use of amphetamines became a hidden part of baseball but before the steroid and PED scandals of the 1980s and 1990s, there was cocaine and marijuana. Both were so-called recreational drugs with certain segments of the population regularly using the illegal stimulants. That did not exclude some major league baseball players.

In 1985, a hearing was conducted in Pittsburgh to determine the depth of the problem. The result was that several players and former players were indicted to appear before a grand jury. Several of those players were suspended by Baseball Commissioner Peter Ueberroth for one year. That number included Keith Hernandez, Dale Berra, Joaquin Andujar, Enos Cabel, Dave Parker, Jeff Leonard, and Lonnie Smith. Others were suspended for shorter periods.

Ferguson Jenkins Ran Afoul of the Law Earlier

The use of cocaine didn't start in 1985. In 1980, pitcher Ferguson Jenkins was arrested for possession of illegal drugs. Canadian customs officials found an estimated five hundred dollars' worth of marijuana, hashish, and cocaine in his luggage. Jenkins was suspended by then- Baseball Commissioner Bowie Kuhn, but the punishment was overturned by arbitrator Raymond Goetz. Later, a Canadian court convicted Jenkins, but the judge erased the conviction citing Jenkins, a Canadian citizen, for years of "exemplary conduct."

Chapter XVII

AMERICA'S PASTIME IS WORLDWIDE

Baseball is democracy in action; in it all men are 'free and equal,' regardless of race, nationality, or creed. Every man is given the rightful opportunity to rise to the top on his own merits.

Francis Trevelyan Miller
Introduction to Connie Mack's *My 66 Years in Baseball*

Shigeo Nagashima

While the game of baseball has held the top spot in the hearts of American sports fans for decades, its growth around the world is something those who still regard the game as number one should take pride. It is certainly not just an American game.

As far back as 1969, when I was in the U.S. Army and had a chance to fill in what we called "dream sheets" that offered a preference for overseas assignments, I wrote in Japan. I did it because I knew they played baseball in Japan. While my assignment was ultimately in Korea, that worked out even better. They played baseball there, too, and I met my future wife. Thanks, baseball!

First Players from Other Lands or Races

The first Cuban in the major leagues was Esteban Bellan. He actually grew up in New York and played for the New York Mutuals of the National Association between 1871 and 1873. He later went back to Cuba and both established and ran the Professional Baseball League of Cuba, which existed until after the revolution in 1961.

From Cuba, baseball spread throughout the Caribbean, thanks in large part to Bellan. The first Mexican to play in the majors was Mel Almada with the Red Sox in 1933. Alex Carrasquel was the first Venezuelan-born player with the Senators in 1939.

Hi Bithorn was the first major leaguer from Puerto Rico. His debut was in 1942 with the Cubs. The first player from the Dominican Republic was Ozzie Virgil, Sr., with the Giants in 1956. The first Nicaraguan was Dennis Martinez with the Orioles in 1976. Humberto Robinson in 1955 with the Braves was the first Panamanian.

After Masanori Murakami from Japan opened the major leagues to Asian players in 1964, representatives from South Korea, Chan Ho Park in 1994 and Taiwan, Chin-Fen Chen in 2002 have continued to make baseball more of a worldwide game than ever before. The first Asian player to make a major impression was Japanese pitcher Hideo Nomo, who joined the Dodgers in 1995 and won thirteen games.

More than fifty nations have been represented in major league baseball by players born on their soil.

Baseball made its debut into the Far East when introduced into Japan in 1872. A school professor named Horace Wilson is given credit. In 1966, the first Japanese player made his debut in the major leagues. Pitcher Masanori Murakami played for the San Francisco Giants for a season in the mid1960s. He played the final month of 1964 and all of 1965, and then he returned to Japan. In the United States, he was 5 and 1 with a 3.43 earned run average in forty-five games, one of them a start. During an eighteen- year Japanese career, he won 103 games.

Best American Players in Japan

Hideo Nomo may have been the first player from Japan to become a star in Major League Baseball, but what about going the other direction? Who was the best from MLB to play in Japan?

There are several candidates, and most of them were hitters. Tuffy Rhodes, Warren Cromartie, Wladimir Balentien, Leron and Leon Lee, Randy Bass, Joe Stanka, and longtime MLB manager Charlie Manuel would all be in the conversation.

Leron Lee and Tuffy Rhodes were around the longest. Lee holds the Japanese Professional Baseball mark for highest career average at .334. Rhodes, along with Sadaharu Oh and Alex Cabrera, were tied for the top single season home run record with fifty-five.

In 2013, Balentien broke it when he hit sixty home runs. The Japanese teams did not avoid pitching to the Curracao native, and vet of major league play with Seattle and Cincinnati. This was a major switch in strategy used against earlier challengers to Oh's record.

Bass hit fifty-four one season and was prevented from getting a shot to tie or break the mark in the season's final game in 1985. The Tokyo Giants, managed by Oh, walked him on every at-bat. Bass also hit .386 in 1986.

Cromartie won a Central League MVP in 1989 when he hit .378 for the Giants. Stanka, a pitcher, won a league MVP and Japan Series MVP in 1964 after he won twenty-seven games in the season and pitched three shutout wins in the Series. He won 100 games in seven seasons.

Japan Has Many Stars Who Never Played in MLB
All baseball fans recognize the name of Sadaharo Oh. The longtime Tokyo Giants star still holds the world record for most career home runs with 868. While his single season mark in Japan fell to Wladimir Balentien in 2013, his career total is amazing, especially when one notes the Japanese season is only 130 games long and his home runs per plate appearance was better than Barry Bonds.

Shigeo Nagashima Was "Mr. Baseball" in Japan
As good as Oh was during his career, he came from Chinese stock and was never as popular in Japan as native-born third baseman Shiegeo Nagashima. Both Oh and Nagashima were teammates on the Giants and both also later managed the team. While Nagashima's wife had attended high school in the United States and had friends there, he was much against Japanese stars abandoning their country to play Major League Baseball. It weakened the game in Japan. Nagashima had several chances to play Major League Baseball himself but always declined. Players from MLB who played in Japan during that period all felt Nagashima could have been an MLB star. For his seventeen-year career in Japan, he hit .305 with 444 home runs.

Sachio Kinugasa Had Longer Streak than Gehrig
On September 6, 1995, Cal Ripkin, Jr., of the Baltimore Orioles played in his 2,131st consecutive game. That broke the MLB record set by Lou Gehrig in 1939. But Ripken didn't have the world record until he surpassed the 2,215 consecutive games played by Japan's Sachio Kinugasa.

Kinugasa played for twenty-three seasons with Hiroshima of the Central League. He hit 504 home runs while primarily playing a corner infield spot on defense. Kinugasa was born to a Japanese woman from an Afro American father in 1947. He never knew his father, who had been a U.S. serviceman stationed in Japan after World War II.

Other Players of Note

Pitcher Masaichi Kaneda fanned 4,409 hitters during his career. Only MLB's Nolan Ryan had more. Victor Sarafin, a Russian-born, Japanese resident, won 300 games.

Before World War II, pitcher Eiji Sawamura had impressed major league hitters who had taken part in good will tours of Japan. In 1934, the eighteen-year-old held the U.S. stars scoreless until giving up a solo home run to Lou Gehrig. That would be the only run of the game. In 1935, during a tour of the U.S. by a Japanese team headed by Sawamura, the Pittsburgh Pirates tried to sign him. He was intrigued but declined the offer.

In a magazine article translated into English, he said, "My problem is I hate America and I cannot make myself like Americans. I'm not good at the language. I cannot eat rice as much as I wish when I am there, and the women are too haughty."

Robert Whiting's book, *You Gotta Have Wa*, features the translation from a Japanese magazine after Sawamura's return from the tour. "In America, you can even tie your shoe strings if there are women around. People like myself cannot possibly survive in an environment where such uncomfortable customs exist."

After the rejection of America and the major leagues, Sawamura won thirty-three games back in Japan in 1937.

The greatness of Sawamura ended with World War II. He was lost at sea after a ship upon which he was serving was torpedoed and sunk. In all, nearly seventy-five Japanese professional baseball players were killed in the war.

Chapter XVIII

PERFORMANCE- ENHANCING DRUGS ARE NOTHING NEW

Steroids don't help you hit a baseball.

Jason Giambi
Veteran Major League player

Pud Galvin

CHAPTER 18: PERFORMANCE-ENHANCING DRUGS ARE NOTHING NEW

Since man has played sports, he has always looked for something to give him an edge over his opponent. For years, amphetamines were routinely given to players who needed a boost after a long road trip or long night on the town. While those "greenies" didn't make anyone bigger, stronger, or faster, they did help to keep players alert. They were definitely an aid.

Most sports followers had no idea players were using pep pills until players like Jim Brosnan and Jim Bouton wrote books. *The Long Season* and *Pennant Chase* by Brosnan and *Ball Four* by Bouton opened some eyes. Both books also tore away other secrets from inside the clubhouse and the players' fraternity. They may have also opened the door for reporters to start feeling that things on the inside should no longer be "off limits" to the pages of newspapers.

The result was that the players built higher walls between themselves and the media. Their union bargained for limits on media access to the clubhouse before and after games. While newspapers themselves started taking reporters off team flights to reduce the appearance of loss of objectivity or being indebted to the teams, the media and players were far more "us" versus "them" than ever before. Things went on that the media had no evidence to report, including the beginnings of steroid use by players.

Often, the public thinks the media should know everything that is going on and if they don't report it, they are intentionally hiding something. It is not that simple. First of all, had media members suspected players were using performance enhancing drugs—and many did suspect just that—they would have had to be 100 percent certain before they ever made any accusations. They would have had to have solid proof. No one did at that time, and no investigative reporting was done.

Players took steroids in secret, even from their teammates. Managers never saw them. Owners and general managers were never on hand. Team trainers were not part of the secret society. All might have suspected—just as some of the media—but no one knew for sure.

Trying to actually make one bigger and stronger really didn't become a part of baseball until the 1970s. Before that, being loose-limbed was of primary importance, and any training other than to keep one's wind and weight in check would be counter-productive. Then the weight room was discovered.

Nolan Ryan and the Weight Room Started Something

In recent years, baseball has had a lot of controversy over players using what have been called performance-enhancing drugs, or PEDs. In the 1990s, according to multiple sources, a large number of players tried various forms of steroids or growth hormones. The use of such products may have been a natural byproduct of more and more players using gyms and weight rooms to gain strength.

Nolan Ryan was one of the first to venture into a weight room. While his career was over before the PED boom, he admitted in his autobiography that his career would likely have been over well earlier had he not started to lift weights. Few players did more than run, throw, and hit to prepare for baseball, but Ryan led a change.

Ryan had discovered a Universal Gym at Anaheim Stadium when he was a member of the Angels in the early 1970s. The gym wasn't there for baseball; it has been installed for the World Football League Southern California Sun. Ryan said he had noticed that so many veteran pitchers tried to keep their arms in shape but not their bodies. It stood to reason that keeping the whole body strong and in shape could prolong a career and make it even better.

Ryan developed his own methods at first and, later, worked with experienced physical conditioner Dr. Gene Coleman. For Nolan, the extra work paid off in a Hall of Fame career that lasted until he was forty-five years old. His efforts also broke the long-held opinion that baseball players should not use weight training in fear of tightening up muscles. Ryan proved that not to be the case, and others followed.

Then it went too far with many players as they were exposed to body builders in gyms that used supplements stronger than vitamins and minerals. It would not be long before some players were using supplements, which were illegal unless prescribed by a physician for a specific need. A lot of players were suddenly much bigger and stronger than would have been allowed by nature and simple, hard workouts. The "Steroid Era" was born.

Breaking the law by using PEDs without prescription was one thing— the drugs would never have been legal for the reasons they were being used. But it was quite another thing on the field itself, when some of baseball's most treasured records fell and fell again, quite likely due to the use of PEDs by many of the players setting those marks. It was an exciting era, but also a dark one.

Eventually, both the player's union and ownership groups came together to clean up the sport, and baseball survived. Baseball has put in rules to keep future players from cheating. The only real controversy now it what to do with the former players that may have inflated their natural abilities into Hall of Fame quality because of the use of PEDs. Will they eventually be forgiven and be selected to the Hall of Fame? That question is still not possible to answer.

Using Performance Enhancers Actually Was Nothing New

While all recent concerns have been with steroids, growth hormones, and other products, the fact is that baseball has been touched by "enhancers" for years. Hall of Fame pitcher Pud Galvin may have been the first.

Before the turn of the nineteenth century, Pud was one of the top pitchers around. But by the late 1880s, the "Little Steam Engine," as he was known, was starting to slow down. He wanted to reverse his decline, so he tried ingesting a concoction that included dried animal testosterone distilled from the testicles of guinea pigs and dogs. Some sources claim the product came from monkey testicles. This wasn't just some wild experiment at the time—there was medical literature that claimed using such a substance would retard or repair damage caused by aging and restore strength. Sound familiar? This was in 1889.

There is no report that Galvin made the so-called Brown-Sequard elixir a regular part of his diet after one widely publicized use. He did win the game he pitched after its use, tossing a two hit shutout, but Galvin won a lot of games. He was baseball's first 300-game winner and finished with 365 victories. But 1889 would turn out to be the last of his ten twenty-win seasons. He was out of baseball by age thirty-five and dead ten years later.

Whether what Pud tried had any effect on anything seems doubtful. But he was the first to try. One hundred years later, the development of PEDs that did help were well documented. What might come next? As longtime pitcher Joaquin Andujar once said, "You can sum it up in one word—you never know!"

Chapter XIX

BASEBALL'S DEFINITIONS AND ITS GREATEST NICKNAMES

I don't mind getting beaten, but I hate to lose.

Reggie Jackson
Hall of Famer

Reggie Jackson

The Language of Baseball Came from
When it was Born

Author Paul Dickson compiled a very good book many years ago, *The Baseball Dictionary*, that he has updated frequently. He traces the history of some of the words and phrases used in baseball and the reasons they are used. Some of them can be figured out just in reading. For instance, earlier we talked of the actual pitcher's box within which hurlers had to stay when making pitches. Hence, "knocked him out of the box" in reference to a pitcher who gave up so many hits that he had to be relieved has a real significance historically.

The word "bunt" originated from the railroad term used to move cars into place. Nautical terms like "on deck" or "in the hold" are in baseball, although the latter has been changed to "in the hole" in modern language. Other terms like "a high can of corn" to describe a high pop fly comes from the old grocery stores that might have cans of corn stored on high shelves.

Two types of hits still commonly used, the "Baltimore chop" and "Texas Leaguer," have stories behind them. The Baltimore chop—to describe balls hit hard on the ground near home plate that take high hops— was actually a part of the old Baltimore Oriole offensive repertoire before the turn of the nineteenth century.

The "Texas Leaguer" is still used to describe a short, low pop-fly that eludes both infielders and outfielders and falls safely. That term reportedly was named after the production of an outfielder named Art Sunday. He had just joined the Toledo team of the major league American Association in the 1880s. His offensive output was impressive early on but featured a number of low pop-ups that fell untouched. Since Sunday had just been called to Toledo from the Texas League, the description of his hits came about and has stuck for over 125 years.

Nicknames in History

One of the distinctions baseball has over most other sports is the historical affinity for nicknames. Because of the age of the sport, which was played in a much less "politically correct" era, the nicknames that set players apart were hardly always complimentary.

"Losing Pitcher" Mulcahy

For instance, do you think "Bald Billie" Barnie, "Blimp" Phelps, or "Losing Pitcher" Mulcahy were always fond of hearing themselves called by those names? What about "Piano Legs" Hickman or "Four Sack" Dusak?

"Piano Legs" Charlie Hickman got his nickname not for his physical appearance but rather the fact that he was a poor fielder at third base. In 1900, he committed eighty-six errors, with the ball often going right through his legs. He likely much preferred his alternate nickname, "Cheerful Charlie," as he was considered one of the more popular players of his day.

"Four Sack" Dusak actually got the nickname after a home run he hit in a minor league game inspired a fan to write a poem about him. It was not disparaging at all, but a compliment.

"Imp" Begley wasn't very big, nor was his major league career. He was 5'6, 145 pounds, and he played in only one big league game on May 28, 1924. Most of his career was in the Pacific Coast League.

"Boob" McNair doesn't sound very smart, but that is not why his nickname arose. He was named after a cartoon character, Boob McNutt, in a Rube Goldberg strip. While the cartoon character was sort of a klutz, McNair was not. He simply had a last name,

249

McNair, which was close enough to McNutt for teammates to attach the connection.

Other nicknames may have been accurate. "Stinky" Davis may have been stinky. "Tomato Face" Cullop suggests a certain coloring. "Harry the Horse" Anderson's nickname could have referenced the shape of his face or something else. "No Neck" Williams was so called because he barely had one. Maybe "Ding a Ling" Clay really was.

"Camera Eye" Bishop really knew the strike zone. He was famed for drawing many walks to get on base ahead of Philadelphia A's sluggers, and seven times he walked over 100 times in a season. He walked eight times in one doubleheader. That is why he was "Camera Eye." "Swish" Nicholson had a big swing. "The Rope" Bob Boyd hit lots of line drives. "Grunting" Jim Shaw gave everything he had.

You think Benny "Earache" Meyer might not have been someone you wanted to sit next to on the bench? And "Bullfrog" Bill Dietrich had that kind of voice.

"Boom Boom" Beck gave up a lot of hits off walls. He also hurled a ball that boomed off the same wall in a game, and his nickname was forged.

Leo "The Lip" Durocher had opinions on everything. "Bow Wow" Arft's name just fit his last. So did "Pickles" Dilhoeffer. "Twinkletoes" Selkirk was a nimble-footed defender. "Stubblebeard" Grimes was rarely clean-shaven.

"Abba Dabba" Jim Tobin is remembered in record books for more than his nickname. He was the first pitcher in modern major league baseball to hit three home runs in one game. He did it with the Braves on May 13, 1942. In the ninetenth century, pitcher Guy Hecker had also done it. As for the nickname, "Abba Dabba," its origin is still a mystery.

How about "Sureshot" Fred Dunlap, "Bloody" Jake Evans, "Scissors" Dave Foutz, "Pebbly" Jack Glasscock, "Prunes" George

Moolic, "Razzle Dazzle" Con Murphy, "Bollicky" Bill Taylor, "Peach Pie" Jack O'Connor, "Dandelion" Fred Pfiefer, "Grasshopper" Jim Whitney, "Voiceless" Tim O'Rourke, "Foghorn" George Miller, "Steam Engine" Pud Galvin, "Monkey" Pete Hotaling, "Smiling" Mickey Welch, "Little Eva" Bill Lange, "What's the Use" Pearce Chiles, and "Dodo" Frank Bird? They had millions of nicknames.

Of course, over baseball history, some nicknames were typecast. If a player had native American background, he became "Chief." If he was of German descent, he was "Heine" or "Dutch." Big fellows almost automatically became "Jumbo." A player with foot speed might be nicknamed "Deerfoot." And a player from the country and who might be lacking in city smarts was often simply "Rube." Baseball has been a game of colorful nicknames and will undoubtedly continue to be.

Chapter XX

THE SECOND SEASON: FIRSTS AND MEMORIES

It's hard to win a pennant, but it's harder losing one.

Chuck Tanner
Hall of Famer

Hoss Radbourn

After the long baseball season comes what is often referred to as "the second season." It is when the champions of leagues or divisions and some other top teams compete for postseason glory. Once called "The Temple Cup" and the Divisional Series, League Champion Series, and now World Series, the competition has provided some of baseball's most enduring memories. With the passage of time, some of those memories have faded. Here in this chapter, many of them are brought back to full lustre.

First Inter-League Postseason Series

From 1884 through 1890, teams from both the NL and AA met in postseason series—the forerunner to the modern World Series. NL clubs won five of the seven. They were the first real postseason matchups in professional baseball history between two separate leagues.

Old Hoss Dominated in 1884

When the precursor to the World Series was first staged in 1884, the NL was easily the strongest league. At least one player was, and that was all that was needed. Hoss Radbourn pitched three complete games, allowing no earned runs in leading the Providence Grays of the NL to a 3 to 0 blanking of the AA's New York Metropolitans. During the regular season, Hoss had started seventy-three games and won fifty-nine of them. In the series, his 3 and 0 record featured seventeen strikeouts and no walks.

Jeremiah Denny: First Postseason Home Run

The first player to launch a postseason home run was Jeremiah Denny in the 1884 series between the Grays and Metropolitans. Denny is still on the MLB record books for something else, too. The barehanded third baseman had a career average of 4.2 defensive chances per game, and that record still stands.

1885 Series Featured Different Rules

When the Chicago White Stockings of the National League met the St. Louis Browns of the American Association in the second postseason matchup between the two leagues, the rules were not the same. During the season, the NL had allowed overhand pitching for the first time as long as the pitcher kept both feet on the ground before release. In the AA, overhand hurling was still not legal.

There were other differences as well. As for the series, it ended up even at three games each with one tie. However, St. Louis had to forfeit game two after Browns manager Charles Comiskey pulled his team off the field in protest of a ruling made by umpire Dave Sullivan.

The 1887 Series Will Never be Matched

Something was tried in 1887 that was not a success and likely will never be attempted again. The postseason series between the two league champs was scheduled as a fifteen-game series to be staged in ten different cities. Because the series booked in advance like a traveling circus, they had to play all the games even if one team had already clinched the championship. Detroit of the NL bested the St. Louis Browns of the AA ten games to five.

When AA Dissolved NL, Top Teams Went for the Cup

In 1892, the National League became a twelve-team loop and played a split season. The next year, in 1893, the Pittsburgh Pirates finished a close second, and club owner William Temple felt a postseason series between the first and second place teams would be a good idea. Starting the next season, those teams would play a series, with the winner taking home a new trophy, The Temple Cup. More important to the players was the winning team would get sixty-five percent of the gate.

254

After the first series in 1894, the players elected to split the money evenly. That wasn't a bad idea because the revenue generated was rather poor. The idea of a pennant winner meeting a second place team did not catch the fancy of many fans. With a twelve-team league splitting into two divisions and having two champions might have helped, but there was not enough support for the idea. After four seasons in which the second place team won the cup three times, the idea was abandoned.

Original Concept Dead, but Not the Cup

In 1900 came the Chronicle-Telegraph Cup. The prize was the same cup originated by William Temple who had sold the Pirates by this time. His old team was in the 1900 series but lost to the Brooklyn Superbas three games to one.

Deacon Phillippe, who would stat in the first World Series between the AL and NL in 1903, tossed a six-hit shutout for the only Pittsburgh win.

No more games for the Cup were ever played. The actual trophy is on display at the Baseball Hall of Fame.

First Meeting of AL and NL in World Series in 1903

The World Series as we know it started in 1903 between the American League and the National League. The AL's Boston Pilgrims beat the Pittsburgh Pirates five games to three. The Pilgrims were led by player- manager Jimmy Collins. The Pirates were guided by player-manager Fred Clarke.

Due to weather problems, the series took nearly two weeks before the teams finished the best of nine series. The Pilgrim's Cy Young threw the first pitch in World Series history but was also the first losing pitcher. He bounced back to win two games and finished 2 to 1 with a 1.85 earned run average. Teammate Bill Dineen won three of three.

The Pirates were playing at a disadvantage. Starter Sam Leever, who had won twenty-five games during the season, tried to pitch with an injured shoulder that he hurt while skeet shooting. He lost both his starts. They had to send Deacon Phillippe to the mound to start five games. He pitched five complete games but couldn't win them all. In addition, shortstop Honus Wagner, a future Hall of Famer, hit just .222 and made six errors. Honus had led the National League in batting during the regular season at .355.

There would be no series the next season as New York Giants' ownership, prodded by manager John McGraw, declined to play the American League champion Boston Pilgrims. But from then on, the series would be played every fall until labor problems in 1994.

First Player to Hit a Home Run in the World Series

Jimmy Sebring of the Pirates homered off Cy Young in the first World Series game ever played in 1903. Sebring had hit four home runs during the regular season, but his career total in five seasons was only six.

The Greatest Series Ever Played?

In 1975, the Boston Red Sox returned to the World Series for the first time since Babe Ruth had been with the team in 1916. Always a baseball hot bed, the success of the Red Sox took over all of New England. They were going to face the underachieving but most-solid team in all of baseball—the Cincinnati Reds.

The Reds won that series four games to three. But the most memorable game was game six, when the Red Sox staved off elimination, thanks to Carton Fisk's extra inning home run that he tried to wave fair as he left the batter's box. The games leading up to the sixth one had captivated the nation like no World Series in years. The Reds did win it the next day but had to overcome a three-run deficit to do it. Baseball was back.

Most Unusual Winner Was Pittsburgh in 1960

The Pittsburgh Pirates beat the New York Yankees four games to
three in the 1960 World Series. Bill Mazeroski's home run in the
bottom of the ninth of the final game was the Series winner. How
the Pirates ever won the Series has mystified fans for years.

In the series, New York outscored Pittsburgh 55 to 27. They
won three games by scores of 16 to 3, 10 to 0, and 12 to 0. The
Yankees had a .338 team batting average with ten home runs.
Pittsburgh hit just .256 with four round trippers. On the mound, the
Yankees' team ERA was 3.54 while the Pirates was 7.11.

How did the Pirates win it? They scored ten of their twenty-
seven runs in the final game and rallied from a 7 to 4 deficit in the
last of the eighth inning. A five-run inning gave the Pirates the lead,
but the Yankees tied the game in the top of the ninth. Then
Mazeroski became Pittsburg's biggest one-game hero of all time.

Sweeps Aren't Always One-Sided

Normally, many postseasons in which one team wins all the games
is not very entertaining. That was not the case in two World
Series sweeps, however. National League teams went down in four
straight in both, but by the narrowest of margins.

In 1950, the "Whiz Kids" Philadelphia Phillies lost to the
powerful New York Yankees in the minimum number of games.
The first three were all one-run New York victories. The finale
went to New York 5 to 2. The scoring margin in four games was
just six runs—just two over the minimum needed, although the
Phillies never had a lead in any game.

White Sox Sweep Over Astros Even Closer

In 2005, the Chicago White Sox took out the Houston Astros in four.
Like the 1950 Series, the winners only outscored the losers by six
runs. But in this one, the Astros had some chances to win.

They lost the opener 5 to 3 and never had a lead. But in game two, Houston led 4 to 2 in the sixth inning before finally falling 7 to 6.

Game three went fourteen innings and was tied from the eighth until the end. The final game went to the White Sox 1 to 0 with no scoring until the eighth inning.

Chapter XXI

THE PAST AND FUTURE OF BASEBALL

A HALL OF FAMER'S PERSPECTIVE: MONFORD MERRILL "MONTE" IRVIN

We don't stop playing because we get old. We get old because we stop playing.

Satchel Paige

Monte Irvin and Greg Lucas, 2014, Houston, Texas

It is fitting to wrap up this mini-tour of the unusual history baseball with some thoughts from someone who has seen it all and been part of much of it: Monte Irvin.

Oh, he can't remember Jim Creighton or Pud Galvin, but he has lived during the development of the modern game of baseball. Monte played Negro league baseball when it was at its peak. He was in the vanguard of the integration of organized baseball. He was one of and played with the greats. He has scouted and worked for the Commissioner of Baseball.

Monte celebrated his ninety-fifth birthday in early 2014. He and I had a conversation in March 2014, less than a month after his birthday. During our conversation, he shared his recollections of the past and thoughts on the future of the sport.

Monte's Baseball Career and Stardom

As one of the first black players in modern major league baseball, Monte was elected to the Baseball Hall of Fame in 1973 after compiling a .293 batting average in an eight-year big league career.

But Monte's baseball career and stardom was even greater and longer as one of the outstanding players in the Negro leagues and winter baseball. He had played ten seasons on that level before getting the call to the major leagues at age thirty in 1949.

Monte won two batting titles in the Negro National League, hitting .395 in 1941 and .404 in 1946. He missed three peak seasons between 1943 and 1945 because he served in the Corp of Engineers in the United States Army in Europe.

Following his major league playing days, Monte continued to work in baseball, except for a period in which he worked with a New York brewery. He got back in the game first as a scout and, later, worked on the staff of the Commissioner of Baseball.

Monte Could Have Preceded Robinson

Before World War II, Negro league owners selected Monte Irvin as the top choice to integrate Major League Baseball, should the opportunity be presented. At the time, Monte knew nothing about it. Newark Eagle owner Effa Manley told Irvin about it a few years later.

He recalled his conversation with Manley. "She said, 'Monte, we had decided that if baseball ever decided to integrate, you were going to be the player we recommended.' I said, 'I'm sorry I disappointed you.'"

It really wasn't Monte's fault that he hadn't had the opportunity. Two obstacles that were out of his control prevented him from being the first black player in the major leagues: military service and money.

He had been surprised to pass an Army physical in early 1943—he'd thought he would likely fail due to frequent water on the knee that resulted from a high school football injury. Monte was in the service from March 9, 1943, until September 1, 1945. However, he still might have become the first Negro in modern major league baseball if money hadn't been another factor.

After Monte had returned from the war in 1945, Brooklyn Dodgers owner Branch Rickey signed Monte to a contract, calling for him to play for St. Paul in 1946. That would be the same season Jackie Robinson would debut for Montreal, the Dodgers' other AAA franchise. Unfortunately, Monte never played for St. Paul because he was released from the contract by Rickey. It had nothing to do with his skills and everything to do with money.

Effa Manley, who had agreed with the other owners years before that Monte Irvin should be the first to integrate baseball, wasn't about to let it happen for nothing. She owned the Newark Eagles with whom Irvin had a contract. She wanted $5,000 from the Dodgers to let Monte play. Rickey would have none of that. He had gotten Robinson for nothing. Jackie had signed a contract with the Dodgers and essentially just resigned from the Kansas City

Monarchs. From the point that Jackie Robinson joined Montreal and the Dodgers the next season, his story is well known as the first black player in the major leagues.

Monte never worried about what might have been. "I didn't dwell on that much," he said. "It would have been wonderful if I could have been the first one chosen, but we fellow Negro league players were happy that Jackie got the chance. We were not jealous but were a little envious."

Robinson was not the top player in Negro league baseball when Rickey selected him. However, he fit the mold: college educated, a former Army officer, good looking, married, and with baseball skills and potential. As Monte pointed out, "Every year in the major leagues, he improved. He became a real star."

Monte returned to Newark to win the batting title in 1946, and then he extended his fame during winter ball in Puerto Rico. In 1949, Monte signed with the New York Giants and was in the major leagues quickly that season.

Monte's Pick for Greatest Hitter Ever

While it is impossible to ever really know because of segregation whether one hitter was the best of all time in all of baseball, Monte Irvin does not hesitate to tell you who he thinks was the best hitter of all time in Negro league baseball.

"There is only one. It was Josh Gibson," he said. "He was a great defensive catcher who loved baseball. As a hitter, he was a natural. When you saw him, you would say to yourself, 'There goes a great athlete.' It got to the point that, as a regular catcher, I thought Roy Campanella might have been a little better defensively, but when Josh and Campy showed up at the same time, there was no question Josh was the best. Campy even said that later on."

Monte still marvels at Gibson's strength. "A right-handed hitter, he was so strong that he could hit an outside pitch as far to right field as a left- hander could. He didn't have to pull the ball. He led ever league he ever played in home runs and batting average. He could run. He could do it all," he said.

Paige and Day Tops on the Mound

Irvin says the most famous Negro league pitcher was probably also the best. "It was Satchel Paige, Leon Day, and some other fellows who were almost as good as they were. There were a number of very good pitchers. There were many other very good everyday players, too, but Gibson was dominant in that area."

Game Was Played Differently in the Old Days

Baseball, particularly in the Negro leagues, was often played with the intent to attract fans. Monte recalled a strategy that made some sense but would never be tried today.

"They did a lot of running and bunting. I know one manager—his strategy was that if he faced a fast ball pitcher for the first five or six innings, he might have the hitter lay the ball down, or bunt, toward the third base line. Then the next hitter would lay it down the first base line, and they'd keep doing that until they got the pitcher tired. Then they started to swing," he said.

"They started to do that with Satchel Paige, and Satchel said, 'The next time you do that, bring a shovel, 'cause you're gonna need to dig your grave if you try to pull that stuff on me.'"

Monte Mentored the Greats

As a youth, Monte grew up marveling at the skills shown by the top players with both the Newark Bears minor league club and the local Negro National League Newark Eagles. Even before Monte got the call to the major leagues in 1949 at age thirty, he became a teacher to young black players who would follow. Two of the most famous were Willie Mays and Roberto Clemente.

Clemente was Just a Pup

Irvin's connection to the future Pittsburgh Pirate star Roberto Clemente was established during Monte's winter ball days in Puerto Rico. In both 1945 and 1946, Irvin was a superstar. Roberto, who was between eleven and twelve years old at the time, idolized him. Monte remembered, "I used to give both he and Orlando Cepeda my suit and equipment bags to carry into the stadium so they could get in for free."

Clemente would watch the game from the bleachers, studying everything about Monte. He especially admired Monte's strong throwing arm from the outfield. "He used to ask me about throwing," remembered Irvin. "I told him, you have to practice. I taught Roberto Clemente how to throw, and he quickly threw better than me."

Monte is right, of course. I never saw a stronger or more accurate arm in baseball. Back when teams used to take pregame fielding practice, watching Clemente cut loose with throws right on a dime was worth the game ticket.

The Willie Mays Project

The Willie Mays connection came about when Willie joined the New York Giants in 1951. Manager Leo Durocher had them share a hotel room on the road.

Monte was immediately impressed by Mays. "He was like Josh Gibson. When you saw him, you knew he was a baseball player, particularly the way he caught the ball, the way he threw the ball, the way he looked, the way he handled himself, the way he ran to the outfield—all of that would tell you that he was a natural," he said.

When Durocher introduced them, he told Monte to show Willie around, to show him how things were done, and to tell him what people and places should be avoided. One of Monte's big projects was to keep the rookie relaxed after Mays started his Giants career by going 0 and 12 in his first major league at-bats.

264

"I told him not to worry about it," Monte remembered telling Mays. You are throwing out everybody that runs, and you are catching everything that's hit out there, and we are winning, so don't worry about that. You're going to be here. Still, he went to Leo and said, 'I don't know if I'm ready to play up here or not.' Leo said, 'Listen, you are my centerfielder as long as I am in charge of the team. Don't worry about a thing.'" In the next game, in the first pitch off Warren Spahn, Mays hit a ball about 450 feet over the left field wall. "That was his start," said Monte.

First in Twenty-Three Years to Steal Home in World Series

The 1951 New York Giants won the National League pennant thanks to Bobby Thomson's famed game-winning home run in the final playoff game with the Dodgers. In the World Series, they would lose in five games to the New York Yankees.

Monte Irvin did his best to keep that from happening. He hit .458 in the series and would put his name in the record books when he became the first player to steal home in a World Series game since Bob Meusel of the Yankees in 1928.

"I was watching how much time it took for Allie Reynolds to release the ball when he was working from a windup. So, I took an extra-long lead and just took off," said Monte. "Yankee catcher Yogi Berra put up a squawk that I was out, but I told him to check the newspaper photos the next day. They would show I was safe."

The photos did indeed show that Monte had been safe. Later, when Monte would run into Yogi, he would always tell him, "You were safe, but Robinson was out." Monte said about Yogi's comment, "He was talking about Jackie's steal of home in 1955. I think Yogi had it right."

Monte Irvin on the Future of Baseball

Monte has seen the good—the development and integration of the game. He has also seen the bad—the labor strikes, drug and gambling scandals, the steroid era, and other major and minor disruptions. But he has great confidence in the future of the game.

As he told me during our conversation, "Attendance continues to increase. I think baseball, in my estimation, will always be number one because all you have to do is keep producing stars— guys who can hit, run, field and throw and hit for power. If you have that kind of excellence on the field, I think it will always be on top or near the top of popularity.

"It's a wonderful game now. It continues to expand. Maybe they'll go to mainland China and Russia and even more places in the future.

"Baseball will always be here. It's the greatest game ever invented. You never know what's going to happen until the last man is out."

That is the very essence of the heart of baseball and why, after all these years and historic moments, it remains a great game. As Monte Irvin said, "Baseball is the greatest game ever invented."

And this author wholeheartedly agrees.

BIBLIOGRAPHY

The sport to which I owe so much has undergone profound changes…but it's still baseball. Kids still imitate their heroes on playgrounds. Fans still ruin expensive suits going after foul balls that cost five dollars. Hitting streaks still make the network news. And hot dogs still taste better at the ballpark than at home.

Duke Snider
Hall of Famer

Duke Snider, 1955

Because this book covered the history of baseball in a very condensed form from a different angle than most, I heartily recommend to fans who wish to read more traditional histories and in greater detail to consider some of the websites and volumes listed in this bibliography. For easy reference, websites are listed by addresses, and books are listed alphabetically by author. Over the years, the research for many items enclosed within these pages started with a story or note contained between the covers of the hundreds of books on baseball that have been written in the past.

There have been some outstanding professional and amateur researchers during baseball's long history. And because of baseball's long history, no writer will ever compose a book that contains everything. If ever finished, that book would be impossible to lift, would need more computer memory than any personal unit could contain, and might take years to read. That is why so many books have been written from so many different angles—and there will be more written as well.

I hope you enjoyed this one, especially some of you who may have recognized something I wrote about from a question sent my direction during my years working on Houston Astro television.

Websites

http://www.baseball-reference.com, modified April 15, 2014, by MSN Network, contains all of the major and minor league stats in great detail for players past and present. It also has team and league information, as well as some biographical information.

http://www.retrosheet.org, last updated July 25, 2009, by Retrosheet, Inc., provides the best place to track down old box scores and unusual information from baseball.

BIBLIOGRAPHY

http://www.baseball-almanac.com, first published in 2000 by Baseball- Almanac, is an easy-to-use site famous for its lists and statistical leaders. It contains some biographical information and more.

http://www.sabr.org, updated in 2014 by the Society for American Baseball Research, is strong for its continual additions of detailed biographies of players. Its members are always updating the site with research and written materials.

http://www.baseballlibrary.com/ballplayers is a good biographical site for basic information, not statistics, on many players from the past.

http://www.wikipedia.com, published 2001 by Wikimedia Foundation, is a great sight to start a search or to use as a cross-check on most players' names or teams.

http://www.mlb.com, updated in 2014, is the official site of Major League Baseball. The site is strong for current information and records.

http://www.milb.com, updated in 2014, is the official site of Minor League Baseball. The site is strong for current information and records.

In addition to these sites, simple Google or Yahoo searches were used extensively to back up or find additional information on players or other historical notes. Much of the information ultimately traces to newspaper accounts.

Books

Adair, Robert. *The Physics of Baseball.* New York: Harper Collins, 1994.

Anderson, Dave. *Pennant Races.* New York: Doubleday, 1994.

Angel, Roger. *Once More Around the Ball Park.* Ballantine, 1991.

Anton, Todd. *No Greater Love.* Rounder, 2007.

Aron, Paul. *Did Babe Ruth Call His shot?* Wiley and Sons, 2005

Aylesworth, Thomas. *The Encyclopedia of Baseball Managers.* Crescent, 1990.

Bak, Richard. *Peach: Ty Cobb and His Time.* Our Sports, 2005.

Berkow, Ira. *The Corporal was a Pitcher.* Triumph, 2009.

Bjarkman, Peter. *The Baseball Scrapbook.* Dorset Press, 1991.

Blake, Mike. *The Baseball Chronicles.* Better Way Books, 1994.

Blake, Mike. *The Incomplete Book of Baseball Superstitions.* Winwood, 1991.

Blair, Sam. *Merle Harmon Stories.* Reid Productions, 1998.

Block, David. *Baseball Before We Knew It.* Bison Books, 2005.

Bock, Hal. *The A.P. Pictorial History of Baseball.* JG Press, 1994.

Borelli, Stephen. *How About That! The Life of Mel Allen.* Sport Publishing, 2005.

Boswell, Thomas. *Why Life Begins on Opening Day.* Penguin, 1981.

Boswell, Thomas. *How Life Imitates the World Series.* Penguin, 1983.

Bragan, Bobby. *You Can't Hit the Ball with the Bat on your Shoulder.* Summit, 1992.

Brickhouse, Jack and Jack Rosenberg. *Thanks for Listening.* Diamond Communications, 1986.

Broeg, Bob and Warren Miller. *Baseball From a Different Angle.* Diamond, 1998.

Brown, Lois. *Girls of Summer.* Harper Collins, 1992.

Bryan, Mike. *Baseball Lives.* Pantheon, 1999.

Buck, Jack. *Jack Buck: That's a Winner.* Sagamore Publishing, 1997.

Burk, Robert. *Never Just a Game.* Chapel Hill Press, 1994.

Cahan, Richard and Mark Jacob. *The Game that Was.* Contemporary Books, 1996.

Cairns, Bob. *Pen Men.* St. Martin's Press, 1992.

Carmichael, John. *My Greatest Day in Baseball.* Barnes and Co., 1945.

Carroll, Bob. *Baseball Between the Lies.* Perigree Books, 1993.

Cateneo, David. *Peanuts and Crackerjacks.* Rutledge Hill Press, 1991.

Chandler, Happy. *Heroes, Plain Folks and Skunks.* Bonus Books, 1989.

Charlton, James. *The Baseball Chronology.* MacMillan, 1991.

Charlton, James. *The Who, What, Why, When and How of Baseball.* Barnes and Noble, 1995.

Clark, Dick and Larry Lester. *The Negro Leagues Book.* SABR, 1994.

Conner, Floyd. *Baseball's Most Wanted.* Brassey's, 2000.

Connor, Anthony. *Baseball for the Love of It.* MacMillan, 1982.

Costello, J. and M. Santa Maria. *In the Shadows of the Diamond.* Elysian Fields Press, 1992.

DeSalvatore, Bryan. *A Clever Base-ballist.* Pantheon, 1999.

Dewey, Don and Acocella, Nick. *The Biographical History of Baseball.* Carroll and Graf, 1995.

Dickson, Paul. *The Dickson Baseball Dictionary.* Facts on File, 1989.

Dickson, Paul. *Baseball's Greatest Quotations.* Harper Collins, 1991.

Durocher, Leo. *Nice Guys Finish Last.* Simon and Schuster, 1975.

Duxbury, John. *The Ol' Ball Game.* Stockpole Books, 1990.

Enders, Erik. Ballparks Then and Now. Thunder Bay, 2002.

Elston, Gene. *A Stitch in Time.* Halcyon Press, 2001.

Fehler, Gene. *Tales From Baseball's Golden Age.* Sports Publishing, 2000.

Fitzgerald, Ed. *The American League.* Grosset and Dunlap, 1955.

Fizgerald, Ed. *The National League.* Grosset and Dunlap, 1955.

Forker, Dom. *Baseball Brain Teasers.* Sterling Publishing, 1986.

Frick, Ford. *Games, Asterisks and People.* Crown Publishing, 1973.

Fusselle, Warner. *Baseball... a Laughing Matter!* The Sporting News, 1987.

Gershman, Michael. *Diamonds.* Houghton Mifflin, 1993.

Gilbert, Bill. *The Seasons.* Citadel Press, 2003.

Gillette, Gary and Peter Palmer. *The ESPN Baseball Encyclopedia.* Sterling, 2008.

Go and Gordon Bell. *The Tao of Baseball.* Simon and Schuster, 1991.

Golenbock, Peter. *The Spirit of St. Louis.* Harper Collins, 2000.

Golenbock, Peter. *Wrigleyville.* St. Martin's Press, 1996.

Graham, Frank Jr. *A Farewell to Heroes.* Viking, 1981.

Gutman, Dan. *Banana Bats and Ding Dong Balls.* MacMillan, 1995.

Gutman, Dan. *It Ain't Cheating if you Don't Get Caught.* Penguin, 1990.

Gutman, Dan. *Baseball Babylon.* Penguin, 1992.

Halberstam, David. *Sports on New York Radio.* Master Press, 1999.

Hamilton, Milo and Bob Ibach. *Making Airwaves.* Sports Publishing, 2006.

Harwell, Ernie. *Tuned to Baseball.* Diamond Communications, 1985.

Helyar, John. *Lords of the Realm.* Villard, 1994.

Hogan, Lawrence. *Shades of Glory.* National Geographic, 2006.

Hollander, Zander. *The Baseball Book.* Random House, 1982.

Honig, Donald. *Baseball: When the Grass was Real.* Coward, McCann & Geoghegan, 1975.

Honig, Donald. Baseball America. Barnes and Noble, 1985.

Honig, Donald. *The National League.* Crown Publishing, 1983.

Honig, Donald. *Shadows of Summer.* Viking Penguin, 1994.

Honig, Donald. *The October Heroes.* Simon and Schuster, 1979.

Honig, Donald. *The Man in the Dugout.* Bison Books, 1977.

Hoppel, Joe. *Baseball- A Doubleheader Collection of Facts, Feats, Firsts.* Gallahad, 1992.

James, Bill. *The Bill James Historical Abstract.* Villard, 1985.

Johnson, Lloyd. Baseball's Dream Teams. Crescent Books, 1990.

Johnson, Lloyd. *The Minor League Register.* Baseball America, 1994.

Kaegel, Dick and Mike Kilduff. *Baseball Chatter.* The Sporting News, 2004.

Kaplan, Jim. *Golden Years of Baseball.* Crescent Books. 1992.

Kaufman, James and Alan. *The Worst Baseball Pitchers of All Time.* Citadel, 1995.

Kavanagh, Jack and Norm Macht. *Uncle Robbie.* SABR, 1999.

Ksicinski, Jim and Tom Flaherty. *Jocks and Socks.* Contemporary Books, 2001.

Kuhn, Bowie. *Hardball.* NY Times Books, 1987.

Lamb, David. *Stolen Season.* Random House, 1991.

Lane, F.C. *Batting.* SABR, 1925.

Lardner, Ring. *Ring Around the Bases.* Scribners, 1992.

Levin, Peter. *A.G. Spalding and the Rise of Baseball.* Oxford Press, 1885.

Lewis, Michael. *Moneyball.* Norton, 2003.

Lowry, Philip. *Green Cathedrals.* Walker, 2006.

Lyons, Jeffrey and Douglas. *Curveballs and Screwballs.* Random House, 2001.

Lyons, Jeffrey and Douglas. *Out of Left Field.* Times Books, 1998.

Mackin, Bob. *Baseball Trivia.* Greystone, 2000.

Mackin, Bob. *The Unofficial Guide to Baseball's Unusual Records.* Greystone, 2004.

Masur, Louis. Autumn Glory. Hill and Wang, 2003.

McCabe, Neal and Constance. *Baseball's Golden Age.* Abradele, 1993.

McCulloch, Ron. *How Baseball Began.* Warwick, 1995.

Miller, Marvin. *A Whole Different Ballgame.* Simon Schuster, 1991.

Miller, Norm. *To All My Fans from Norm Who?* Double Play Productions, 2009.

Montville, Leigh. *The Big Bam- Life and Times of Babe Ruth.* Doubleday, 2006.

Morris, Peter. *A Game of Inches.* Ivan R. Dee, 2006.

Nadel, Eric and Craig Wright. *The Man Who Stole First Base.* Taylor Publishing, 1989.

Nash, Bruce and Allen Zullo. *Believe it or Else.* Dell Sports, 1992.

Nash, Bruce and Allen Zullo. *Baseball Confidential.* Pocket Books, 1988.

Nash, Bruce and Allen Zullo. *The Baseball Hall of Shame Vol 1-4.* Pocket Books, 1986-1990.

Nash, Bruce and Allen Zullo. *The Baseball Hall of Shame's Warped Records.* Collier, 1991.

Nash, Bruce and Allen Zullo. *The Baseball Hall of Shame Blooperstown.* Lyons Press, 2012.

Nelson, Kevin. *Greatest Stories Ever Told About Baseball.* Perigee Books,

1986.

Nemec, David. *The Rules of Baseball.* Lyons and Burford, 1994.

Nemec, David. *The Great Encyclopedia of 19th Century Baseball.* Donald I. Fine, 1997.

Nemec, David. *Players of Cooperstown.* Publications International, 1993.

Nemec, David and Scott Flatow. *Great Baseball Feats, Facts and Firsts.* Signet, 1989-2008.

Nemec, David and Pete Palmer. *Fascinating Baseball Facts.* Signet, 1994.

Nemec, David and Saul Wisnia. *Baseball-More than 100 Years.* Publications International, 1997.

Okkomen, Marc. *Baseball Memories.* Sterling Press, 1992-1994.

Okrent, Dan and Harris Lewine. *The Ultimate Baseball Book.* Houghton Mifflin, 1979.

Okrent, Dan and Steve Wulf. *Baseball Anecdotes.* Harper and Row, 1989.

Parrott, Harold. *The Lords of Baseball.* Longstreet Press, 2001.

Pearlman, Jeff. *Love Me, Hate Me.* Harper Collins, 2006.

Peary, Danny. *We Played the Game.* Hyperion, 1994.

Pepe, Phil. *Talkin' Baseball.* Ballantine Books, 1998.

Plaut, David. *Speaking of Baseball.* Running Press, 1993.

Pollack, Alan. *Barnstorming in Heaven.* University of Alabama Press, 2006.

Ray, Edgar. *The Grand Huckster.* Memphis St. University Press, 1980.

Reichler, Joe. *The Baseball Record Companion.* Collier Books, 1987.

Reidenbaugh, Lowell. *Take Me Out To the Ballpark.* The Sporting News, 1986.

Reidenbaugh, Lowell. *Cooperstown- Where Legends Live Forever.* Crescent Books, 1997.

Ribowsky, Mark. *The Power and the Darkness.* Simon and Schuster, 1997.

Rickey, Branch. *Branch Rickey's Little Blue Book.* MacMillan Moutain Lion, 1995.

Riley, James. *The Biographical Encyclopedia of the Negro Leaguers.* Carroll and Graf, 1994.

Ritter, Lawrence. *Lost Ballparks*. Viking, 1992.

Ritter, Lawrence. *The Glory of their Times*. Vintage, 1984.

Ritter, Lawrence and Don Honig. *The Image of their Greatness*. Crown Publishers, 1979.

Robbins, Mike. *Ninety Feet from Fame*. Carroll and Graf, 2004.

Rogosin, Donn. *Invisibile Men*. Atheneum, 1970.

Ryan, Nolan and Jerry Jenkins. *Miracle Man: Nolan Ryan*. Word Publishing, 1992.

Salin, Tony. *Baseball's Forgotten Heroes*. Master's Press, 1999.

Schaap, Dick and Mort Gerberg. *Joy in Mudville*. Doubleday, 1992.

Scheinen, Richard. *Field of Screams*. W.W. Norton and Co., 1994.

Schlain, Bruce. *Oddballs*. Penguin Press, 1989.

Schlain, Bruce. *Baseball Inside and Out*. Viking Penguin, 1992.

Schlossberg, Dan. *The Baseball Book of Why*. J. David Publishers, 1992.

Schlossberg, Dan. *The Baseball Catalog*. J. David Publishers, 1983.

Seidel, Michael. *Streak: Joe DiMaggio and the Summer of '41*. Penguin, 1988.

Shannon, Mike. *Tales From the Dugout*. Contemporary Books, 1997.

Shapiro, Michael. *The Last Good Season*. Doubleday, 2003.

Shatzkin, Mike and Jim Charlton. *The Ballplayers*. William Morrow, 1990.

Silverman, Jeff. Classic Baseball Stories. The Lyons Press, 2003.

Smith, Allen and Ira. *Three Men on Third*. Breakaway Books, 1951.

Smith, Curt. *Voices of the Game*. Diamond, 1987.

Smith, Curt. *Storied Stadiums*. Carroll and Graf, 2001.

Smith, Robert. *Baseball in the Afternoon*. Simon and Schuster, 1993.

Solomon, Burt. *The Baseball Timeline*. Avon, 1997.

Sullivan, Neil. *The Dodgers Move West*. Oxford Press, 1987.

Sullivan, Neil. *The Minors*. St. Martin's Press, 1990.

Thorn, John. *Baseball in the Garden of Eden*. Simon and Schuster, 2011.

Thorn, John. *The National Pastime*. Warner Books, 1987.

Thorn, John. *A Century of Baseball Lore*. Galahad Books, 1976.

Tygiel, Jules. *Baseball's Great Experiment*. Oxford Press, 1983.

Vincent, Fay. *The Last Commissioner*. Simon and Schuster, 2002.

Von Goeben, Robert. *Ballparks*. Metro Books, 2000.

Wallace, Joseph. *The Autobiography of Baseball*. Abrams, 1998

Wallace, Joseph. *The Baseball Anthology- 125 Years*. Abrams, 1994.

Ward, Geoffrey and Ken Burns. *Baseball: An Illustrated History*. Knopf, 1994.

Ward, John Montgomery. *Ward's Baseball Book*. SABR, 1888.

White, G. Edward. *Creating the National Pastime*. Princeton Press, 1996.

Will, George. *Men at Work*. MacMillan, 1990.

Wolff, Rick, et al. *The Baseball Encyclopedia 9th Ed*. MacMillan, 1993.

Wright, Craig and Tom House. *The Diamond Appraised*. Simon and Schuster, 1989.

Zimbalist, Andrew. *Baseball and Billions*. Basic Books, 1992.

Zoss, Joel and John Bowman. *Diamonds in the Rough*. MacMillan, 1989.

Zoss, Joe. And John Bowman. *The American League: A History*. Gallery Books, 1986.

Zumsteg, Derek. *The Cheater's Guide to Baseball*. Hougton Mifflin, 2007.

Photography Credits

A special thank you to the National Baseball Hall of Fame Library for historic photographs. To see more stories and images collected in the archive, visit www.baseballhall.org.

ABOUT THE AUTHOR

Greg Lucas began his career in sports by giving play-by-plays of college basketball games as a student at Butler University in Indianapolis. More than 45 years later, Greg Lucas has recounted plays for fans as a widely recognized sportscaster of 25 different sports in more than 3,000 games. His specialties have included major league and collegiate baseball, professional and collegiate basketball, and collegiate football. He was mainly affiliated with the network formerly known as HSE or Fox Sports Southwest/Houston.

In addition to sports broadcasting, Greg has worked as a television host, actor, researcher, narrator, and writer. His television credits include "Tales of the Game" (1987-2012), "Houston Sportbeat" (2005-2008), and several commercials. Movie credits include *Glory Road* (2004) and *Tyson* (1996).

Greg's writing credits include work as an online columnist for Fox Sports Online (2000-2002) and Fox Sports Houston (2008-2012). *Baseball: It's More Than Just a Game* is his first book.

In honor of his work, Greg was elected to the Texas Baseball Hall of Fame in 1994. He is also a three-time Telly Award winner, two-time Texas Emmy nominee, and a recipient of the Army Commendation Medal.

Today, Greg is an active member of American Sportscasters Association, Screen Actors Guild/AFTRA, and Society for American Baseball Research. He resides in Houston with his wife, Yong Ae, and has one son. He is already working on his next book.

For further information about Greg as a speaker, spokesman, sports broadcaster, author, researcher, show host, narrator, and actor. Find him at:

www.gregclucas.com
FaceBook (www.facebook.com/AuthorGregLucas)
Twitter (@GregCLucas)

Printed in Great Britain
by Amazon.co.uk, Ltd.,
Marston Gate.